CW00924782

The Great War-plane Sell-off

The story of Croydon's Aircraft Disposal Company and its aeroplanes 1920-1931

by

Arthur W. J. G. Ord-Hume

GMS Enterprises

in association with

Aero Book Company

First published 2005
by GMS Enterprises
67 Pyhill, Bretton, Peterborough,
PE3 8QQ, England
Tel/Fax +44 (0) 1733 265123
email: gmsimons@btconnect.com
www.gmsenterprises.net

ISBN: 1-904514-18-9

Printed and bound for GMS Enterprises by
Woolnough Ltd, Express Works, Irthlingborough, Northamptonshire.

Other Aviation titles by Arthur W. J. G. Ord-Hume:
On Home-Made Wings (1997)
Flight on Frail Wings (1998)
British Light Aeroplanes (2000)
British Commercial Aircraft (2003)

The above works are all published by
GMS Enterprises
in association with
Aero Book Company

Contents

<u>*Note to Readers:*</u>
Throughout this book, reference numbers in square brackets, *i.e.* *[7]* or 'Jackson *[10]*' refer to a reference in the Bibliography.

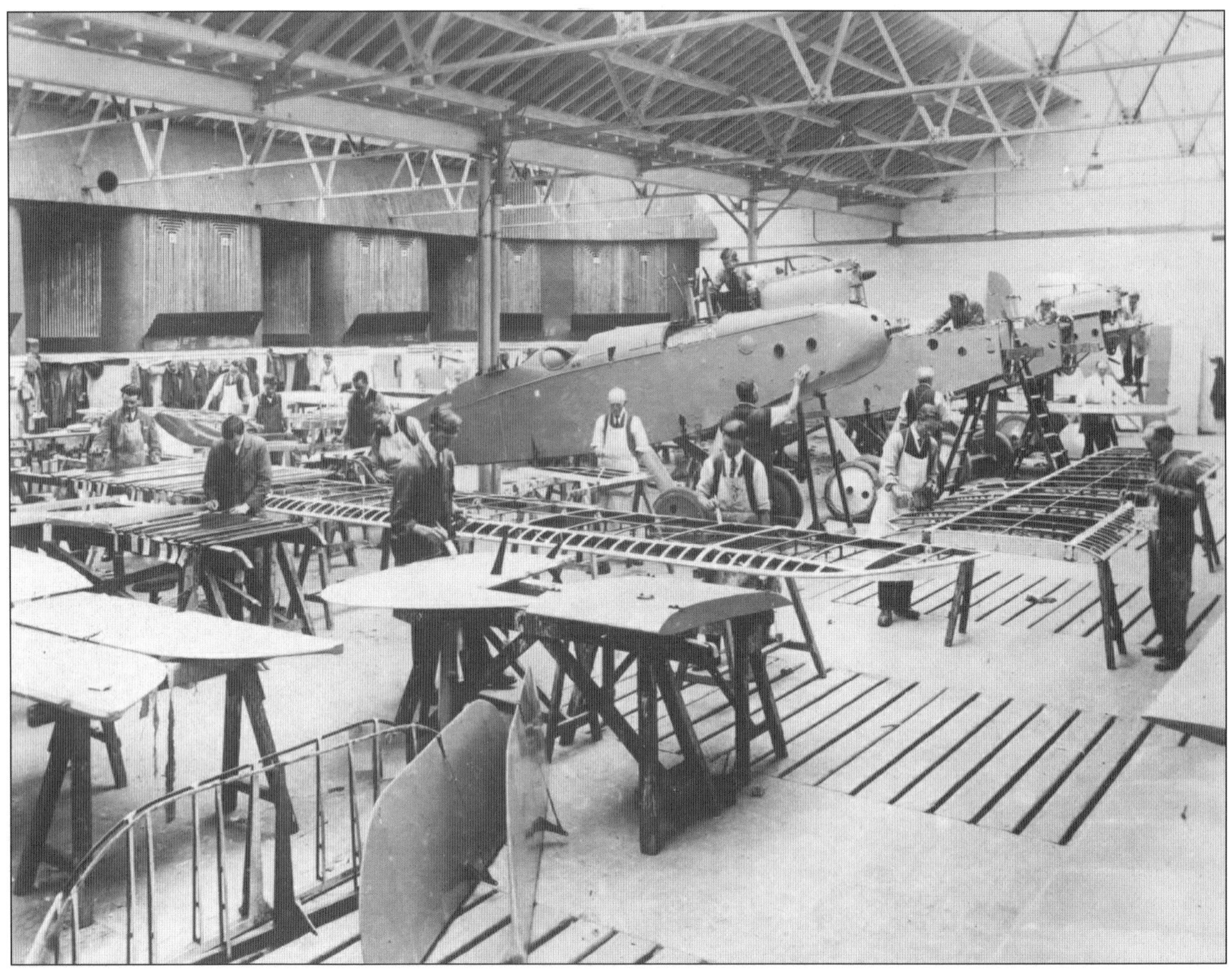

A view of the dope shop of the Aircraft Disposal Company's factory at Waddon showing Nimbus-powered DH.9 aircraft being assembled in the background while wings are being prepared for fabric-covering in the middle. The foreground shows tail surfaces that have been covered and doped.

Acknowledgements

THIS story is based on a lecture given before the Croydon Airport Society on July 20th 1999 entitled 'Croydon Airport and The Aircraft Disposal Company'. In presenting this considerably expanded version of that monograph I would like to express my acknowledgement to that Society which today is charged with preserving the memory of what will always remain the most famous aerodrome in Britain if not the whole of Europe. This story also derives from part of my major work, *British Light Aeroplanes: Their Evolution, Development and Perfection 1920-1940,* produced in 2000, and its companion volume, *British Commercial Aircraft: Their Evolution, Development and Perfection 1920-1940,* both published by GMS Enterprises.

I wish to place on record the invaluable assistance I have received from the Brian Cocks photographic archive and also from Graham Simons without whose enthusiastic co-operation this book might have been impossible. Co-publisher John Farley of Aero Book Company has also played a significant part in getting this work off the ground. My thanks also go to others who have contributed material and pictures, in no particular order Richard T Riding, Michael Oakey of *Aeroplane,* Michael J Hooks, Lydia Matharu, the late Maurice Brett and John Murray, and Desmond Langton, Simon Peters, George C Cull, and Peter Green. The Croydon Airport Society, founded by people who recall with happiness the better days of that now derelict aerodrome, has been of great help, in particular the assistance of Tom Samson and Geoff Morris, and the knowledgeable co-operation of Society Archivist, Peter Skinner. The enthusiastic assistance of these gentlemen I warmly acknowledge. I am also pleased to be able to reproduce the rare picture postcard that Brian Cutler managed to find showing the tug-of-war competition winners from the National Aircraft Factory in 1918.

Many of my other illustrations are from my own collection of contemporary newspaper and picture agency photographs which I have collected over the years on the open market. In most cases the original copyright holders may no longer be traced. To those that I may have overlooked, my gratitude and apologies.

Were it not for Croydon Airport, none of this would have happened, so this list of acknowledgements has to include the historic site itself.

Ask any old-lag aviator and he will be the first to admit that all airfields are haunted. Redolent with spirits from a past age, aerodromes have seen the extremes of human emotion from excitement and happiness through, unfortunately, to sorrow and loss. Between those extremes there is a welter of other emotions, private, personal and commercial.

Amidst the phantoms of Croydon Airport there are the spirits of people and businesses that once thrived at the place. Imperial Airways of course, together with the personalities and pilots that represented it and every other European airline. But beyond this there are ancient visions of a once-famous business. The people that made that business are the ones we really should be acknowledging.

One of the almost-forgotten aircraft manufacturing concerns of the First World War was Sage Aircraft of Peterborough. The aircraft may have gone, but the building remains! *[Simon Peters]*

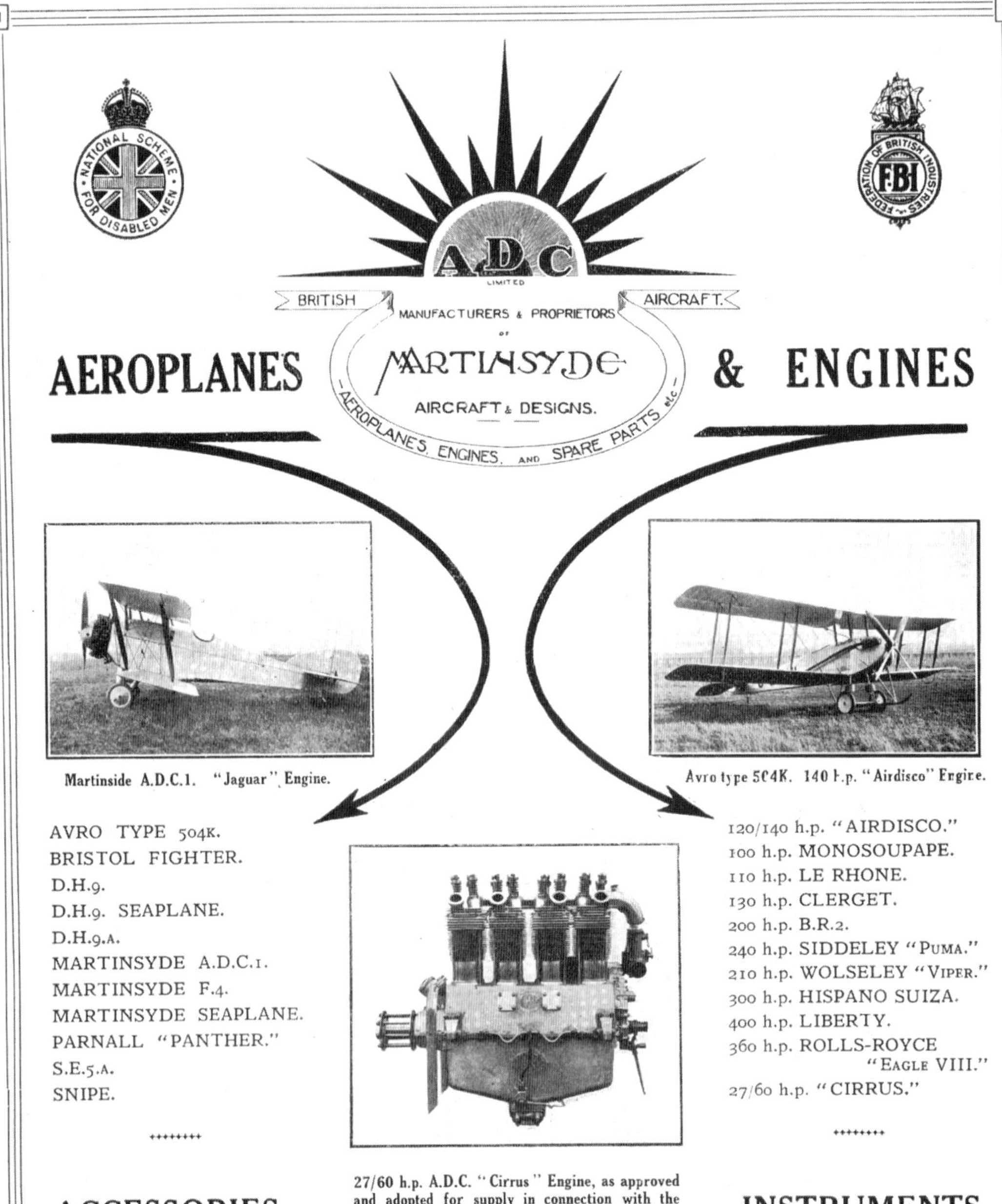

SPARE PARTS FOR THE ABOVE MACHINES AND ENGINES AVAILABLE IN LARGE QUANTITIES FROM STOCK.

We have a competent designing staff, highly skilled mechanics, an approved inspection department, and a well-equipped factory, all of which ensure first-class work being carried out to our clients requirements.

AIRCRAFT DISPOSAL COMPANY LTD.,

REGENT HOUSE,

Telephone: Regent 6240.

89, KINGSWAY, LONDON, W.C.2.

Telegrams: "Airdisco, London."

[Janes AWA 1925]

Introduction

What are we going to do with all the new aircraft which we don't want, which are redundantly surplus to establishment and so forth? In 1919 we were making aeroplanes, paying for the material, paying the factory hands, and then wheeling the machines out of the works and burning them in sight of the people who had made them, and, funniest or saddest of all, in sight of the A.I.D. Inspectors who had certified that they were war-worthy.

C G Grey, letter published in *'The Aeroplane',* August 3rd, 1945

NOT so long ago, a good friend of mine presented a fine pictorial book on Croydon Airport which drew from one reviewer the rather petulant observation 'Do we *really* need *another* book on Croydon?' This reminded me of the old joke of the wife contemplating a Christmas present for her husband and a friend, trying to be helpful, suggesting 'What about a book?' to which the reply was 'No, he's already got one of those!' Knowledge and information comes in convenient packages which is probably as well since no one author might ever be able to write a definitive book on any historical subject because exposure to knowledge invariably shows that there is yet something new to learn.

Now here comes yet another book on Croydon Airport! I can be certain, from past experience, that at least one reviewer will let out a groan and seek out alternative pleasures from the pin-ball machine of life. Every author claims – a few with greater justification than others – that their books are one way or another different from all the others. It is usually a vain quest for getting one's work mentioned in reviews and, more importantly, cited in other writers' lists of bibliographic references.

But, with humble temerity, I present this book as 'something different' with, I hope, particular justification. I want to set down the extraordinary story of a private business that was created to disperse the many thousands of Government surplus aeroplanes and parts that existed at the end of the First World War. Although it was at its time a momentous and far-reaching undertaking that touched absolutely everybody in aviation, both military and civil, the story has never before been told. This could be because several of the people

The great dynasty of de Havilland aircraft began with the Airco DH.I built by George Holt Thomas's Aircraft Manufacturing Company at Hendon. This aircraft, seen here on the roll-out of the prototype in January 1915, may have looked rather archaic but it featured two advanced design concepts. First was the use of an undercarriage sprung by both coil springs and oleo struts. Second was the use of air brakes, a radical step that, for the DH.1, proved something of a leap too far for they were found to be unsuccessful and removed after early flight trials. They can be seen in this picture as a horizontal airfoil on the fuselage side behind the pilot. One was mounted on each side and each spanned about three feet. A lever in the cockpit could rotate them at right-angles to the airflow. When at any significant angle to the air stream they are likely to have caused turbulent flow over the tail surfaces even at low speed. Only 73 DH.I aircraft were produced at a cost of £1,100 each plus £522 10s for the 70 hp Renault engine.

Left: the Airco DH.1A seen here with a 120 hp Beardmore engine was already outmoded by the time it entered service. As a two-seat reconnaissance biplane with forward-firing Lewis machine gun, it was slow and vulnerable. In November 1915 this example, 4606, was sent to Egypt to combat the Turkish threat to Egypt and the Suez Canal. None survived the war and while the Aircraft Disposal Company had large numbers of DH.2 and DH.4 parts – which represented only a marginal development of this Royal Flying Corps dinosaur – it was spared trying to sell off this very primitive type.

The Airco DH.2 was mostly played out by the end of the War although large quantities of spares remained that the Aircraft Disposal Company had to take along with other and more marketable products. This example is one of a batch of 100 numbered from 5916 to 6015 and built at Hendon by the Aircraft Manufacturing Company Ltd (Airco) at Hendon. This firm also built a second batch also of 100 that were numbered from 7842 to 7941. While admittedly photographed straight off the production line, the superior finish of the fabric covering is notable.

Pictures of the DH.2 in flight are hard to find. The curious aspect of the fuselage tail booms when viewed from the front provides a strange perspective as seen in this shot of No.24 Sqdn's Major Lanoe George Hawker flying at St Omer in February 1916. The flight leader's pennant flies from the starboard rear interplane strut.

involved were at the highest levels in government and industry and they may have considered it best, for them at least, that a veil be drawn over the whole miserable enterprise.

The idea behind this business was to minimise the waste of taxpayers' money by converting redundant ex-military aircraft into some return for the Chancellor of the Exchequer. With thousands of aeroplanes being built at the time of the Armistice plus the vast numbers in service, getting rid of all this expensive hardware needed delicate strategy if the British taxpayer, a historically vociferous animal when faced with even a suggestion of subterfuge, was to be placated. Certain Members of Parliament were already on the warpath regarding what they saw as the peacetime misappropriation of public funds.

Like so many good ideas, especially those that are overtly brokered by politicians, the plan was not thought through particularly well and the outcome was rather different from that expected. True, it was a huge success and the taxpayer's investment was to a large extent vindicated. But it was such a success that it became a hydra – an enterprise that swamped the world market with fully reconditioned and new aeroplanes at a low price. While these prices reflected the world economic doldrums of the early 1920s, the enterprise sealed the fate of many aircraft manufacturers and sub-contractors who suddenly found that their factory-gate prices were higher than the cost of surplus wartime aeroplanes.

It was a disaster of colossal magnitude. It put a brake on both civil and military aircraft development that continued well into the mid-1920s. It fostered company closures and bankruptcy, financial ruin for some and unemployment for many. It can honestly be said to have shaped the birth of civil flying, both commercial and private, in the first decade following the end of the Great War, and it had a far-reaching effect on the then-very new Royal Air Force.

The irony was that the formation of this firm, The Aircraft Disposal Company, was the result of an idea that came from within the aircraft industry itself. It was no lesser person than Frederick Handley Page, pioneer aeroplane-maker and builder of huge bombers, who founded the business, putting his brother and himself at its helm.

What actually happened was that the fledgling organisation grew to such huge proportions that not only did it suck the life-blood out of the industry that had spawned it, but it also turned on its founders. It generated a strategic management team that actually threatened to put the man who started it, none other than Frederick Handley Page, out of business. And it created a rift in the Page family as Handley's own brother became swept along in the company's expansion.

While The Aircraft Disposal Company grew stronger and stronger, the British aircraft industry became weaker and weaker, not helped by the fact that the Royal Air Force (the wartime creation and expansion of which had created much of the surplus in the first place) was scheduled to be disbanded, its duties returned to the Army. What little of the RAF survived was considered too small to justify the placing of orders for new aircraft.

As the aircraft industry slowly bled to death, the rampant child in its giant factory at Croydon came of age and with time and maturity gradually changed. After the initial flush of truculence regarding its powers and success, it began contributing to the industry that it had practically annihilated. It

Above: the DH.4 was one of the most outstanding aircraft of its time. This is the prototype pictured at Hendon in August 1916. Originally designed for the 160 hp Beardmore, this was switched before completion to the new and equally outstanding 230 hp Beardmore-Halford-Pullinger, known as the BHP. This engine was marginally taller than the first-specified engine and this accounts for the small step in the nose profile at the forward centre-section pylon struts. From this view, the short undercarriage feature, carried forward into the DH.9, can be appreciated. When the DH.4 entered mass-production, the then-new Rolls-Royce water-cooled engine was preferred and so the machine was modified to take this heavier motor. In the second picture here, A7995 shows how the wings had to be moved forward and the undercarriage revised. Both aircraft are seen here fitted with twin two-bladed propellers,

Below: No.49 Sqdn Royal Flying Corps DH.4 serial number A7694 pictured at Bellevue Aerodrome, France, about November 1917. One of the first aircraft flown by Sqdn-Ldr A H Curtis, it was powered by a 200 hp RAF.3A engine.

designed new engines and gave the world the famous Cirrus and Hermes series of aero engines that were later to be taken up by separate companies and, later still, by the engine division of Blackburn Aircraft Ltd. Through its genius engine designer, Frank Halford, it can also be said to have some responsibility for the later Gipsy series of de Havilland engines.

Its contribution to aero-engine development was enormous yet today it its achievements are totally forgotten: ignored by most historians and under-estimated by the few that do make any reference to its work. Its Cirrus engines became famed the world over and many flew just that — the world over. Another of its engines – the Airsix – was truly a pioneering project being Britain's first six-cylinder in-line air-cooled aircraft engine.

The premises of the Aircraft Disposal Company's factory were far larger than the premises of any other aircraft manufacturer in the country. At its peak, the company exported fully-reconditioned aircraft to most of the countries in what was then known as the civilised world. It encouraged many of these nations to 'buy British' when they might not normally have given such action so much as a thought.

And when, in the fullness of time, having exhausted its stocks of rebuilt and revamped war surplus, its activities gradually subsided and the end came quietly. Airdisco, the telegram address by which it was commonly known for most of its life, had run its course and peacefully went out of business. As the years had advanced, an aeronautical respectability had

Above: Designed and built to fulfil the demand for a low-cost trainer, the DH.6 was aerodynamically unsophisticated and structurally utilitarian. The prototype, seen here at roll-out early in 1916, had a RAF.1A engine and the structure was entirely cable-braced.DH.6 rudders were pointed, unbalanced and angular on all production aircraft built by Airco. This is one of the two prototypes that featured a balanced curved fin and rudder reminiscent of a much later design from Geoffrey de Havilland. The engine is the 90 hp RAF.1A eight-cylinder air-cooled 'V' motor attached to the top longerons with no cowlings. Two thousand two hundred and eighty-two of these practical and multi-purpose machines were built and large numbers ended up surplus with the Aircraft Disposal Company.

Below: This side-on view of the prototype DH.6 reveals the curious low-cost centre-section wire bracing. The airframe cost £841 10s plus £522 10s for the engine. Some examples were fitted with the Curtiss OX-5 which cost £693 10s.

The DH.9 was developed from the DH.4, in fact the prototype was created from a modified DH.4 and was well into flight trials by July 1917. Unfortunately it demonstrated all the signs of premature introduction for it was plagued with engine-reliability problems. It had been designed around the new 230 hp BHP, originally styled the Galloway Adriatic, which had been rushed into production by the Siddeley-Deasy Car Company. With order for 2,000 engines placed with Siddeley-Deasy, component part castings had to be ordered in large batches and it was found too late that more than 90 percent of the cast aluminium cylinder blocks were defective. It is interesting to note that the engine that resulted from this involved parentage became known as the Siddeley Puma of which the first batch were rated at 300 hp, but later de-rated to 230 hp due to the below-standard nature of the cylinder blocks. The Puma thus originated from Frank Halford, did the rounds before returning as surplus to the Aircraft Disposal Company – and being re-worked by Frank Halford! Here we see D1651, a standard production DH.9 built by Mann, Egerton & Company. Very early on in the life of the aircraft, in an attempt to cure a curious roll tendency experienced in sharp turns and identified as caused by fuselage flexibility, an additional 15 cwt strain bracing wire was installed from the lower chin to the top of the first interplane strut.

cloaked its existence and many actually rued its eventual disappearance.

By the time of its closure, The Aircraft Disposal Company, now called ADC Aircraft Ltd, had adjusted its position in the aircraft industry. It had dropped the word 'Disposal' from its name and it was an ordinary aircraft and engine supplier. Nevertheless irrevocable damage had already been done. It had left the weaker businesses long since dead in its wake.

In the lean times that following the cancellation of lucrative war-production contracts, even the strong had become vulnerable. Among those that it consumed was Martinsyde, at one time one of the largest aircraft manufacturers in the country. As Martinsyde writhed in its death agonies, Airdisco confidently took over its aircraft stock and assumed design rights to make new 'Martinsyde' aircraft variants from the company's bankrupt stock.

When finally the business had run its course and chose voluntary liquidation, its vast stocks of parts that remained were acquired by other businesses. As we shall see, World War One components, bought by the Aircraft Disposal Company after that war had ended, were still to be found on the market well into the 1950s, while its enormous factory and warehouse premises survived the millennium only to be razed from the face of the Surrey countryside in the year 2000-2002.

The history of The Aircraft Disposal Company, Airdisco or simply ADC, is inextricably tied up with the early years of Croydon Aerodrome and its personalities but, curiously, its roots lay elsewhere. The precursor of ADC began its days nearer to London's Regent's Park Zoo in those old tented and timbered storage depot buildings that older readers will recall had for so long spoiled the appearance of this famous Royal Park. Wartime use of the Royal Park was accepted but the straggling shanty-town remained well into the 1920s by which time, as the public was quick to point out, it was nothing to do with the military but the responsibility of a civil profit-making company! ADC, as I shall relate, got off to a bad start virtually from Day One!

To tell the story of ADC in isolation is to present bald facts that many of those who may not have been privy to the wider canvas may have difficulty in understanding. Because of this, I have chosen to present a

Popular though the DH.4 was, it suffered from having the pilot's cockpit under the top wing. Apart from the matter of seriously reducing both upward and rearward visibility, it was also considered a hindrance to easy evacuation should an emergency arise. Its development, the DH.9, overcame this objection by placing both cockpits well aft of the wing. The prototype, C6051, is depicted here powered by a 230 hp Siddeley Puma driving a fine-pitch wooden airscrew. Large numbers of DH.9 and 9A aircraft were sold off by The Aircraft Disposal Company including examples fitted with the ADC Nimbus engine.

No.49 Sqdn Royal Flying Corps DH.9 serial number C6114 pictured at Conteville, France, shortly before being shot down by ack-ack fire on June 7 1918. The observer, Lt P T Holligan, later DFC, is seen in the picture and the pilot was A H Curtis. The engine is the 230 hp BHP. The Aircraft Disposal Company reconditioned and factored a large number of these machines.

more complete picture by relating the circumstances that led up to the public scandal that was resolved by the formation of ADC. This means that there is something about the vast enterprise created to build thousands of aircraft in time of war and how hard it was to bring this gigantic operation to a halt once the Armistice was signed in November 1918.

We also have to understand why ordinary people and Parliament were so sensitive to problems of surplus disposal and accounting for taxpayers' money. This means we have to take a glance at the scandals of the time – like the decision to make aircraft wing-spars out of cypress (which caused the scrapping of many aircraft), and the matter of four million yards of best-quality Irish linen for wing-covering that suddenly flooded the market and almost ruined the trade in quality cloth.

The need to dispose of finished and part-built aeroplanes is, therefore, only some of the story. There was also a huge operation in hand at the end of the war bringing damaged or crashed aircraft back from the Front for salvage. These had to be 'dismantled' for usable-parts salvage. How the King's Royal Park in London became a spares and surplus dump is also of relevance as is the early history of the old Croydon Airport, its building and its unique railway branch line and sidings.

At the same time, it is interesting to note how different was the British attitude to war surplus aircraft from that of the French and Italians. And what happened to all the German surplus military aircraft? After all they had at least as many aircraft in service and construction as we did. How did these nations dispose of their huge inventories of government surplus aircraft? I shall try to fill in as many gaps as possible.

This book was begun in 1999 but although it had reached final draft stage, the unearthing of much more material suggested a Homeric intermission while this fresh material was evaluated. One of the immediate benefits of this wise recess has been the discovery of many more related photographs and a quantity of other material. The result is, I hope, a bit more than just 'another book about Croydon Airport!

Arthur W J G Ord-Hume,
Guildford,
Surrey.

DH.9A aircraft were the product of the decision to create a new airframe to suit the engine that America agreed to provide as part of her contribution the war effort. Announced on August 12th 1917 by the American Secretary of War and named the Liberty, the engine was designed by Maj J G Vincent of Packard and Maj J G Hall of the Hall-Scott company. It was, remarkably, completed just 28 days after drawings were begun. A 12-cylinder version of the original 8-cylinder prototype was put into production and Westland Aircraft Works undertook the production of the airframe initially as a conversion of the DH.9. The Liberty engine was ultimately successful but was not without its teething problems, much of it being centred around its use of coil ignition. This is the first Liberty-engined example, C6122. A large quantity of these machines remained for disposal at Waddon and a number were successfully sold abroad.

Dramatis Personae

Brief Biographical Notes concerning the Key Personalities whose names appear in the following story.

BARRETT-LENNARD, Lt-Col John.
Appointed by the Bank of Scotland to the Board of Handley Page Limited at the infamous Board Meeting of March 1921, Barrett-Lennard was additionally appointed a director of The Aircraft Disposal Company as well as its general manager. After the financial fracas that deposed Handley **PAGE** and his brother from the Board of the company, Barrett-Lennard became joint managing director with Maurice Ormonde **DARBY.** In 1927 with the change of name to ADC Aircraft Ltd and the formation of Cirrus Engines Ltd, he and Darby were also joint managing directors of the two companies. He resided at 234 Kew Road, Kew, Middlesex, and died in March 1935.

BLACKBURN, Robert.
Born on March 26th 1885, Robert Blackburn designed, built and flew his first aeroplane in 1909 and produced an all-steel military monoplane in 1911. He operated a school of flying at Hendon for eighteen months before taking over the Olympia Works in Leeds and forming his aircraft company in 1814. He designed and produced a large number of aircraft for Service use, concentrating initially on naval types especially torpedo aircraft. Robert Blackburn became chairman and managing director of Blackburn Aeroplane & Motor Company Ltd as well as North Sea Aerial and General Transport Ltd. He subsequently became director of Cirrus-Hermes Engineering Company Limited whereupon he shifted the whole enterprise to Brough. In 1937 the company name was changed in 1937 to The Cirrus Engine Division of Blackburn Aircraft Ltd. The Cirrus name was well known into the 1960s by which time the name had become Blackburn Engines Limited following the name-change of the parent company to Blackburn Aircraft Limited in 1936. After the 1939-45 war, the company merged with General Aircraft Ltd to become Blackburn & General Aircraft Ltd. Robert Blackburn died of heart failure in 1955.

Robert Blackburn

BRAMSON, Mogens Louis.
The Danish-born Mogens Louis Bramson (*b.* Copenhagen. June 28th 1895) combined the duties of chief test pilot and sales director, a position in which his useful command of French, German and Scandinavian languages, in addition to English, would have been useful. He had worked with skywriting pioneer Major John Clifford 'Jack' Savage as European manager and pilot as well as collaborating with him in the design and development of the Savage-Bramson Anti-Stall Gear launched in 1927.

CASSAM, B.
Served as sales manager to The Aircraft Disposal Company based at Waddon.

COURTNEY, Francis (Frank) Thomas.
Born in Ireland on August 6th 1894, Frank Courtney became one of the most significant test pilots and early airline pilots of the 1920s and 1930s. Parental pressure dictated that he enter the world of banking and learn international commerce. He became a clerk in a Parisian bank but quickly became captivated by the rising tide of interest in aviation that swept Europe in the years before the outbreak of the First World War. He broke free and found his way back to England where, between 1913 and 1914, he was apprenticed to the Grahame-White Company at Hendon. He passed through every division of the company and gained his Aero Club Aviators' Certificate No.874 at Hendon on August 20th 1914 flying a Grahame-White Biplane. Now his apprenticeship was cut short by the subsequent events of 1914 and so, in 1915, he joined the Royal Flying Corps as Air Mechanic and Pilot. Commissioned in March 1916 he became test pilot to the Royal Aircraft Factory undertaking experimental work of all descriptions. He became Flight Commander, No. 45 Sqdn in 1917 and after the War worked on the Kennedy Giant at Northolt which he eventually 'flew' on its one-and-only very short hop. Largely freelance, he flew for Armstrong Siddeley, Boulton & Paul, Airco, and Central Aircraft before joining Airco as chief test pilot in 1920. Joined Aircraft Transport & Travel Ltd as pilot, organised Air Post of Banks Ltd, succeeded in winning the Aerial Derby in 1921 before flying for Instone Air Line from June 28 1922 until August 28 that year. He did occasional flying for the Aircraft Disposal Company and was

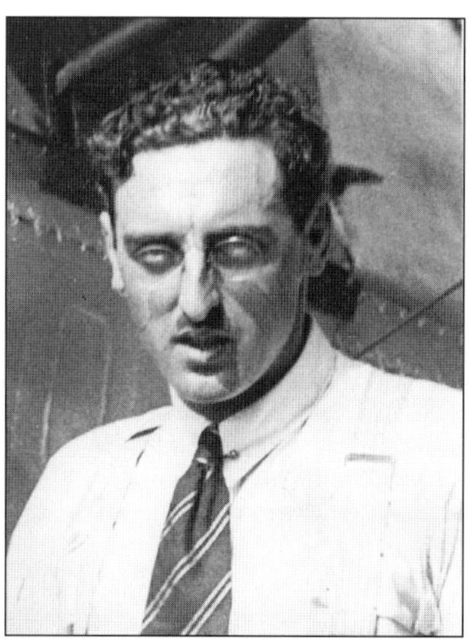

Frank Courtney

also an ADC test pilot. His skill in test-flying earned him the nickname 'the man with the Magic Hands' and it is related that he made more than 10,000 test flights in over one hundred different aircraft ranging from flying boats to Cierva's autogyros. Courtney's amazing and varied flying career was all the more amazing when it is recalled that he had congenitally poor eyesight and had to wear 'bottle-bottom' spectacles that gave his eyes a curious aspect to the observer. Furthermore his pilot's licence was endorsed 'fit for day flying only'! As the age of the peripatetic test-pilot passed into history, Courtney saw out his days in America where he died in 1982.

DARBY, Lt-Col Maurice Ormonde.
Darby, (*b.* London, April 1886; *d.* June 13th 1961, ran both The Aircraft Disposal Company's London office at Regent House, 89 Kingsway, WC2 and the Regent's Park depot. He held the position of joint managing director with John **BARRETT-LENNARD.** He lived at Rose Walk, Purley, Surrey.

GRANT, John R.
Between its foundation in 1920 and 1925, Major Grant was in charge of aircraft reconditioning for The Aircraft Disposal Company Ltd at Waddon. Grant, plagued by serious infirmity caused through an accident while destroying unused bombs after the Armistice, had lost an eye besides incurring other major injuries when a piece of ordnance exploded close to him. A man who was exceedingly popular with all who worked under him, he was always ready with advice and thoughtful help as well as going out of his way to help anyone in difficulties. Following his death on March 15th 1927, *The Aeroplane* wrote: 'The fine condition in which the old Aircraft Disposal Company [by this time ADC Aircraft Ltd – AO-H] delivered machines to various foreign Governments was bought about largely by the quality of Major Grant's work and this policy has been ably carried on by Capt Roy Walker, his successor'.

GREY, Charles Grey.
Charles G Grey was born in London on November 13th 1875 but undertook most of his education in Dublin at the Erasmus Smith School. He then studied engineering at the Crystal Palace School of Engineering after which he joined the editorial staff of *Autocar* in 1908. The following year, with Wilfred Aston, he co-founded a magazine called *The Aero* in partnership with E V

Charles G Grey

(later Sir Victor) Sassoon. Two years later the magazine title was changed to *The Aeroplane.* This he ran outstandingly well until his retirement just before the outbreak of war in 1939 following which he remained a regular contributor for many years. In 1916, after the death at the age of just 50 years of Fred T Jane (John Frederick Thomas Jane, *b.* August 6 1865; *d.* March 8th 1916), Charles Grey succeeded him as editor of *All the World's Aircraft* which he ran both successfully and autocratically until 1941 when, after a falling-out with his management, it was taken from him and given to Leonard Bridgman, his collaborator and joint editor. CGG's often acerbic style of writing concealed a deep feeling that the leadership of this country was lacking in comprehension of the need to re-arm in the late 1930s. To emphasise his point he made frequent references to Germany and the strength of the Luftwaffe (of which he had been an occasional guest). He spoke praising Hitler's farsightedness in understanding the need for supremacy in the air. These words were seen as non-patriotic and the irony was not understood in high places. Matters came to a head with the 1940 edition of Jane's *AWA* when so strong were the objections to some of his words, in particular certain picture captions, that the entire edition was withdrawn and re-printed – at the cost of CGG's editorship. A few 'review copies' escaped the recall: they are valuable curiosities today. Always outspoken yet always fair, CGG is remembered for his gentle manner and warm friendship, characteristics that were quite at variance with his style of journalism that, it is said, was feared as much by civil companies as by the Air Ministry and the Royal Air Force. It was said that when CGG criticised, the aviation world trembled! A lifelong friend was his occupational arch rival, Stanley **SPOONER** of *Flight:* they celebrated their family occasions together. Towards the end of his days, CGG continued to write for *The Aeroplane* as a correspondent and contributor but, while he never lost his gift of words, his failing memory (or, some would say, his increasingly-eccentric way of interpreting facts) frequently led to extended correspondence regarding 'fact-correction.' His home was 'The Clone', Kingston Hill, Surrey.

Frank Halford

HALFORD, Maj. Frank Bernard.
Born in Nottingham on March 7th 1894, Frank Halford was educated at Nottingham University after which he learned to fly at Brooklands taking his Aviators' Certificate No.639 on October 2nd 1913 on a Bristol Boxkite. He became an instructor at Brooklands the following year after which he joined the RFC and later RAF, serving until 1919. During this period the Air Ministry loaned him first to William Beardmore & Company. It was at this time he became closely involved with the Royal Aircraft Factory at Farnborough where he first met and got to know Capt Geoffrey de Havilland, so embarking on a friendship that would have far-reaching consequences for the British aviation industry in years to come. From there, he was transferred, again as an Air Ministry loan, to Ricardo & Company 1918-19. Here he was responsible for the design of the BHP engine — Beardmore-Halford-Pullinger. His interest in engines encouraged him to embark on an independent career as a designer joining The Aircraft Disposal Company Ltd where he produced the Cirrus, Airdisco and

Nimbus engines. He also had considerable input in the design of the Airsix completed after he had left the company to work with Napier on the 'H' type series of engines including Dagger and Rapier. He also worked with Geoffrey de Havilland to design the first Gipsy engines. He ultimately joined the company and, in 1944, took over as head of the De Havilland Engine Company. He died aged just 61 years on April 16th 1955 at his home 'Monkbarns', Sandy Lane, Northwood, Middlesex.

ISAAC, Godfrey.
Brother of Lord Reading Godfrey Isaac. Director of Marconi and a long-standing family friend of Frederick Handley **PAGE.**

KENWORTHY, John.
Born in Darlington in December 1883, Kenworthy joined the Royal Aircraft Factory in 1911 as designer after which he went to the Aeronautical Department of the Austin Motor Company in 1918 as designer and chief engineer. Here he was responsible for the design of the Austin Kestrel. He became assistant chief designer to Westland Aircraft Works in 1922 and the following year joined The Aircraft Disposal Company as chief designer, a position he carried into the era of the revamped ADC Aircraft Ltd. Responsible for the design of all ADC aircraft and modifications. On the winding-down of ADC he became managing director and chief designer of Redwing Aircraft Company Ltd. He lived at 'Hildene', Anglesey Court Road, Carshalton, Surrey.

John Kenworthy

LANE, John Kenneth.
Born in Bristol November 17th 1900, Kenworthy's aviation career began in the drawing offices of the Blackburn Aeroplane Company in 1920. The following year he

John Lane

joined Westland Aircraft in a similar capacity and in 1923 transferred to The Aircraft Disposal Company Ltd where he became assistant designer and worked on the redesign of the Martinsyde F.4 as the ADC.1. In 1929, as ADC Aircraft Ltd began to wind down its airframe development work, he joined Redwing Aircraft Company, designers of the Robinson Redwing biplane, as chief inspector and assistant designer, later becoming managing director and later chairman of the company. He died on August 2nd 1981 leaving behind a useful small book on the design and development of the Redwing.

OLNEY, Ernest Stephen.
Works superintendent of Aircraft Disposal Company. On the formation of Cirrus Aero Engines Ltd on February 16th 1927, Olney assumed a similar role with the new business.

PAGE, Frederick Handley.
Born at Cranham Villa, Cheltenham, Gloucestershire, on November 15th 1885, Frederick Handley Page was the second of four sons of Frederick Joseph Page and his wife Ann Eliza, *née* Handley. This explains from whence the name 'Handley' came, for it was a Christian name. Frederick unofficially adopted his second Christian name as part of his surname but the family name remained that of Page. He founded the company that bore his name in 1909 and went on to build the first successful large bomber of the 1914-18 war. In 1919 he formed Handley Page Transport Ltd and operated a pioneering airline until 1924 when it was one of the four core operators united to create Imperial Airways Ltd. Although a true pioneer, Page was not himself a regular pilot and left that job to better-qualified and experienced flyers than himself. In 1920 he was the founder of The Aircraft Disposal Company and had responsibility for all aircraft sales until he was ousted by ADC and the Bank at a meeting in 1922. He was knighted in 1942 and, with Sir Roy Fedden, was instrumental in founding the College of Aeronautics at Cranfield, today known as Cranfield University. For two decades the name 'Handley Page' equated with big aircraft: it even entered the dictionary as a term for a large aeroplane. He died on April 21st 1962. He is widely remembered for his invention of the wing leading-edge slot, or 'slotted wing' (ever known as 'the Handley Page slot') that contributed greatly to the reduction in the risks of stalling at low speeds. His home was 'Limes House', Stanmore, Middlesex.

Frederick Handley Page

PAGE, Theodore.
A younger brother of Frederick Handley [*qv*] and initially a director of The Aircraft Disposal Company.

PERRY, Herbert Howard.
Capt Herbert Howard Perry (*b.* Harrow, July 3rd 1892) gained his Royal Aero Club certificate No. 1620 at Northolt in July 1915. He served in the Royal Flying Corps as an engine fitter from 1912 until 1915 and later became a sergeant pilot until demobilized in 1920. He then joined Handley Page Ltd specifically as a cross-channel pilot and undertook a flight to Romania and back in 1920. With the formation of The Aircraft Disposal Company he began to undertake occasional assignments for the company, joining full-time in 1922 as chief pilot and test-pilot. He remained with ADC until 1927 after which he joined Imperial Airways at Croydon becoming a senior captain. He lived at 'Sinaia', Cosdach Avenue, Wallington.

RYDER, John Herbert Dudley.
(the Earl of Harrowby). A partner in Coutts and Company's Bank.

SEELY, Maj-Gen John Edward Bernard.
On completing active service, Seely was appointed Deputy Minister of Munitions and on January 11th 1919 he became Under-Secretary of State for Air, and later vice-president of the Air Council. It was his initiative that pressed through the Air Navigation Bill during the second half of February, a measure that paved the way for civilian flying to become legal on April 1st After a very busy and fruitful year in office. he resigned on November 12th 1919 (due to an internal wrangle over the Air Ministry's – and hence Winston Churchill's – anomalous attitude regarding the exclusion of the Admiralty's involvement with the Secretary of State both for War and Air) to be replaced, mid-December, by Maj G C Tryon. His appointment proved to be short-lived for, following a post-Easter (1920) Air Ministry re-arrangement, he was swiftly moved sideways to the Pensions department and the Marquess of Londonderry (Sir Charles Stewart Henry Vane-Tempest-Stewart) took over as Under-Secretary of State for Air.

Maj-Gen J E B Seely

SPOONER, Stanley.
Born in Rosherville, Kent, in 1855, Stanley Spooner was one of the most influential writers over the burgeoning days of aviation yet today he is largely forgotten. When on April 3rd 1940 he died in his 85th year in University College Hospital, London, his obituary in the magazine that he founded contained the sentence: 'a man who believed in aviation at a time when few shared his views, and who lived to see the vindication of his faith.' In 1896 he started a motoring journal named *The Automotor Journal and Horseless Vehicle,* later shortened to

Stanley Spooner

Automotor Journal, then *Auto.* From around 1900 onwards, *Auto* began to take an interest in flying and for several years had an aviation section. Through his friend Griffith Brewer (the aviation inventor and patent agent), Spooner kept in close contact with the aviation world and its personalities from the Wright Brothers onwards. In 1908 Spooner believed the time was right to create a separate aviation magazine and, inspired by the success of the monosyllabic 'Auto', chose the name *Flight.* This drew a caustic response from Claude Johnson, then managing director of Rolls-Royce Ltd. 'My dear Stanley' he wrote, 'How in the world can you think of wasting your time and your money on a flying paper beats me. Obviously flying can never amount to anything serious'. Spooner went ahead and, with his own money, launched the first issue of *Flight* on January 2nd 1909. The magazine went from strength to strength, achieving its greatest days in the 1930s and war years. Spooner, never quite on the same level as the younger, more outspoken and flamboyant 'CGG' of rival magazine *The Aeroplane,* was nevertheless an excellent journalist, contemporary historian, commentator and, above all, debunker of that form of rubbish frequently spouted under the guise of parliamentary debate. Spooner, never the man of the moment, was a quiet and observant man who, though of a personality that tended to keep him from the limelight so openly courted by his younger rival, wielded a pen that was both powerful and tempered with wisdom and devotion to his beloved world of aviation. In 1934, he sold the magazine to his friend Lord Iliffe and retired, vacating his chair in favour of the quietly-spoken Danish-born Carl Marcus Poulsen. Stanley Spooner is remembered fondly by the older generation of aviation buffs as a gentleman first and foremost, and an 'elder statesman' in an industry that he enjoyed seeing develop around him. What charisma he may have lacked (when compared to 'CCG') he more than made up for by his mature ability to focus and pronounce on his subject when others were 'unable to see the wood for the trees.'

SYKES, Maj-Gen Sir Frederick Hugh.
Chief of the Air Staff at the end of the War, Sykes (*b.* July 23rd 1877; *d.* September 30th 1954) held office as Controller-General of Civil Aviation between the Armistice and 1922 under Prime Minister David Lloyd George. He learned to fly in 1911 gaining Royal Aero Club Aviators' Certificate No 95 on a Bristol biplane. In April 1918 he had succeeded Sir Hugh Trenchard as Chief of the Air Staff. He survived the first-ever commercial aircraft crash on May 3rd 1919: AT&T's Airco DH.9 H9273 (G-EAAD) fell to the ground taking off from Kenley en route for Paris killing pilot 20-year old Capt E Middleton Knott. A popular man, as first director of civil aviation his watchword was that Britain must foster, not force, civil aviation. Much of the legislation he was instrumental in creating formed the basis of subsequent international air law. When Lloyd George was succeeded by Bonar Law as PM, Sykes' future in politics was already proven – and secure, not just from his record of achievements but because, on June 3rd 1920, he had married Isobel, daughter of Law who, at that time, was Leader of the House of Commons.

Maj-Gen Sir Frederick Sykes

TRIBE, Maurice O.
Company secretary to The Aircraft Disposal Company Ltd and, later, ADC Aircraft Ltd. Nothing is known of his background or achievements, let alone subsequent career after ADC.

Chapter 1

War and the Demand for the Mass-Production of Aeroplanes

THOSE far-off skies of the early twentieth century were to become the hunting grounds of the pioneers. From the time that the Wright Brothers first flew in a powered heavier-than-air machine, progress was extremely rapid as Man achieved the unlikely goal of emulating the birds. Man could now fly! Even so, by the start of 1910 aeroplanes and their engines were still largely experimental. They were also in short supply because they were all hand-built one at a time.

This did not hamper the growth of the aviating bug for there seemed no shortage of people that wanted to learn to fly. From ones and twos, the numbers grew. By December of that year the Royal Aero Club had issued 36 Aviator's Certificates and the Aero Club de France a further 14 to British flyers making a total of 50 licensed flyers. During 1911, the number of licences would rise to 168.

From earliest times, flying schools, such as they were, had to be adept at rebuilding their own aircraft, in many cases building them from both scratch and scrap. Original identities blurred and bits of one machine were used to keep another in the air, a practice that occasionally produced a curiously original outcome. It was a rich period of recycling as typified by Hendon's Hall School of Flying which continually repaired and replaced so many bits of its aircraft that the end result was a 'wholly-new' machine that consisted of Caudron wings and a fuselage created from other bits and pieces.

Professional aircraft manufacturers, such as they were, consisted of little more than those experimenters who had built and successfully flown an aircraft to their own design. Once they had been asked to make one like it for a friend or customer, they became 'manufacturers'. Still, however, aeroplanes were hand-made one at a time. The 'aeroplane factory' was no more than a glorified barn often with an earth floor.

On top of this there were the products of the experimenters. Generally, but not exclusively, this faction of the burgeoning business of flying comprised the young well-to-do blades that gained their money by that most satisfactory, remunerative and least labour-intensive of methods – inheritance. Some were mere Public School-educated croquet-playing frivolities or university rowing-eight drop-outs: others were deadly serious, extremely poor, and took their self-induced responsibilities extremely seriously. Flying may have been the province of the well-heeled, but there were a few good and solid impecunious visionaries who gambled what little money they had on possible success but mostly had to accept failure. If the flying side was sometimes seen as the province of the Hooray Henrys, then the hard work and innovation was the product of devotion and associated poverty and hardship.

Up and down the country these were the ones that never quite made the history books as aviators, yet still they designed and constructed flying-machines. The bitter disappointment that followed attempts at flight generally did not diminish their enthusiasm and only sometimes their Bank-balances. These were aircraft-builders even if their handiwork was denied the opportunity to prove itself in the skies.

Between 1910 and 1914 there were growing numbers of 'private aircraft' and makers such as Grahame-White and Bristol, not to mention Bl'eriot, Farman and the brothers Voisin, offered to build aeroplanes for sale to intrepid individuals or anybody else who wanted one. There was, as some customers learned to their cost, no guarantee that these confections would or even could fly. And the newly established flying schools that were springing up were turning out 'trained' aviators, complete with licence, on a daily basis.

Even in the face of so many licensed flyers, this scarcely-regulated, unbridled sort of flying can hardly be considered as

A more unlikely-looking civilian aircraft than the SE.5A would be hard to find, yet the Aircraft Disposal Company successfully traded every one of the military examples on its books, virtually all to foreign air forces. Its civilian conversions, as we shall see elsewhere, were less successful other than for skywriting. Note the style of marking the serial number: when expressed in a single line, the letter was separated from the numerals by a dart-shaped apostrophe. The wrinkled finish of the fuselage fabric on this Farnborough-built example is due to the lacing which seldom managed to look neat yet did allow the quick removal and replacement of the covering for service and repair.

One of a batch of 100 SE.5A aircraft built by Wolseley Motors of Birmingham in 1918, F904 was among the last new aircraft to enter service. It is seen powered by a 200 hp Hispano-Suiza engine. Because the aircraft is trailing pennants from its interplane struts this suggests that it was the machine of a flight leader. Total production of the type was an astonishing 5,205 of which at the time of the Armistice 1,407 were in store with several hundred others with various contractors.

representative of a properly organised aviation movement. But before the pre-war British experimentalists could progress to the point where they had produced a practical flying machine, events dictated that they all enrolled into the Government war-machine for the collective good of the nation. Thanks to the enthusiastic pioneering work of Cody and others, military experimentation had been proceeding since as early as 1910 through the endeavours of the Army Balloon Factory at Farnborough.

While the numbers of military aircraft had increased by 1913, they were still pretty few in all. The Army, still horsebound in combat, had difficulty in seeing any possible military purpose in flying machines. Balloons, on the other hand, were thought invaluable as observation points in the sky, and the Army had unshakeable faith in them as an indispensable aid to manoeuvres. Thoughts that might have united the concepts of gunfire and sitting ducks were not allowed, save by the poor junior ranks encouraged to drift over enemy lines displaying the same degree of invisibility as a Day-glo red tent parked in the snow.

When the First World War, also known as The Great War (historically 'the War to end all Wars'), broke out in 1914, the Royal Flying Corps had more vehicles than aircraft, with 95 of the former and 63 of the latter. It also had 105 officers. By comparison, the German air force could muster at least 260 aircraft. The British may have ridiculed 'Kaiser Bill' and the pointed tin helmets of the aristocracy that ran the German armed forces, but they proved more astute than we did in detecting a military value to aviation very early on. We were still using spherical hydrogen-filled observation balloons while the growing German air might was being methodically established as a combat force.

In terms of progress and development in aviation, it was always believed that Britain captured an early lead over the French leaving Germany some way behind both nations. It is now clear that this was incorrect and the belief in (and acceptance of) such a proposition was a crucial blunder in the politics of war. In terms of sheer numbers, Germany had the superior air force. To begin with, we were totally unprepared for practical aerial combat. We were also blissfully unsure what to do with aeroplanes in time of war if – and when – we actually had them.

Not for the first time would Britain be found lacking in resources. As the war progressed, the value (more likely no more than usefulness) of aircraft on the front line increased. As battle-line observers and gunnery direction-finders they could do things that most men on horse-back were not quite so good as. And once aircraft came to be employed in the serious business of shooting, bombing and killing, everybody metaphorically grasped the nettle in both hands. And everybody wanted aircraft.

At the start of the war in August of 1914, the deficit in our entire field of armament was embarrassing to say the least. Our anodyne Prime Minister, Herbert Henry Asquith, took a studied but totally indifferent approach to armament elsewhere than in the hands of the ground-based British Army and its gas-filled observation balloons. Consequently, and amidst the widely-held belief that the conflict would 'be over by Christmas', little was done to alleviate the situation. Indeed, politicians (the majority of them) thought any such action quite unnecessary and therefore unjustified.

The beginning of 1915 brought the gradual realisation that the war might last

Royal Aircraft Factory Farnborough SE.5 A8907 was one of the first production aircraft built in March 1917 for delivery to No 56 Sqdn at London Colney before being taken over to France. This shows the early 'glasshouse' canopy of the semi-enclosed cockpit as well as the gravity tank on the port upper wing root. The curious form of the early Service serial number shows the arrowhead apostrophe inserted after the letter 'A' when it was displayed in one line. The aircraft was designed by Henry Philip Folland, John Kenworthy and Maj Frank Widenham Goodden. Goodden, born in Pembroke in 1889, was head of the Experimental Flying Department at the Royal Aircraft Factory, and lost his life in an air accident on January 28th 1917. Kenworthy went on to join the Aircraft Disposal Company in 1923 as chief designer.

longer than the pundits had postulated and that unless we improved our position, the unthinkable could happen and Great Britain might just lose out to the enemy. Industry slowly got into its stride and began turning out more guns and shells, increasing numbers of rifles, wagons and lorries, as well as ships and aeroplanes.

At the point when War was declared, the British aircraft industry consisted first and foremost of the Government's establishment at Farnborough, known rather regally as the Royal Aircraft Factory (*see* picture on page 55). This was the preferred source of aeroplanes as far as Government, the armed services – and the Civil Service – was concerned. Like most things official, it was over-staffed, expensive – and not very efficient.

Parallel to this aeronautical oligarchy (despite its efforts it was not quite a 'closed shop'), were the private or independent makers who were disparagingly referred to by the bureaucrats of the Army, Navy, and Government as 'the Trade'. They comprised just nine reasonably well known names – A V Roe & Company Ltd; Sopwith Aviation Company Ltd; Handley Page Ltd; British and Colonial Aeroplane Company Ltd (later to become The Bristol Aeroplane Company Ltd); Grahame-White Aviation Co Ltd; Blackburn Aeroplane and Motor Co Ltd; Aircraft Manufacturing Co Ltd; Martin and Handasyde Ltd; and Short Brothers Ltd.

As well as these there were the armament firms of Vickers Ltd and Coventry Ordnance Works Ltd. Others of then-lesser importance included the boat-builders J Samuel White Ltd and S E Saunders Ltd along with a dozen or more minor constructors such as Hewlett and Blondeau Ltd, White and Thompson Company Ltd, H J Mulliner Ltd, Pemberton Billing Ltd, or the foreign licensees, the British branch of Blériot Ltd and the British Caudron Company Ltd.

The total labour force amounted to barely 1,000 men. Within a short space of time the workforce was doubled as were the number of makers. However it was only the Royal Aircraft Factory at Farnborough which had widely ranging design and construction experience plus the ability to tackle aerodynamic and structural problems in a scientific manner.

After just five months of war, tremendous endeavour and recruitment in the industry had resulted in fewer than 200 landplanes and 50 seaplanes being built. Of that total about 60 ought to be regarded as experimental. Yet it was already clear that aircraft would be needed 'in hundreds and scores of hundreds'[1] unless victory was surprisingly and quickly attained. As time wore on it was clear this was not going to happen.

Prior to the outbreak of war, the attitude of the Government was anything but air-minded and displayed little respect for our own industrial ability. Consequently it had considered it adequate to do no more than keep the British aeroplane and aero-engine 'Trade' ticking over with minimal orders.

Demonstrating an irresolute lack of faith in our national aptitude, Government nurtured the belief that if there was any emergency then the already-strong, well-established French aircraft industry could satisfy all of our needs. After all, France had real aeroplane factories rather than mere scattered collections of sheds.

Sir Walter Raleigh, in the first volume of *The War in the Air*, describes what ensued:

> In October 1914 a Flying Corps officer was sent to Paris to organize a department to deal with purchase of French aircraft supplies. The Paris office, which dealt through the French Ministry of War, became known as the British Aviation Supplies Department, and in December a representative joined the Department to watch the interests of the Naval Air Service and place orders on behalf of the Admiralty Air Department. The Paris office did not work smoothly. From the outset the War Office and Admiralty representatives were, by nature of their different allegiance, in competition. Each was there to get all he could for his own Service, and the consequent friction led to disappointments which, because many of the high performance aeroplanes used by the RFC were French, had repercussion in the field. The result was that Maj-Gen Trenchard [at that time Lt-Colonel at Farnborough with the task of building up the strength of the Royal Flying Corps] found it essential to make many personal visits to the French firms, accompanied by the Flying Corps representative in Paris. French manufacturers were in no real position to meet British demands, but were themselves in need of essential materials which we could supply, such as steel in the raw and treated, aeroplane cable, ball-bearings, and Davis guns. The matter therefore became one of bargaining, or, to use a more polite word, of reciprocity.

Despite the snub from high places, British manufacturers were commendably wiser. They knew that they could meet whatever challenge the war was to set for them and they struggled to gather the left-over crumbs from the French contracts. In their bulldog way, the companies were steadily overcoming difficulties and expanding to meet the envisaged demands. As Penrose (*op.cit*) highlights, their outlook was ably expressed by that great automobile engineer and aeronautical theorist,

Dating from the beginning of the War, this 1914-era RE.7, 2400, was built by the Siddeley-Deasy Motor Company Limited and was powered by a 150 hp RAF.4A engine. This two-seater was allocated to the Machine Gun School at Hythe. Some 250 examples were built at a cost of £1,886 10s for the airframe and £836 for this particular make of engine (six different engines were to be installed in the type). Thoroughly outmoded by the Armistice, none survived into surplus disposal.

1. Penrose *[24]*, p.10.

Built by Sir W G Armstrong Whitworth & Co Ltd at Gosforth, these RE.8 aircraft served in Mesopotamia in 1917 and Palestine in September of 1918. Some 4,077 examples were built of which more than 1,900 survived the War. Generally speaking, these were too obsolete for extensive civilian use and the majority were reduced to produce at Hendon and Waddon. The complete airframe, less armaments, cost £1,232; the RAF.4 engine £836 or the Hispano-Suiza £1,040.

Frederick William Lanchester (1868-1946), who in the 1914 Christmas issue of *Engineering* had written:

> The supremacy of British aircraft can only be maintained by the adoption of a thoroughly progressive constructional policy, guided constantly by the most recent scientific discovery in research and by utilizing to the full information and experience gained in the Services. The day is past when technique or craftsmanship can be permanently bottled, and the trade or art in question monopolized by any single nation, as was at one time the case. Under present-day conditions the lead can only be obtained and held by mobility and progress in which the motive power is a combination of brains, energy, and material resources.

Typical of such progressive outlook was the Aircraft Manufacturing Company which had been constructing a pusher fighter designed by Geoffrey de Havilland on the basis of the FE (Fighter Experimental) design developed at the Royal Aircraft Factory from his privately built and ultimately successful second biplane. Instead of receiving the 100 hp Green for which it had been redesigned, de Havilland was brusquely told in December that all these engines were diverted to the twelve FE.2a escort fighters at that time nearing completion at the Royal Aircraft Factory, Farnborough. Instead he was offered a 70 hp Renault. As it was only just sufficiently powerful for experimental flights, DH reluctantly fitted this heavy engine to the DH.1 nacelle. This typified the official way of dealing with what was still disparagingly known as 'the Trade'.

There was clearly a need for dramatic expansion in aircraft building. That this need quickly came to be met marked one of the more extraordinary manufacturing achievements of the Great War. The success of the transition from apathy to a nation capable of both defending and attacking from the air can be measured by the fact that at the end of the war in 1918 the aircraft industry employed some 350,000 people and had a production capability of more than 32,000 aircraft per year: in 1918 it delivered an average of 2,668 aircraft per month giving the new Royal Air Force a combat strength of 2,630 aircraft by the middle of that year.

First we should go back to 1917, a grim year as regards losses on all sides. Regarding German air force losses, it was reported in the *Daily Chronicle* at the end of November 1917 that:

> '...the 100 machines per month destroyed by the French, and those similarly disposed of by the British, are far from neutralizing the output of German factories, and the importance of Allied superiority in this essential arm of modern battle remains.'

What the paper could not reveal was the tremendous numerical increase in British aircraft produced during 1917. The Air Board had good cause for congratulation for at last British production fully matched anything the Germans could do. From an average of 50 aircraft a month in the first six months of war, deliveries in 1917 would total almost 30,000. Single-seat fighter production had increased every week of the year, from 893 in the first quarter, to nearly 2,000 in the next, 3,000 in the next, and over 4,000 in the last quarter, giving a tremendous total of 10,000 of which many were being destroyed in fighting or through accidents.

Two-seat construction was nearly twice as great, achieving nearly 19,000. Seaplanes,

Farnborough's Royal Aircraft Factory should have learned that an aircraft destined to serve as a fighter had to possess the degree of manoeuvrability only possible with a design that did not court inherent stability. While this was a noble characteristic of the BE.2c when employed on reconnaissance and observation, it was a positive hindrance in a dog-fight. Discovered too late to change significantly, the RE.8 entered large-scale production in 1917 and 1918 as a flawed design that would be withdrawn at the end of the war and scrapped. It was one of the first machines to be used in supercharging with the RAF.4 engine as early as 1916. Cockney rhyming slang directed that the RE.8 was known to pilots and ground-crew as the 'Harry Tate' after the contemporary popular music-hall artist (real name Ronald Hutchinson, born 1872, killed in an air-raid 1940). B5106 was built by Daimler at Coventry in late 1916.

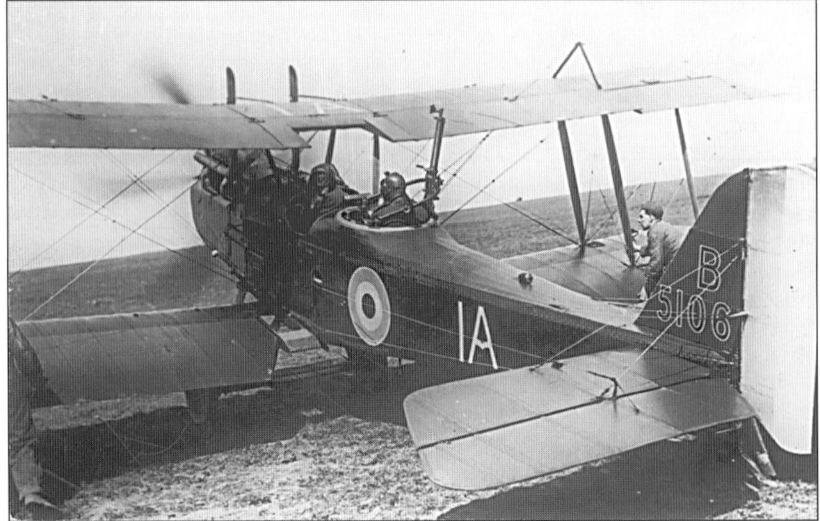

Above: The Vickers FB.9 was one of a short-lived breed of curious designs generated by this maker that were characterised by having tailplanes of far greater chord than the main wings. Used predominantly for training, only about 50 were built of 95 serial-number allocations. This example is one of possibly two that were fitted with a non--standard, lengthened nose and a 110 hp Le Rhône engine. None survived the end of the war.

Below: Another Vickers design of obsolescent appearance was the FB.26 dating from the winter of 1917-18. A strutted pusher, it had the refinement of a fully-cowled 200 hp Hispano-Suiza inline engine and incorporated a special triple Lewis gun-mounting firing through the nacelle nose. This was designed by Capt Leon Ernst Eeman at Orfordness. The prototype (it is thought only three were ever built) is remembered for being the machine in which Harold Barnwell (brother of the Bristol Aeroplane Company's Capt Frank Barnwell) lost his life. Here is a rare view of B1484 displaying its curious fuselage side truss vertical struts with their streamlined fairings. Although all three examples saw service, none is known to have survived after the Armistice. Eeman, incidentally, is remembered for the immense improvement in fire-power achieved by his invention of uniting three machine guns to one sight and one trigger. First tried on a Martinsyde Elephant, the Eeman principle was adopted too late in the War for it to have any major influence. In 1919 Eeman patented a novel system of hinged or pivoting floats for seaplanes to reduce the 'hammering' associated with choppy water.

with their more localized demand, were a long way behind with 910 completed, supported by 147 new flying-boats. Only 30 twin-engined bombers had been built by Christmas, most of them in the latter part of the year. Giving scale to the unremitting endeavour in designing aircraft of better and better performance [Penrose, *op.cit*] were 69 experimental machines, of which 25 were completed in the last quarter, including a major redesign of the BR.1 Camel to accommodate the larger diameter BR.2 engine: this was the Sopwith 7F.

Speaking in the House of Commons on April 25th 1918, and being careful not to quote sensitive information that might be useful to the enemy, the Minister of Munitions Mr Winston Churchill told Parliament:

> In 1917 the principal great new task which was entrusted to the Ministry of Munitions in 1917 was the construction of aeroplanes and aeronautical appliances of all kinds. Since that date we have delivered more than twice as many aeroplanes as have ever been made before. We are now making in a single week more than we made in the whole of 1914. We are now making in a single month more than we made in 1915. We are making in a single quarter more than we made in 1916, and we are going to make this year several times what we made last year.[2]

This enormous expansion in production, described by Churchill in the same speech as 'the geometric progression... of the supply is most impressive when viewed in figures', was largely due to the efforts of one man, Sir William Weir. Churchill described him as 'a man with war intuitions of a very high order, a man... to express the swiftly changing war conceptions which a Service like this provides in terms of a great and expanding mechanical supply'. Weir, later Lord Weir, was to have a distinguished career in aviation and to play a significant part in the development of the Cierva Autogiro.[3] The only blot on this otherwise unblemished service to aviation was his misguided backing (and consequent ordering into mass-production) of the truly awful ABC Dragonfly engine – a scenario that might just have cost us the outcome of the War.

The years had brought with them a softening of official attitude to makers other than the RAF at Farnborough and the wider spread of contracts had paved a solid path to the crucial mass-production that war demanded.

The phenomenal expansion first shown in 1917 and continued into 1918, was realised by two different strategies that were independent of the resources of the established aircraft manufacturers. First was the sub-contracting of aircraft manufacture to a large number of suitable businesses that hitherto had not been involved with aviation but had the necessary skilled workforces to adapt easily. Among these were piano-makers, organ-builders, boat-builders, shop fitters and cabinet-makers. The second stratagem was the creation of the National Aircraft Factories.

One has to remember that by 1917 the war had settled into a pattern of steady attrition and there seemed no immediate end in sight. Merely sustaining the war, quite aside from winning it, demanded the continual input of ever more resources in manpower and equipment. It was the classic stalemate situation from which every possible resource, human and material, continued to drain away remorselessly.

News of the creation of the National Aircraft Factories came in the summer of 1917 as a means of meeting the hugely-enhanced Service demands. The

2. *Flight*, May 2nd, 1918, p.489.
3. Ord-Hume *[22]*, p.552.

The FE.9 was designed in 1916 probably as a replacement for the FE.2b as a two-seat fighter-reconnaissance aircraft powered by the 200 hp Hispano-Suiza engine. A curious transitional machine – it had a neat oleo--sprung undercarriage and an SE.5-style pivoting tail-skid that was rudder-governable – the FE.9 had massive ailerons on its top wings, these demonstrating a large overhang from the shorter-span lower wings. The prototype, seen here, was A4818 (written as A'4818) and of the 27 machines ordered, only three were completed. Here, then, was one design that never made the post-war surplus market.

Government had approved a War Office recommendation that the Royal Flying Corps should increase its strength from 108 operational squadrons to 200. This would call for the mass-production of aeroplanes on a scale never before attempted in Britain. That was on July 2nd 1917.

For the Ministry of Munitions this posed an apparently insuperable problem for existing manufacturing facilities were already operating at their maximum ability. The only option was to create fresh factory premises of such an enormous scale that present production capacity could virtually be doubled. Whatever measures could be taken had to be achieved in a time-period of a mere few months.

By October plans had been detailed for the setting up of three vast new production facilities for which a budget of £1,500,000 was agreed. This was to involve the construction of brand-new plants at Croydon, Liverpool and Richmond (Surrey). The Liverpool site was adjacent to the Aintree Racecourse and the Croydon one was at Waddon. In each case, a deciding factor in the choice of site was the proximity to a main railway line. Crucially, the three factories were to be finished and equipped within an eight month time-span and the production target from each factory was 200 aircraft per month, a target to be achieved within the shortest possible time after commissioning.

As it turned out, the availability of a partly-built factory of suitable size at Heaton Chapel, Manchester, meant that this was substituted for the Richmond site and no other Surrey factory was built.

The Croydon factory – National Aircraft Factory Number One – was to be erected close to the existing RFC/RAF aerodrome at Beddington on virgin farm-land on the west side of Coldharbour Lane, later to be renamed Purley Way. This was to be the National Aircraft Factory flying ground and would be known as Waddon Aerodrome. A particular benefit of the site was that it was close to the London Brighton & South Coast Railway (later re-named the Southern Railway) from which a spur could be laid with factory sidings for the transport of material and components.

The Air Board gave its approval to the project on September 16th and four days later building contractors Holland, Hannen & Cubitt Ltd took over the 240-acre site. After a frenzy of surveying, just four days later the first turf was cut. By November 12th 1917 the contractors had prepared the factory area and begun construction. Despite a particularly hard winter, they completed the task on time just eight months later.

By a curious and seemingly rash Government decision, the contractors that built the factory were also appointed to run it. Although as building contractors one could not fault Messrs Holland, Hannen & Cubitt Ltd, and while they had carried out some sub-contract work for the Ministry (they produced bomb-fuses), the business possessed no manufacturing experience when it came to the matter of 'finished goods' Similarly they had no aircraft manufacturing experience. It was to be an extremely steep learning curve.

What would come to be known as NAF No.1 comprised more than fifty separate buildings besides the main factory building and totalled almost 650,000 square feet of covered area. There was no 'official' completion for as each structure was completed it was equipped and occupied.

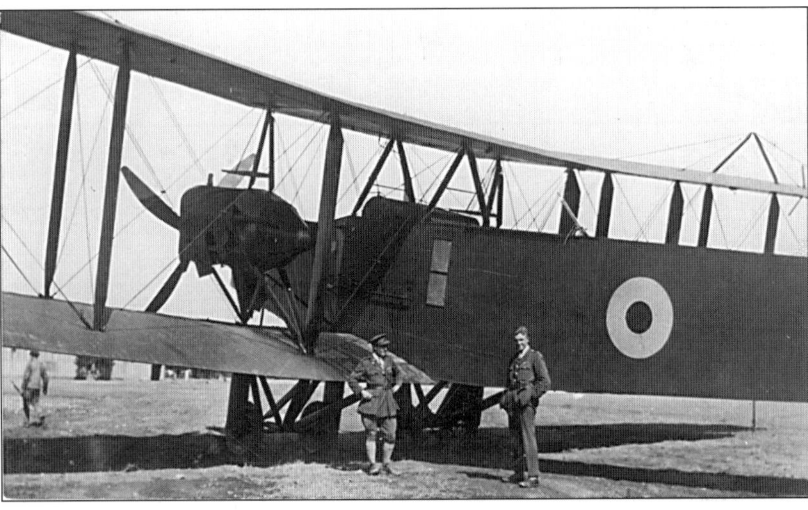

Handley Page O/400 heavy bombers like this were to make up the first generation of civilian airliners but even so a number of these bombers existed on the books of The Aircraft Disposal Company. The engines seen here are the 320 hp Rolls-Royce Mark III, later to be named Eagle.

Constructed by the British Caudron Company Ltd, D8345 was one of a 50-strong batch of Handley Page O/400 heavy bombers. At the end of the war a number of these went to Waddon for disposal although Handley Page Transport Ltd obtained the best examples for its own airline use.

The first was in production by January 15th 1918. By late summer the full plant was up and running.

An examination of the quantity-surveyor's tally reveals just how big the project was. Five million bricks, a quarter of a million square feet of glass, 2,000 tons of steel, 90,000 feet of timber – and half a mile of twin railway track!

Fifty-eight days after commissioning the first building – March 14th 1918 – the first complete aircraft (an Airco DH.9) was handed over to the Director-General of Aircraft Production, bluff 51-year-old Scot, Sir William Weir (later The Rt Hon the Lord Weir of Eastwood). It was then flown away by Capt Franklyn Leslie Barnard.

The 1914-18 war laid to rest two of the accepted 'traditions' of aircraft-building. The first of these bastions of the art was that aeroplanes were always hand-made, and the second was that they were always hand-made by experts. These two maxims went out with the needs of the time which quickly altered all that.

The adoption of production machining during the war was no vast new leap into the unknown for precision woodworking machinery had been around for many years. It had first come to the notice of the curious during the building of the Crystal Palace in 1851 when millions of feet of timber glazing bar was accurately spindle-moulded and shaped to precisely the correct form and length by steam-powered forming tools.

The most precise woodworking machinery, however, was to be found in the manufacture of keyboard musical instruments, in particular the harmoniums and reed organs popular in the late Victorian homes. These instruments with their highly-complex labyrinths of windways precisely cut in hardwood were produced on largely automated production lines first in the United States of America during the 1870s and then in Britain, France and Germany by the turn of the century.

It was this type of machinery, still, in the majority of instances, driven by steam or water power, that brought the first automation into aircraft factories at the time of the First World War. Routing and shaping wing spars and struts was, by comparison, a straightforward operation. Metal-working was also a process in which mechanisation was just entering use. Automatic, screw-cutting and turret lathes were already well-established which the tools of the forge and casting-floor were already based on over a century of experience.

Sheet-metal handling and the fly-press likewise formed standard engineering shop workbench techniques while the weaving of highly flexible steel control cables and the extruding of cast wire (the so-called 'piano-wire') marked industrial processes refined in the late Victorian years.

As regards the craftsmen-builders, aeroplanes, like boats, were built by skilled

Bristol F.2B Fighter Mk.II J6586 (275 hp Rolls-Royce Falcon III) was built by The British & Colonial Aeroplane Company, Bristol. It was actually post-war production but represented a then-more up-to-date version of aircraft that were being offered for sale at Waddon.

Around 160 Sopwith Triplanes saw War service, N5492 representing the type, yet curiously it was an aircraft never officially declared surplus and none is known to have civilianised. Even rarer is the Austin AFT.3 Osprey (bottom) designed to the same specification as the Sopwith Snipe. With many clever features including fully-interchangeable wings and simple construction for field repair, the triplane form imposed penalties of drag and made rigging complicated. Only one was built – X15 seen here.

labour but the Great War taught that unskilled labour, properly directed, might perform all but the most demanding operations provided that the design was completed with construction by unskilled production workers in mind from the beginning. This radical approach was begun at the Royal Aircraft Factory, Farnborough, where it was proved that women, seldom seen in any sort of factory at that time and then restricted to the mills and cloth-weaving industry, could be trained to build aircraft. During the First World War that alone was a demonstration of radical thinking.

Besides the expected 'soft' work of fabric-covering, sewing and stitching, doping and painting, women trained as welders, lathe-operators and wire-workers. By 1918, as more and more able-bodied and older men were called to the Front, women assumed a vital role in virtually every wartime commodity production. In the aircraft factories they accounted for more than 10 percent of the workforce in 1917, and 12 percent a year later.

Production of aeroplanes was one thing. Suitable engines for aircraft represented another. The story of engine development, production and availability was that of another crisis which Gen Sir Douglas Haig, Army commander in chief, had to resolve as part of his plans for increasing British air power.

> If the British aircraft industry was small in 1914, the aircraft engine industry did not exist. What there was of it in 1917 had grown up during three years of war, and now, when maximum demands were being made on it, it was short of materials and, above all, of skilled men. The three major manufacturers, Rolls-Royce, Sunbeam and Beardmore, were producing 600 engines a month: the expansion called for by Haig would need 2000 – and more powerful than any yet developed. The result was terrifying: a 90 per cent fault-rate on cylinder-block castings; inadequately-tested engines going straight into operational aircraft; and, worst of all, engines known to be faulty being put into aircraft regardless. Once again, the Admiralty's independent policy rebounded to their advantage, and to the country's: the 8000 French-built Hispano-Suizas which they ordered – against the advice of the Air Board –more than made up for the 1719 Sunbeam Arabs which the company failed to deliver in 1917.[4]

On April 1st the Royal Flying Corps became the Royal Air Force. The demand for aircraft was ever greater especially since the life expectancy of an aircraft in service was a maximum of eight weeks[5]. In that short time it might have been rebuilt up to three times in field workshops – special open-air encampments some distance back from the lines where crashed or damaged aircraft could be delivered by road, repaired and flown out to re-enter service as quickly as possible. But losses were mounting and deliveries from the factories were barely maintaining the numbers, let alone catering for the demands of continual expansion. Factories worked a regime that was quite new to Britain, namely 24-hour shifts six days a week with normal single-shift work on Sundays. And still the totals fell short of demand.

That summer turned out to be one of the bloodiest of the whole conflict. War-weariness had long since set in and both sides strove, in their different ways, for an early end to the conflict. The burden of War bore ever heavier on the ordinary people of Britain and Germany. A time was approaching where it might just prove too much... But it was Germany who cracked first. The capitulation of Germany came suddenly and with little warning. An Armistice was agreed. The Great War was effectively over.

And still the factories were turning out aeroplanes in ever-increasing numbers. They had to be stopped somehow – and quickly!

4. Popham, *[26]*, p.68-9.
5. Public Records Office, Kew, [Doc.AIR1/1139/204/5/2305]

Chapter 2

The Royal Flying Corps and the Royal Air Force

THE expansion of flying activities during the First War effectively marked a transition from the limited, restricted applications of 1914 to the widespread utilisation that characterised 1917 and 1918. To set the scene for what was to come we must look at what was happening with the fledgling Royal Air Force. The events of the immediate post-war years also had a significant bearing on much that followed.

The Royal Flying Corps had been formed as the result of a Government White Paper published on April 12th 1912. The new Service was divided into five sections – the Military Wing, the Naval Wing, Reserve, the Central Flying School and the Army Aircraft Factory. Initially seven squadrons, each having a strength of 12 aeroplanes, were set up. The whole enterprise was therefore administered in the main by the Army, with the Royal Navy to take command of the Naval Wing.

In June of 1914, the RFC Military and Naval wings were officially separated. The Admiralty announced the formation of the Royal Naval Air Service with its flying school at Eastchurch. War broke out the following month and the RFC's 63 small wooden aircraft flew across the Channel to France while their associated horse-borne transport infrastructure went by sea.

The RFC was thus seen at this time as a division of the British Army and to this end all staff carried Army ranks and initially dressed the same way. As a fighting aid, as distinct from a fighting part, the field of operations was clearly France where the battlefields were established. There was, it was believed, no need to keep fighting aircraft in Britain. This was a grave mistake for it denied Britain an aerial defence capability. Later it allowed Zeppelin raiders to drone across our skies without hindrance. The first bombing raids on British soil were conducted by these

The BE.2 design underwent a number of changes during its lifespan. It was also used in experiments some of which were rather curious. This early example pictured in May 1913 shows a somewhat agricultural style of undercarriage comprising independently-mounted forward skids combined with main wheels and legs fitted with oleo-spring compression. The manner in which the two components are linked using slender free-pivoted tubular-steel trusses that transfer all drag loads from the cross axle forward to the skid trusses is curious. Just as odd are the 'cuffs' attached to the upper portions of each interplane and centre-section strut. In an endeavour to increase the side area of this large but slender aircraft, aerodynamacist Edward Teshmaker Busk devised what he termed 'fin struts' to increase the side area of the aircraft by $4^{1}/_{2}$ square feet. Experience would show that this type of fragmented surface addition could be expected to contribute little more than 45 percent of the aerodynamic effect of one single or continuous surface. In other words, a fin adding two square feet of side area would have been more effective – and less than half that at the distance of the rudder from the centre of pressure would have been just as good. Busk, seen here in the cockpit, was killed on November 5th 1914 when the machine he was flying caught fire in the air. A note with this photograph says that this was the experimental aircraft, upgraded to BE.2c and numbered 601, in which he met his death at the age of 28 years.

No account of the BE.2c would be complete without reference to one of the most interesting of the many engine installations employed with this versatile if slow fighter. When the machine was used by the Belgians they powered it with the 150 hp Hispano-Suiza, an eight-cylinder upright 'V' engine. However, the cowling design chosen for this motor incorporated a flat circular radiator that economised in drag and complexity. The outcome was a curious radial-type cowling as seen here. Other changes made to Belgian aircraft included placing the pilot in the front cockpit and providing him with a synchronised Vickers gun firing forwards through the propeller. This change was also to give the gunner, now in the rear cockpit, a wider field of vision with his Lewis gun.

elephantine monsters of the air.

In June of 1917 and again the following month, German bombers penetrated our non-existent air defences and for the first time dropped bombs on London. In the public outcry that followed there was clamour for the establishment of a separate air defence force to protect us from attack from the skies. That November Parliament joined the public in demanding action to form a third Service. On February 21st 1918, Major J L 'Johnny' Baird, Under-Secretary of State to the Air Ministry, addressed the House of Commons and confirmed that an Air Force was to be created.

In June 1914 the prototype BE.2c took to the air for the first time at Farnborough. In the end, 1,793 examples were built of the style and, despite its grim reputation as being a sitting target for the enemy Fokkers, it gave a good account of itself. By October 31st 1918, though, only 474 remained on strength and it was in the main BE.2e models that were stacked, wingless, in rows down at Waddon. However, this picture shows one of the very first production BE.2c machines from 1914. It was described as having an unduly complicated structure and increasing simplification characterised the varieties that followed. Here, though, one can appreciate the complex cable bracing of the undercarriage and the cable-bracing (rather than streamlined or RAF-wires) of the wings. Because the thin wing-section was prone to flex in a dive, a curious inter-bay lift wire featured on this and other very early models: it extended outboard from the first bay forward interplane strut's base up to the front spar at the third rib position. It was once said that there was more bracing wire in this design than in the whole of the Bristol Boxkite – an assertion seemingly stemming more from a marked case of 'rigger's pique' than sober accuracy.

The announcement immediately brought forth an interesting exchange headed by that vociferous and sometimes cantankerous MP, the Member for Hertford East. This was none other than Noel Pemberton-Billing (1881-1948) who entered the House as an Independent. Pemberton-Billing was already well ahead in the aviation field having set up his own aircraft business as early as 1912. Under the leadership of the noted flyer and speedboat-racer Hubert Scott-Paine, this was later to become Supermarine. For the moment, though, Pemberton-Billing was bothered about engines. He began with a statement and followed it with a pointed question. 'The Germans have standardised on four types of engine with success while we have 'standardised' on 44 types without success; and will he see that the spare parts for these engines which are of no further use are not occupying the time of munition workers.' The answer from Baird was one of those time-honoured stock political retorts: 'I cannot confirm'!

Standardisation or otherwise, the Government had acted and in the Air Force Memorandum of March 1st it set out its 'Conditions of Service'. There was unease in military and naval camps as the die-hards saw no benefit to splitting a defence budget other than in two directions. But the

To many people, there is a strong visual similarity between the Armstrong Whitworth FK.3 and the BE.2c. The reason for this is not hard to find. Armstrong Whitworth was awarded one of the earliest production contracts for the BE.2c but when they received the manufacturing drawings from the Royal Aircraft Factory at Farnborough they described them as excessively complicated and not conducive to rapid production, adding the rider that they could design a better aeroplane to the same specification. Fortunately, they were taken up on their offer and Frederick Koolhoven schemed out the FK.3. In the end at least 500 were built and they subsequently excelled in the training role fitting in easily between the DH.6 and the BE.2c. It was, however, victim to the ultimate success of the Avro 504 which became the standard training aircraft. The aircraft cost £1,127 10s plus £522 10s for the RAF.1A engine. This example, B9554, was one of a batch of 300 built by Hewlett & Blondeau. Many survived the war to enter the surplus market while some came onto the Civil Register. Few, though, lasted more than one C of A but of these E D C Herne's 'fleet' based at Hendon completed a worthwhile joy-riding season at Porthcawl, Glamorgan. Edmund Donald Colrick Herne (*b.* October 13th 1889) was a most accomplished pilot later to make the first flights London-Berlin and London-Warsaw (January 1920). He was also a pioneering aerial photographer/mapper using an 80 hp Renault-powered Avro and is remembered as being the first pilot to complete two return flights to Paris in a day.

decision had been taken and The Royal Flying Corps and the Royal Naval Air Service amalgamated to form the Royal Air Force on April 1st 1918. For the Navy, many die-hard senior officers breathed a sigh of relief to be rid of the responsibility of flying-machines which were, to this unfortunate majority, very hard to justify in pure Naval terms.

This brought forth a most amusing letter from one of the well-known motor industrialists of the time – Frederick R Sims of Simms Motor Units Ltd, Rathbone Place, London. He wrote:

> Sir: I have just read that in future the Flying Services will be joined under the name Royal Air Force. This name is certainly a very good and forceful one, but why not 'Royal Airy' which would be synonymous to Royal Army and Royal Navy?'[1]

We should be thankful that Fred Sims' tongue-in-cheek words were appreciated as the satire he intended rather than the implication proposed!

When, less than eight months later, the end of the war came on November 11th, 1918, the new Royal Air Force had 30,122 officers, 263,410 other ranks and 33,000 aeroplanes. There followed a necessary halt to this growth followed by a dramatic reduction in size, strength and capability.

What would actually happen when the War ended had occupied the thoughts of many people as the conflict continued with seemingly little hope of short-term victory. So it was that *The Times* specifically addressed the aircraft industry and its prospects in its April 1918 Trade Supplement. In a compelling article by Bernard Isaacs under the title 'The Future of the Aircraft Industry', he stated that there was a general assumption that there would still be a 'heavy demand' for aircraft once the war ended. This popular belief he refuted asserting that there would be little demand for the first twelve months after the end of the war.

Significantly, Isaacs was the only one to forecast a 'temporary slump' in the fortunes of the aircraft industry. But did anybody take note of his words – anybody in industry perhaps? Even if they did, they made little in the way of plans for the uncertainty ahead. An understandable explanation was that they were all too busy with the War Effort and meeting ever-increasing production demands.

While 'the Trade' was left to look after itself, the Public Purse had to be secured before those inevitable awkward questions might arise.

First under scrutiny, then, was the Royal Air Force. Amidst a huge programme of Government cost-cutting, this great enterprise was not only mutilated – pruning is too gentle a word to describe what took place – but there was actually a scheme to abandon the Service altogether and again divide Service flying activities between the Army and the Admiralty.

There was a degree of notable dismay that such a dramatic proposal was quite widely welcomed. Alongside compelling arguments asserting that such absorption would lead to great spending economies, public opinion had clearly turned. Many of the very people who demanded an air force in 1917 now pressed for its abolition. This campaign for dissolution begun with the ending of the war and gained impetus over the next four years.

In every sphere, 'the war to end all wars' had had a profound effect on public feeling, but in 1919 the Cabinet formulated a 'rule' (for it was stronger than a mere devout belief) that there would be no major

1. *Flight,* March 28th 1918, p.356.

Top: The British Aerial Transport Co. Ltd of Willesden, better known as BAT, designed the FK.25 Basilisk as a fighter in 1918. Remarkably small – it spanned 25 ft 4 in – it was let down by its ABC Dragonfly engine. Claimed to be the fastest single-seater of the great War, only two were built.

Above: Specifically designed for use on ships, the Sopwith Camel 2F.1 had a two-piece fuselage and a wider centre-section. Powered by a 150 hp Bentley BR.1, armament was a single port-offset Vickers gun and a top-wing Lewis gun. Of 129 built, none seem to have reached surplus.

Right: Another lost fighter contender from the closing days of the war was Westland's Weasel. Another Dragonfly-driven fighter, only four were built.

The standard production BE.2c fitted with the air-cooled V-eight RAF.1A engine. The exhaust pipes tended to vary in length and position between various contract manufacturers and the sharp right-angle bend seen here is likely to have caused some not inconsiderable back pressure. The alternative would have been straight side pipes but these would have had to terminate behind the pilot's cockpit requiring almost three times as much steel manifold tube. This aircraft has painted on its side the legend *Presented by 'The Indian Nobles'*, the full meaning of which is no longer known.

Built in 1916, 9990 was one of a batch of 50 BE.2c aircraft built by Blackburn Aeroplane & Motor Co Ltd of Leeds whose logo is discernible on the fin. The engine is the 90 hp RAF. The Aircraft Disposal Company had a large number of this type on its books.

war for ten years. As the base-date for this assumption continually moved forward (until it finally expired in the early 1930s), the national goal was to reduce our warring capability. Others, more perceptively, saw it as the stripping away of our very ability to defend ourselves should, Heaven forefend, another conflict flare up.

The first task of the peace-seeking wreckers was to undo, dismantle, break up and return to grass all that only months before we had been labouring long and hard to develop, establish and consolidate.

The Fleet Air Arm passed back to an ambivalent Navy in the autumn of 1922 and this was viewed by many as the precursor of the inevitable end of a separate RAF. It was almost a foregone conclusion that the Army would demand an Army Air Force. The Royal Air Force, already reduced by ninety percent from its war-time strength, would thus have been left with a mere handful of expensive squadrons to maintain scattered about the world: remember that at this time we had important air force presence in places such as Egypt, Iraq and India.

It is today difficult to appreciate by how slim a margin the Royal Air Force survived during those immediate post-war years. Still unconsolidated and with its ranks borrowed from the Army, it preserved a makeshift atmosphere about it through to the end of the war. Now, as a Draconic programme of demobilisation was inflicted upon it, it seemed certain to be denied any possibility of *sui juris*. By the autumn of 1919, its 200 squadrons had been whittled down to just twenty-five-and-a-half.

Prime Minister Bonar Law appeared virtually certain to axe the fledgling Service and was supported in his judgment by many senior fellow politicians. The Royal Air Force's eventual salvation was the work of a minority campaign led by two of the most powerful supporters of aviation at a time when aviation seemed to have become a dirty word. These were 59-year-old Hugh, Viscount Trenchard (later Air Chief Marshal Sir Hugh Montague Trenchard) and 42-year-old Sir Samuel John Gurney Hoare. These two men faced their darkest hour in 1922/23 when it seemed inevitable that the RAF was at an end. Salvation came on June 20th 1923 with Cabinet approval to re-form the Service and increase its strength by creating 34 new squadrons and trebling its strength over five years.

As demobilisation of the new Service personnel continued, aircraft ordering was naturally non-existent. Disarmament had reduced the aircraft industry to so low a state that it needed years to recover. By 1922, the aircraft-manufacturing industry was frantically looking for work. Only 2,500 men and women remained in the aircraft industry and the few firms engaged on making aeroplanes and their engines were on the verge of closing down.

Sir Samuel Hoare told the House, during the Air Estimates debate on March 2nd 1923, that Britain had only sixteen first-line aeroplanes equipped and ready for home defence and that all our squadrons in India had been grounded for lack of spares: they had received no new engines for seven years and were forced to touring local bazaars to buy materials for patching up their obsolete equipment.

The eventual re-forming of the Royal Air Force on a peacetime basis was the major achievement of 1923. Even so, this was to be a monumental and costly task. Demobilisation had removed from the Service the majority of its mechanics and other engineering staff. Its pilots had gone back to civilian life and the whole structure of the Service had been undermined. The RAF had sold off most of its aerodromes for next to nothing and was now faced with having to buy them back at market prices.

It even had to buy back, at commercial prices, some of the aircraft it had disposed of as surplus just two and a half years earlier. But that was almost five long years since the end of the war. What had happened in the intervening time was a wholesale denuding of our aviation assets and incentives. This brief history of the events surrounding the Royal Air Force will help focus on the reasons for the extreme privations of the industry.

It is now necessary to return to the days that followed the signing of the Armistice and look at the aircraft production and manufacturing scene.

The BE.2e was immediately distinguished from the earlier models by the unequal-span single-bay wings and the revised tail. This example, C7001, was the first of a batch of 100 built in 1916-17 by Barclay, Curle & Company of Whiteinch, Glasgow. The engine is the 90 hp RAF.1A and the cowlings are notable for their neat appearance. Some of these aircraft were to end up as unlikely candidates for Waddon disposal after the War.

The eleventh month, the eleventh day and the eleventh hour! November 11th 1918 and the Great War was over!

To be strictly true, that was not quite the way it happened and it may come as a surprise to some today to learn that the First World War did not come to an end with the signing of the Armistice on November 11th, 1918. It is true that on that day all hostilities ceased but the word 'Armistice' means no more than a short truce. While the immediate effect was to stop all the fighting and bloodshed, Britain chose to keep her options open just in case anything went wrong.

As far as the general public was concerned, though, the war was at an end. But in the corridors of the War Office, the Armistice was merely a cooling-off period during which the enemy could be observed to see what he was going to do next. Because of this the armed services felt that they should remain alerted just in case hostilities were resumed.

Although both sides were only too willing to seize with both hands the chance to stop fighting, nobody actually said 'the war is over'. With the signing of the Treaty of Versailles between the allies and Germany on June 28th 1919, and that of Saint Germain by Austria on September 10th, the conditions imposed by the ten-month long Peace Conference in Paris were put in place. Yet still nobody actually said 'the war is over Perhaps it was all a bit of an anti-climax. France, however, decided on her own that loose ends needed tidying up, even if the British didn't think it necessary. Consequently France decided that October 23rd 1919 would be a good day to declare the cessation of its own hostilities with Germany.

The British government remained taciturn over such matters. It maintained parts of its defence system for a while to come. The anti-aircraft station next to the Serpentine in London's Hyde Park was still maintained in action state as late as November 1919 while the big military vehicle transport depot at Putney was not run down until more than a year after the Armistice had been declared. It was officially proclaimed that the war between Britain and Germany was at an end on August 31st 1921 – almost three years after the commonly accepted date.

It was this uncertainty over the immediate future that caused great problems in the defence manufacturing industry. The vast wartime aircraft production orders took

After the Porte/Felixstowe F.2A came the F.3 and the F.5, the prototype of which (F90) is pictured here. Never as popular as the earlier machine and constructed under the pressure of material limitations, the F.5 was introduced too late for operational service and, while retained in small numbers as the RAF's standard post-war flying boat and remaining in service until replaced by the Southampton in 1925, a number ended up for disposal in 1920.

Designed by the Air Department of the Admiralty in the autumn of 1915, the two-seater AD Flying Boat was intended for patrol duties. It was also one of the earliest to be designed, under Harris Booth, by Lt Linton Hope. The boat entered limited production in 1917 and some twenty-seven were built at a cost of £2,853 8s each plus £1,004 for the 200 hp Hispano-Suiza. This one, N1522, was one of a batch of ten built by Supermarine Aviation (then Pemberton-Billing Ltd) of which three became civilian Supermarine Channel Mk.I passenger boats. The Aircraft Disposal Company handled very large quantities of engines for these machines as well as spares.

a while to cancel. Some were more or less cancelled immediately but others took a lot longer. The run-down in war production, in particular aircraft production, was undertaken in two stages and in conformity with two time-scales. Sub-contract work – work put out to specialised non-aircraft industry such as piano-makers[2] and shop-fitters – was summarily cancelled with immediate effect. Large contracts for completed aircraft were stopped 'with effect from a convenient point', generally interpreted as upon completion of whatever was already on the production line.

This was the reason why it took some while to slow down and stop the war machine. Inevitably, despite the provision for phased cancellation of work, much was scrapped save for finished aircraft upon which the Government would honour contract payments.

One of the diarists of the time was the renowned Theodore Stanhope Sprigg, later to become editor of magazine *Air and Airways* as well as *The Aeroplane* in post-Second World War years. Like Churchill and many others of his time, he relished in applying comparisons to the aircraft industry. He wrote:

> …the average monthly delivery of aeroplanes during the first 12 months of the war was 50 per month, whereas during the last 12 months of the war the average deliveries had risen to no less than 2,700 per month. By the date of the armistice the British aircraft industry's capacity of output had grown to approximately 3,500 complete machines per month.
>
> Altogether, no less that 73 different types of aeroplanes were used by the RFC and the RAF at home and overseas between August 1914 and October 1918, and the grand total of machines supplied during that period amounted to approximately 39,592 exclusive of aircraft used by RNAS units, prior to the formation of the RAF.[3]

If stopping the construction of aeroplanes was one thing, stopping the production of components presented another problem. Items such as sparking plugs, magnetos and fuel-pumps were batch-produced by the thousand and inevitably huge stocks were allowed to accumulate before Whitehall could move in to stop them.

So what happened at Waddon's National Aircraft Factory Number One? Well, the factory had been completed on time and work begun but, as related in Cluett *[4]*, all was not exactly right. The demand to get into production quickly meant that non-economic methods had been introduced and the continuing clamour for more production had allowed neither the time nor opportunity to revise these methods. On top of that, although the workers were apparently paid above-average wages, there were continued labour disputes resulting in strikes.

None of the National Aircraft Factories proved economical in any respect. Each was a huge burden that never had the chance to break even. Had the war continued for several more years, then there might have

2. One of the principal London piano-makers, Broadwood, was approached by the War Office in August 1915 to manufacture 4-bladed aircraft propellers, complete in transport case, at £33 7s each. In due course, the firm also made Maurice Farman fuselages and skids. By May 1917, Broadwood (which was already well in with Airco as a principal supplier) began making DH.4 and DH.6 fuselages. In November 1917 an order was received from Airco for 100 DH.9 fuselages and this was followed by further DH.9 contracts from the National Aircraft Factory No.1 (Cubitts) at Waddon. By March 1918 Broadwood had aircraft contracts worth £90,000 and the following month Airco put in an order for yet another development, the DH.9A 'complete with undercarriages, cowling, bomb cells &c @ £125 each'. The company's fleet of lorries was fully stretched ferrying completed aircraft parts to Hendon as well as Croydon. *See Broadwood by Appointment: A History,* David Wainwright, Quiller Press, London, 1982, pp.277-288.

3. T(heodore) Stanhope Sprigg: *'Veterans of the War',* article in *Air and Airways,* June 1932, pp.99-102.

The Norman Thompson Flight Company of Bognor Regis, Sussex, was established on October 4th 1915 out of the original White & Thompson Limited founded in 1909 by Douglas White and Norman Thompson. Its NT.2B flying boats were popular and ordered, by the RNAS, in such large numbers that the work had to be farmed out to other manufacturers for licence-building. This example, N2294, is fitted with a Sunbeam Arab engine having originally flown with a Beardmore. After the end of the war, Norman Thompson Company was bought out by Frederick Handley Page and closed down, the stock of 51 surplus machines being disposed of by the Aircraft Disposal Company. A curious feature of the NT.2B was that, in order to offset the increased torque of the larger engine, it had to be mounted several inches starboard of the centre-line.

been a chance for production to be rationalized. As it was it was a bitter and expensive lesson proved by the estimate[4] that the average price of military aircraft provided by 'private' aircraft manufacturers was £1,350 while each Bristol Fighter produced by NAF No.3 (at Liverpool) was estimated to have cost the taxpayer £5,000. If capital costs are added into the equation, then the cost of each aircraft produced by the NAFs may be doubled[5].

The concept of the NAFs was admirable but the reality was nothing short of disappointing. Jones[6] observes that:

> The excursion of the Government into the aircraft industry must, so far as it concerns the manufacture of aeroplanes, be written down as a failure... It is possible had the War continued into late 1919 or 1920 the National Aircraft Factories would have justified themselves in the matter of output, cost of production and general efficiency.

Although aviation was still a very young activity, the western world had been force-marched by War into leaping from the fragile, slow, temperamental and experimental fine-weather machines of pre-1914 days to the regime of tough, fast and largely dependable combat aircraft. Things official, however, always move at their own pace. Since before Nelson's time, Admiralty shipyards had managed to turn out vessels that cost the public purse more than those bought from private yards. For all their perceived efficiency and equipment, during the short existence of the NAFs they merely proved that private enterprise (the dreaded 'Trade') was, in the final analysis, both cheaper and more efficient.

Waddon's day of reckoning came on Saturday January 11th 1919. On that fateful day some 1,500 employees were dismissed while the 600 that remained had their wages reduced. The union shop steward, addressing a gathering of employees that had promptly marched on Croydon's Town Hall, told them:

> Two thousand of you have been chucked out of work when, at little expense, and with a little knowledge, the whole caboose of you could have been employed in making articles of a commercial and productive nature, remunerative to the State. But by trickery and subterfuge these factories are going to be handed over to private enterprise at little or no cost – the Government is going to create a further monopoly for vested interest.

The shop steward, a Mr E Miller, was probably not to know that similar speeches would be made up and down the country by his opposite numbers in countless factories as more and more labour was thrown on to the market. It was hard, but reality was staring everybody in the face. The factories and their production were not wanted. And, sadly, neither were their workers. Their products – the aeroplanes for which the nation had united to boost production – were no longer part of the equation.

4. Jones, H A: *The War in the Air,* Oxford, 1937, vol. 6.
5. *Op.cit.*
6. *Op.cit.*

The Porte/Felixstowe F.2A N4477 of 1917 was developed from the first Gosport-built flying boat to employ John Cyril Porte's revolutionary hull design. It actually started life as a Glenn Curtiss design ordered in 1915 and known as the Curtiss H.8 or 'Large America' powered by a pair of 160 hp Curtiss engines. Porte had the engines replaced by two 250 hp Rolls-Royce Eagle I engines and the aircraft became styled the Curtiss H.12. But the hulls were not seaworthy and leaked badly. Assisted by Lt (later Maj) John Douglas Rennie (later designer of Blackburn's series of flying boats). Porte redesigned the hull and the aircraft became the successful Porte/Felixstowe F.2. Later examples were fitted with the 346 hp Rolls-Royce Eagle VIII and revised tail units to become the F.2A. This faded, grainy picture from 1918 shows the broad shape of the hull and represents one of a number of machines that the Aircraft Disposal Company had on its books.

The Felixstowe F.2A with its wide hull was acclaimed as a successful and safe flying boat. Orders for 161 were placed in March 1918 but deliveries were delayed due to extreme shortage of the Rolls-Royce Eagle engines. At the end of the war, the Aircraft Disposal Company offered a number of these for sale. The example seen here has clearly met with an unfortunate accident and has been beached broadside on. The starboard underside of the hull has been stove in at the nose. This probably accounts for the emergency mooring ropes attached to the wooden propeller-blades.

Above: Norman Thompson NT.2B N2569 was delivered in December 1917 fitted with a 200 hp Hispano-Suiza engine driving a two-bladed wooden propeller. This was the standard production form of this interesting little flying boat seen here coming in to alight.

Left N4230 was the first of a batch of fifty Felixstowe F.3 flying boats to be built by Dick, Kerr & Company Ltd of Preston – one of four contractors to receive production orders in 1917. One of these machines was used in experiments with an 'automatic landing' device thought up by Maj Arthur Quex Cooper who is remembered for his involvement with the ill-fated Cooper-Travers Hawk Monoplane of 1924. A number of F.3 machines survived the war and ended up at Waddon.

Below: An advertisement from *Jane's All The World's Aircraft 1918.*

In the fullness of time, shop steward Miller's predictions regarding the Waddon factory would come true and in so doing adding fuel to the rising undertow of argument about 'taxpayers' money' and 'what about all this surplus stuff?'

There was an interregnum, fortuitously as it turned out, for the decision was taken to convert the great and still-new factory into a salvage operation where both completed aircraft and broken ones returning from France and elsewhere could be properly scrapped. The official parlance, still used to this day, is to 'reduce to produce'. It is less emotive than 'smash up', but the end result is the same. It entails removing everything that can be removed that may be of value and destroying the irreducible remainder. In the case of Waddon, it served to unfabricate a large number of aircraft. More or less finished aeroplanes went in one end and a pile of engines, instruments, metal parts, seats, turnbuckles and wire emerged from the other. It was nothing short of production-line dismantling.

The *Wallington Advertiser* for January 24th 1919 commented on the turn of events that had overtaken the great building. 'It was National Aircraft Factory No. 1 and one of the wonders of the neighbourhood. Now by a stroke of the pen, so to speak, it has fallen from its high estate to the comparatively lowly position of being the National Aircraft Depôt No. 3'. The paper omitted to record the most important word in the new title – one that was officially ensconced in parenthesis. The proper title was National Aircraft [Salvage] Depôt No. 3 and somehow had a slightly more humiliating ring to it than the title the newspaper used.

Chapter 3

Waddon and the National Aircraft Factory

WAR is an awesome event. On the homefront it is a disaster that, in 1914-18, was to touch almost every family in the land. On the battleground it robs generations of their successors. It does not discriminate between officers and men, or the sons of a nation: it takes the honest manual toiler alongside the cerebral genius, the practical mechanic with the advanced concept designer, the artisan with the artist, and the man on the Clapham omnibus alongside the political reformer.

The end is inevitably a pyrrhic victory within which the celebrations mix freely with the tears of grief.

But war is also an economic disturber. One day vast quantities of munitions are sought and supplied with fervour; the next they are unwanted, too new to be of any more use and insufficiently old (and far too numerous) to be curios. The accoutrements of war now become an embarrassment. The problem is that the conversion of swords into ploughshares is neither inevitable nor simple. You are left with enormous stocks of war merchandise that has been paid for by the National purse (meaning the taxpayer) and now you have to get rid of it all as best you may.

One key effect of the Great War, 1914 to 1918, was that the skills of aircraft design and the practice of aeroplane manufacture had been honed and fine-tuned. The outcome could be described as a gigantic leap for aviation.

Incidental to this, but nonetheless important, was that it had taught the whole nation (not just at home but in every major country of the world) that aviation was here to stay and that it was a reasonably practical method of emulating the birds. If people in general were still not quite sure as to what use aviation was other than for attacking the enemy in times of war, it paved the way to suggesting that Man could fly for purposes that might just be considered both useful and pleasurable.

With the Armistice of November 1918, there was a noticeable interregnum in the new world of the aeroplane. Up to this point there had been neither proper civilian flying nor organisational control for aviation.

The progress made through the aegis of War was phenomenal. Now in 1918 there was an end to the conflict and the impetus to make war machines no longer existed, so what next? As Frank Courtney *[6]* wrote:

Forgotten faces from a distant past. A postcard picture showing the winning team in the Tug-of-War from the National Aircraft Factory sports activity. The placard is dated September 7th 1918 and the back of the card identifies all the people. Left to right, standing: Chas Seadon, G L Churcher, N R Boswell, G Thomas, N Keiller, H L Wicks (coach); Middle row, seated: N Elliott, J Bourne, K Keiller, H Stevens; Foreground: C Hales, E Nowles. The Keiller girls would appear to be twins. Within three months most if not all of these would be out of work. The original of this card belongs to Croydon Airport Society member Brian Cutler. The National Aircraft Factory was very strong in social activities for its workers.

By the time this A V Roe-built Avro 504K bit the dust as the result of spinning in from a great height, the war was virtually over. H2482, one of a batch of 500 aircraft, probably ended up reduced to produce never to fly again – at least as a whole aeroplane.

Aviation had gone into the war with nothing that could seriously he called a warplane, and it had come out of it with nothing but warplanes.

It wasn't that there was a shortage of aircraft. Indeed, there was a great surplus of all types of military aeroplanes, especially the two-seat observer and fighter types. Huge manufacturing contracts which had been placed with capable industrial businesses up and down the land meant that many furniture-manufactures, piano-makers and car-producers were engaged in turning out aeroplanes in their dozens, night and day. Winding down such an enterprise was no simple matter and the stocks of finished and part-manufactured components were truly enormous.

As we have seen the largest of the National Aircraft Factories was the brand new one at Waddon where production had started in January of 1918. With a work-force of about 2,100 men and women, the production target was 200 DH.9 aircraft a month. That it never attained this figure and that it was nowhere near as efficient a manufacturing plant as even the lowly sub-contractors and 'the Trade' is another matter. At the Armistice, one might imagine that production was promptly halted. Stopping a vast mechanism that had built up its momentum to peak performance was not quite as easy to achieve.

The reality was spelled out in a series of official documents that followed the end of hostilities. The Report of the Select Committee on National Expenditure, published on June 12th 1919, contained some pretty stark information. It turned out that on November 11th 1918 – Armistice Day – there were 25,000 aeroplanes on order and the immediate task was to decide what action should be taken to stop work on these machines. Simply shouting 'stop!' was not an option!

At a meeting of the Air Council on November 15th, attended by the Director-General of Aircraft Production, the Secretary of State stated that the Air Ministry should not take delivery of a single machine that they could get out of

DH.4 B7747 was one of 500 various types of aircraft that were rebuilt from scrap and spares and then given a fresh identity by No.1 (Southern) Aircraft Repair Depôt, South Farnborough during 1917 and sent back to fight again – or crash again as in this case. The place was Bellevue Aerodrome, France, and the date February 16th 1918. The pilot, Lt A H Curtis, is standing on the left by the cockpit with observer 2nd Lt V Gordon leaning on the trailing edge of the wing. The mishap was caused by engine failure on landing causing the machine to undershoot and wipe off its undercarriage against a grassy bank beside a road. Note that the two uppermost blades of the propeller are intact confirming that power was off at the moment of impact.

[receiving]. The report stated that the Air Council had agreed that 'the most rigorous and drastic steps' must be taken to shut down production of four obsolescent types of aircraft at once and that the output that could not be cancelled should be sent directly to store and not made over to the Royal Air Force.

Decisions in Committee and published in Reports often bear little relationship to harsh reality and so it comes as no great surprise to find that on December 6th the Director-General found it necessary to write to the Minister of Munitions (who was present at all the committee meetings but who would seem to have broken his note-taking pencil-point) that:

Right: The Armstrong Whitworth FK.3 was designed by Frederick Koolhoven for the Royal Aircraft Factory as a simplified replacement for the BE.2c for both the RFC and the RNAS. Used in many roles including observation and bombing, at home the FK.3 made an ideal trainer. The best trainers in the world, though, pale into insignificance when confronted by an immovable object as A1479 was to discover when it met a tree. At least 500 FK.3 aircraft were ordered but in the end they were superseded by the Avro 504 series and a number ended up for disposal at Waddon.

Below: Built by Boulton & Paul Ltd, this Sopwith IF.1 Camel was delivered to No.5 TS(AFC) at Minchampton where, following a test on June 8th 1918, it was found to be tail heavy with slack wires vibrating. Something somewhere had 'let go' for the landing by Lt A H Curtis was neither as planned nor as expected and F1343 ended up like this so creating another repair job for the maintenance section. The Aircraft Disposal Company would later have huge numbers of both Pups and Camels on its books.

Left: In time of war, airworthy aircraft were extremely scarce, hence very valuable. This Avro 504A, built in the summer of 1916, was involved in a training accident when it overshot on landing and went through a hedge minus its undercarriage. This was repaired and flying again in under a week.

Below: With its fuselage and port wings badly shot-up, this unidentified late series DH.2 was brought down by enemy action over the Western Front, wiping its undercarriage off on an abandoned trench. It seems likely that in this case the pilot was at least badly injured because the cockpit area has been shot up. If they could be rescued, aircraft downed under such circumstances would be dismantled and collected by transport and taken to a field maintenance unit for salvage or repair. Where this was not feasible they would be destroyed on site.

> The Air Council desire to make it clear that under present conditions further deliveries are not... required by them.

There were problems, though. Huge production runs from vast labour-forces in massively-extended wartime factories behaved a bit like one of today's oil-tankers at sea: they took a long time to slow down, let alone stop. The Air Council, already up to its knees in unwanted aeroplanes, conceded that:

> ...labour and other considerations may prevent the Ministry of Munitions from arranging a complete cessation of further deliveries, and for this reason the Air Council are prepared to continue to accept aircraft and engines of which continued production is required by these considerations. But they desire to be furnished as early as possible with full particulars of the machines and engines which they will be expected to accept, and they desire to be consulted with regard to each specific type of aeroplane for which it may be proposed to place entirely new orders.

Part of the difficulties behind this was that an agreement had been reached that labour was not to be dispersed until after Christmas 1918. This meant that machines that were not wanted were taken from contractors and, as the National Aircraft Factories were also to be kept going, it was necessary to find work for the people there. The result was that machines delivered in good faith from contractors were sent to the national factories in order to be destroyed in order to keep the people there employed.

The Ministry of Munitions felt it had some responsibility for the well-being of the workforce and was not prepared to chuck them all out of work in the run up to the first peacetime Christmas for four gruelling years. Although all the workers in the factories, both National and private, were weekly servants and could therefore have been discharged at a week's notice, it was a form of 'thank you for your wartime effort' that work had to be found until the end of 1918. After that they could be sacked with impunity to join the gathering thousands of unemployed that were to herald the 1920s.

After that Christmas, however, immediate steps were taken to cancel contracts. At the time of the Armistice, aeroplanes, spare parts and so forth were on order to the extent of £150-million. This was cut down to about £65 millions and the 25,000 aeroplanes on order quickly reduced to 13,432.

The piano-makers, organ-builders, furniture factories and so on that had been roped in to produce aircraft under licence were relieved to resume their chosen work. They merely had to dispose of excess

Sopwith's Cuckoo was designed as a torpedo-carrying landplane with folding wings to operate either from shore stations or from the nascent aircraft carriers then being experimented with. A late project evaluated at the Isle of Grain in July 1917, first production orders went out the following month but, of 350 ordered, only ninety had been delivered. Unlike other Sopwith types, the Cuckoo was seen as an important adjunct to the peacetime Services and so did not make it onto the surplus market. This particular example, N8003, was one of a batch of 100 ordered from the Blackburn Aero & Motor Company of which only 32 were delivered in 1919. Used by No.1 Training Flight, 210 Sqdn Gosport in 1921. This incident occurred on June 6th 1922 following engine-failure on take-off. The crow's-foot trailing-edge fairings for wing-folding are clearly visible on the upper wings behind the inner rear interplane strut attachment points.

workers and arrange for their stocks of work-in-hand to be taken away. For the workforce it was one long and unmitigated tragedy.

And so it was on that January Saturday when some 1,500 employees of Waddon's National Aircraft Factory were dismissed while the remaining 600 or so had their wages reduced. The effect on the local community can be imagined as this vast number descended on the local Labour Exchange to register for what was coyly termed 'out-of-work wages' amounting to £1 5s 0d per week.

The whole of this enormous factory was stilled and the site now officially became the National Aircraft [Salvage] Depôt Number 3, Aintree assuming the rôle of Number 1 and Manchester becoming Number 2.

Like all production factories, these places were filled with 'work in progress' – incomplete aircraft and stocks of component parts waiting their turn on assembly lines that were now shut down. Besides that there were the huge numbers of aircraft actually in service or undergoing repair.

It was almost a tradition before the war that any aircraft damaged in an accident should be repaired where at all possible, a rule understandably based on the realistic preposition that, except in instances of fire, at least some serviceable pieces would survive a crash. When this Aircraft Manufacturing Company-built DH.4 hit the ground in a training mishap, it is quite likely that some of the wreckage ended up at a maintenance depot and thence to Waddon for redemption. The DH.4 airframe cost £1,424 10s to build and its RAF.3A engine an additional £1,210.

The railway siding to Waddon delivered a huge quantity of broken aircraft for salvage by the Ministry of Munitions' Disposal Board workforce in 1919-1920. Many were damaged machines salvaged from France – the ones that had escaped on-site burning. Others were the returns from maintenance units and depôts around the country where the need to rebuild broken aircraft had suddenly ceased. This pile of parts appears to include bits of one or more DH.4 aircraft.

Technically, all were surplus to requirements but in truth, somebody wisely realised that if they got rid of the lot, the new military service, the Royal Air Force, would effectively cease to exist. A relatively small percentage of machines was retained while a number of the newly-formed squadrons were wound up. The youngest Service, consequently, would resolutely progress with its flying and its aeroplanes even if, as many commentators were disparagingly quick to point out, it was now a minuscule Service.

But that still left a vast stockpile of aircraft parts, engines and finished machines to be cleared. Most of the redundant but airworthy aircraft were kept at the landing field at Aintree where part of the racecourse had been requisitioned early on in the war as an aerodrome. At disposal dumps around the country (but mainly in the South), colossal stocks of unfinished or semi-manufactured components were offered to the public. The National Aircraft Depôts now became salvage dumps where the eager public could buy whatever they liked literally for a few coppers. Propellers and wings were priced at 6d each, while a complete fuselage cost between a shilling and half-a-crown.

Farmers found wings particularly useful for fencing, although later it was found that the dope on the fabric poisoned chickens when wings were employed in making a run. Fuselage trusses and even complete fuselages frames were ideal for supporting roofs and numerous barns were strengthened or restored using these lightweight yet very strong parts to hold up corrugated iron.

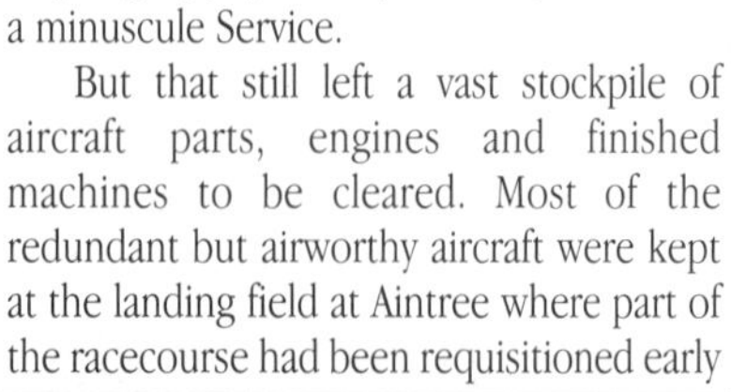

Noted cabinet makers Marsh, Jones & Cribb of Leeds and London, were founded in the 18th century. Famed for 'arts and crafts' style furniture, they built 100 DH.5 aircraft and 175 Sopwith 1F.1 Camels. Here is a nameplate from one of their aircraft. Other sources have misquoted their name as 'March'.

Furniture makers eagerly bought up ash and mahogany – timbers that had become increasingly hard to buy on the open market after 1916 – but eschewed the softer spruce which was mainly used for fencing as was piano wire and flexible control cable.

The Aircraft Disposal Board came into being as part of the enormous Government Disposal Board set up at the beginning of 1919. It had the formidable task of clearing work in progress, recovering salvageable material from crashed or otherwise damaged aircraft returned from the Front, and disposing as best it could of complete aircraft and spare parts including engines. It was a mammoth task in view of the enormous volume of unwanted material that nevertheless represented taxpayers' money.

In the manner in which it had been set up, the brief of the Disposal Board was an almost unattainable goal: as far as disposing of aeroplanes was concerned it would prove impossibly uneconomic.

Chapter 4

Peacetime and the Birth of Civil Aviation

IN virtually every walk of life, as any invention or technology develops so it ultimately demands reclassification as it divides naturally into sectors that originally were either non-existent or, at best, unnecessary. Retrospective re-classification ranges around us to differentiate between the old and the new from things like '*stainless* steel' to '*pre-decimal* currency'; from the tautologist's '*two*-wheeled bicycle' (and, Heaven forefend, '*three-wheeled* bicycle'!) to '*subsonic* flight'; '*organic* potatoes', '*black-and-white* television'. '*electric* train' – the list is endless yet demonstrates that as the event or object is developed, it becomes necessary to qualify it in comparison and relation to its predecessors. All electronic computers have processors, but today the particular type of processor has to be given a name!

And so all aircraft builders were, in the beginning, amateurs and private individuals, and every aeroplane was a hand-made creation. The concept of 'private' or 'civil' flying, then, did not even arise because that was the only type of flying that existed. Before the First World War, virtually all heavier-than-air flight was an *ad hoc* affair to which the adjectives 'private', 'civil' or 'military' were as unnecessary as was the need to place the word 'gas' before 'light'.

The military interest in flying that resulted in the creation of the Royal Flying Corps, the Royal Aircraft Factory and the Royal Naval Air Service thus developed on the backs of amateurs and pioneer aviation. And when those that built aeroplanes began to receive enquiries from others regarding the construction of a flying machine in exchange for money (or goods), the change from home-built to factory-produced machines was neither immediate nor really definable. It just happened and before long the idea of a factory-built aeroplane and with it the implications of a commercial enterprise inevitably arose from the mêlée of experimenting individuals. Cody was an amateur, yet built aircraft that were

A curious piece of civil aviation history is represented by this FE.2b built in early 1918 by the Suffolk-based firm Garrett & Sons of Leiston. Awarded its Certificate of Airworthiness on August 8th 1919, it was legal to fly with the former military serial displayed in large characters on the fuselage. Operated as a three-seater by J Carter Smith it operated from Bournemouth Aerodrome where this picture was taken. In March 1920 it was sold to Bournemouth Aviation Company Ltd and became G-EAHC. It was withdrawn from use on the expiry of the C of A on August 7th 1921. Although a number of FE machines were acquired by The Aircraft Disposal Company, it seems that they were well aware of their extreme obsolescence and merely reduced them to produce rather than attempting to sell them on.

A V Roe tried to buy back all Avro aircraft from the Ministry of Munitions' Disposal Board and was later to take The Aircraft Disposal Company to Court to prevent the sale of any aircraft that were not of its manufacture. The outcome was coloured by the discovery (by the judge who heard the case) that historically many Avro aircraft were not made by A V Roe at all, having been constructed by sub-contractors! A V Roe operated its own aircraft in joy-riding. One example enjoyed a short(ish) life: Avro 536 (ATC.2) was registered K-104 on April 30th 1919. Before it could be painted with its 'new series' registration G-EAAQ, it was destroyed in a bizarre crash. While flying at 3,000 feet over London on September 9th that year and carrying two passengers (one of them a woman), 'a cylinder burst' (according to *The Daily Graphic* report) and the pilot, RAF-trained Lt E A Sullock, attempted a landing in Southwark Park. As this somewhat poor newspaper picture shows, it all went rather wrong yet, thanks to the robustness of the Avro's construction, nobody was killed – shaken rather than stirred!

evaluated by the Army.

It was largely due to this rather unregulated nature of aviation in the days immediately preceding the outbreak of the First World War that the Royal Aircraft Factory emerged. Out of this arose the first re-classification of aircraft when the military and the Government established a differentiation between RAF (Royal Aircraft Factory) work and 'the Trade' which embraced everybody else in the aeroplane-making business.

There was an interesting dichotomy regarding the making of military aircraft. Largely for historical reasons, the RFC developed alongside the Royal Aircraft Factory (originally the Royal Balloon Factory) on which it was largely dependent for its machines. The Royal Naval Air Service, also for historical reasons, had from the first preferred to work with individual manufacturers – the much-maligned 'Trade'. Popham *[26]* highlights the intimacy that existed between the Eastchurch Wing and Short Brothers, a policy that proved invaluable for it encouraged some of the most enterprising firms in British aviation to develop and experiment, in particular, in the early days. As an aside, it was this 'Trade' co-operation that began to give the Navy an advantage over the Army, transforming a 'generous rivalry' into 'deplorable and extensive competition' *[op.cit]*. As an aside, one result of this was that it often happened that the RNAS had aircraft sitting in reserve while the RFC was short of replacements for its first-line squadrons.

To return to the opening premise of this Chapter, the relevance of all this is that there did not exist the concept of civil or private flying in the days that led up to the War, yet by the time the war had ended, there clearly had to be a division between military flying – meaning the RAF (which now meant the Royal Air Force) and the Royal Naval Air Service (which, along with the RFC, had actually ceased to exist when the RAF was created on April 1st 1918) – and those that might want to fly privately or for hire-and-reward.

While government surplus aircraft marked military machines that had been the product of war production, peacetime brought with it the matter of allowing private (meaning civilian) flying to re-start and allow the now distinctly possible idea of commercial aviation to be developed. Early in 1919, just a few months after the November 1918 Armistice, the newly-created Air Ministry (formed at the recommendation of the South African

The Rolls-Royce Eagle-powered DH.4 design was outstanding in many ways. The first successful day bomber, de Havilland's design first flew in August of 1916 and gave sterling service in time of war. It was still providing cost-effective and practical service right up to 1930 in some quarters. Large numbers of the DH.4 and the 4A (pictured here) were withdrawn from the Royal Air Force after the Armistice and very many ended up stacked in rows at Waddon to await sale. The British Government gave ten to South Africa as an Imperial Gift – and The Aircraft Disposal Company sold hundreds more around the world.

Aptly registered, Avro 504K G-EAIR had an unusual history. Formerly E4164, it was bought directly from the Air Ministry by Aircraft Transport & Travel Ltd and got its first C of A on November 28th 1919. It flew for a year with the company but, on expiration of the C of A, was stored until August 1921 when it was bought by Surrey Flying Services and joined the 'barnstorming' joy-riding circuit. The old Avro gave good service until August 21st 1923 when it crashed at Hayling Island. It is pictured here operating from a field near Portsdown Hill north of Portsmouth.

General, Jan Christian Smuts) had announced plans to re-start non-military flying activities which, of course, had been banned since the outbreak of war. It was thus the end of the war that gave rise to civilian flying as a new operational category of aviation.

The Civil Air Navigation Act came into being on May 1st 1919 and now 'aviation' had been pigeonholed and categorised. And so it was that on that first peacetime May Day, civil flying began its new and post-war life.

To those who had followed the progress of aviation, the new civil flying age was completely different from that which they may have known in the pre-war days. By this time, the pioneers were already ancient history and most had migrated into that other new category – aircraft manufacturers. They were now 'the Trade' as the authorities had disparagingly named them. By the same token there were military pilots and private pilots, although the majority in both categories were flyers trained by the Services.

The new civil aviation era thus began with ex-military aircraft. There were no specific 'civil' aircraft designs (in truth there were but they failed to receive orders and consequently were abandoned). Ex-military aircraft were hastily converted for private flying, for joy riding (this was the new fad), and for the burgeoning air-transport industry.

It is axiomatic that any machine that is made for one purpose cannot directly be made to fulfil another while retaining the same degree of practicality. So it was with military aircraft. Good fighters made bad private runabouts, good bombers made

Midland Aviation Service was formed in 1921 by H W Barrett and based at Alexandra Park flying three Avro 504K aircraft and this DH.6, G-EARR (B3067). Barrett is seen standing by the engine, hands in pockets, while pilot Claude Hudson stands on the wing. The third person, by the wing leading edge, is unknown. This aircraft had been bought from the Disposal Board in 1920 in the famous auction held by No.1 Aircraft Salvage Depôt at the Hyde, Hendon, and was one of the half-dozen examples that sold from between £60 and £100. G-EARR was withdrawn from use on expiry of its one and only C of A on May 27th 1921. It was a DH.6, albeit rather a non-standard rebuild, that was the first aircraft to take a civil registration – K-100.

Of the Handley Page O/400 bombers that were successfully civilianised, J2250 was channelled by its designers into service with Handley Page Transport Ltd without ever officially entering the surplus market. Built by contractors The Birmingham Carriage Company Limited as one of a batch of 50 ordered in October 1918, few were actually constructed due to the end of the war intervening. J2250 was one of the 30-odd approaching completion when the contract was abandoned. Completed as airworthy, it was flown to Cricklewood for finishing off and fitting out upon which, as G-EAKG, it attracted its Certificate of Airworthiness on September 6th 1919. It was used for a year until the C of A expired after which it was scrapped in favour of the new W.8 series of airliners being then introduced. Theses were Handley Page's first attempt at developing bomber technology into airline sufficiency.

spartan airliners, and Service trainers made bad joy-riding machines.

There were diverse reasons for this. The most obvious concerned the fundamental differences in operating conditions. Service aircraft did not have a need for much in the way of creature comforts; consequently they tended to be uncomfortable, draughty and cold. Engines did not as a rule have mufflers or silencers to their exhausts and such considerations as fuel consumption, ease of maintenance and cheapness of running were aspects which, despite the perennial pleas behind the second of these, had no place in aeroplanes originally intended for military applications.

An early outcome of all this was that service trainers, being two-seaters, were hastily altered for joy riding. Open cockpits presented the poor civilian first-timer with the unavoidable necessity of donning an unflattering leather overcoat or Sidcot flying suit, helmet and goggles. Heavy bombers such as the lumbering Handley Page O/400 and the Vickers Vimy were converted with a few seats to provide the first generation of commercial airliners.

This matter came up in the House on March 2nd 1920 when Viscount Curzon asked the Under Secretary of State to the Air Ministry how long was required to convert a bombing, observation and scout machine, respectively, from war to peace purposes. Major Tryon rose to the challenge, responding that:

> The time necessary for the conversion of a war machine to use for peace purposes depends entirely on the degree of comfort required by the pilot and passengers, as the removal of war fittings can be effected within a few hours. I regret that I am not able to... reply to the last part of [the] question, as the time would vary with each particular type and design of a peace machine.

Another member, perhaps with a little more foresight than most, asked if he was 'satisfied that every step is being taken by

The Martinsyde A.1 was one of the Woking company's post-war designs. Incorporating a number of F.4 components, the Falcon-powered two-seat long-range machine was created to compete for the Australian Government's £10,000 prize for the first flight from England to Australia. Fitted with an enlarged rudder and painted pale blue, G-EAMR left Hounslow on December 4th 1919 piloted by Capt C E Howell with Cpl George Henry Fraser as navigator. Five days later the machine was forced down into the sea off Corfu and both men drowned, the sole example of the A.1 going to the bottom.

INSTONE AIR LINE

"AERIAL TRAVEL-DE-LUXE."

THE REGULAR AIR SERVICE between

LONDON and PARIS

of the INSTONE AIR LINE

has been augmented by the addition of new and commodious Vickers-Vimy (Rolls-Royce) Limousine Aeroplanes de Luxe.

These majestic and trustworthy machines are similar in construction to the Aeroplanes which made the historic flights across the Atlantic and to Australia. They are sumptuously fitted and contain the latest improvements and conveniences.

Wireless Telephony, Luggage Compartment, Lavatory Accommodation, &c.

INSTONE AIR-LINER "CITY OF LONDON".

Each of these machines has a capacity of 11 passengers or 1¼ tons of goods.

FARES (LONDON-PARIS)—

Passengers—Single Journey, £12. Return, £21.

Goods, per lb., 1/9.

LEAVE LONDON MONDAY and THURSDAY. RETURN from PARIS, TUESDAY and FRIDAY

Special Trips and Circular Tours arranged.

Special Facilities for the transit of Articles of value.

INSURANCES EFFECTED.

Write or 'phone for illustrated booklet to: Instone Air Line (S. Instone & Co. Ltd.), 22, Billiter Street London, E.C. 3 (Avenue 3616), 1 and 2, Rue des Italiens, Paris (Inter: 740), Brussels, Genoa Cardiff, Newcastle, etc.,

or usual Booking Agents.

An early airline, Instone, operated a specially civilianised version of the Vickers Vimy carrying 11 passengers in a new purpose built wider wooden fuselage.

the Air Ministry to encourage civil aviation, and thus to provide an adequate reserve of machines for use in time of war'. This excellent point, touching on such vexed aspects as airline subsidies, fostering private flying and sustaining the capabilities of the Royal Air Force, was deftly parried into touch.

Even flying low and slow, the airline passenger of 1919 had to be a pretty hardy type to withstand the noise, the cold and the sheer discomfort of sitting in a Lloyd Loom wicker-basket chair, devoid of anything even as basic as a lap-strap, being tossed about by the unavoidable turbulent air in an unupholstered and non-sound-proofed plywood and fabric box to which draught-exclusion was merely an afterthought.

Private flyers were a different class of people. They both understood and accepted the inconveniences and the problems of flight and aircraft. They went in for it because they chose to. They even liked it! Noise, discomfort, draughts and cold, not to mention a thirsty engine, all were part of the romance of aviation. Such considerations as comfort and economy of operation didn't concern them.

The first generation of civil aircraft, then, was predominantly comprised of unsuitable military conversions, some generated by the manufacturers themselves in an endeavour to keep abreast of what was quickly identified as a useful new market. Among these were machines such as the Armstrong Whitworth FK.3 and FK.8, the Armstrong Whitworth Siskin, Blackburn Velos and a number of others covering the whole gamut from training aircraft to fighters: flying boats to bombers.

Some of these were developed for specialist categories of the civilian market such as racing and competition, and machines such as the Siskin, for example,

Civil DH.9 aircraft came in a number of guises. The Aircraft Manufacturing Company (Airco) and the de Havilland Aircraft Company both made conversions but so, at a later date, did the Aircraft Disposal Company with the result that often no two conversions looked alike. Generally, an enclosed rear passenger cabin was provided but, in the DH-built G-EAYU, this was removed altogether and the aircraft was operated in this manner by the company. G-EAYU is thought to have been the example with which some of the earliest experiments in aerial crop-spraying were undertaken in Kent during June of 1922. G-EAYU was registered on January 10th that year but on November 3rd 1924 it was sold together with several military DH.9 machines (probably from the Aircraft Disposal Company) to the Hedjaz Government in the Arabian Peninsula. In an unfortunate armourer's confusion over bomb-fusing, this aircraft and its Russian pilot were blown to smithereens before they ever reached the rebel tribesmen in the area now known as the Kingdom of Saudi Arabia.

This image from the summer of 1919 comes as a picture postcard from the seaside. Described as 'The Beach & Palace Pier from East-Brighton', it shows a typical crowded beach scene on this first summer after the end of the war. The latest holiday attraction is a joy-ride around the piers and seafront in an Avro seaplane operated by A V Roe & Company of Manchester. Judging by the disturbed water, it had just driven at speed up the beach.

By 1919 more than 50 joy-riding firms had been set up around the country by ex-RAF pilots anxious to keep flying. Most were short-lived operations that made their money by carrying passengers at a guinea a time from small fields and many closed with the slump of 1921. In Scotland one such outfit was Aerial Photos Ltd of 81a George Street, Edinburgh. Founded in June 1919 with a share capital of £18,000, it offered to provide aerial pictures and 'cinematographic images' but the main income was joy-riding. Run by Capt R S G B Andrews, Charles Henry C Smith and O Hardie, they bought three Avro 504 aircraft direct from the Disposal Board in August 1919 – G-EAHU (E1611); G-EAHV (H2297) and G-EAIG. On Sunday March 20th 1921 they held an event at Turnhouse Aerodrome outside Edinburgh which they promoted with these hand-made photographic prints – an expensive promotion even then. It was to be the firm's last season.

Below: In case anybody questions why these joy-riding concerns only went in for small aircraft, besides the fact that the fields they usually flew from were small there were also the physical problems involved in operating a large aircraft. Here we see the manpower and equipment commonly needed to erect a World War I bomber.

Top: After the Handley Page O/400, the Cricklewood-based company designed the first of its purpose-built airliners – the W.8. This proved so popular that the Belgian company SABCA obtained a license to build several examples for SABENA. Here we see a SABENA W.8b sneak in for a short landing on Croydon's expanse of grass airfield in 1926. Even then, the proximity of homes to the landing and departing aircraft was causing some concern. *[Mike Hooks.]*

Below: Delegates attending the Government's first Air Conference at Croydon mingle with the aircraft in October 1920 – but on that occasion were not permitted to see the hangars of The Aircraft Disposal Company! *[Mike Hooks.]*

Bottom: The early days of Croydon Aerodrome as [pictured from the first control tower. Viewed over the roof of the Customs Shed (left foreground) with two luggage carts outside – one of which is marked 'Instone Air Lines' – and the wartime Bessoneau hangars centre distance. *[Mike Hooks.]*

eminently distinguished themselves in this limited field over subsequent years. Meanwhile the Avro training biplanes soldiered on, taking wartime standards well into the peacetime market.[1]

Civil flying, then, did not start from a clean slate in these immediate post-war years. While it is generally accepted that Britain led the world in establishing the successful light aeroplane and its markets, leading the French and, incidentally, the Americans as well, it was nevertheless several long years more before the industry offered a serious challenge to the market. Its success, however, came in spite of the cruelties of an uncertain economy which produced a numbing slump in the early 1920s and, less than a decade later, the world economic crash of 1929-31.

With aircraft available on the market at generally affordable prices, many aspiring aviators saw a chance to get themselves into the air. Most, of course, didn't.

But there was another class of person who fervently hoped he could find a use for aeroplanes. This comprised those military pilots and other aircrew that were themselves now described, like their aircraft, as 'surplus to requirements'. They were the people who had been exposed to the hubris of flying in time of war and now found that they didn't want to give it up – or couldn't. They were those young men – exclusively young men, for there had been no wartime women flyers – who had been called up straight from school and knew no work other than aircraft and flying. Young men who might have yearned for the masculine pride of a motorcycle but now had experienced something very different and even more exciting. For many of them, flying had become part of their lives and they simply could not stop with the end of the war.

Aircraft were bigger, they were faster, and they were practical. Besides that, the man on the Clapham omnibus saw aircraft and, particularly, the men who flew them in time of war, as saviours and heroes. Aviation

1. Civil flying may have demanded courage, determination and a hardiness of spirit but nowhere was this better demonstrated than by Miss Standen and Mr Hamilton who got married at Chorley Wood (Hertfordshire) at the end of June 1919 – and then flew from a meadow next to the churchyard to Fowey, Cornwall, for their honeymoon in K-134, the prototype Avro 504M with a curious rear enclosed cabin-cockpit. This Avro became G-EACX but was withdrawn on C of A expiry on May 23rd 1920.

This fine air-to-ground picture was taken in the mid-1920s by Surrey Flying Services and shows what was then described as the London Terminal Aerodrome at Croydon. It reveals the site of the original aerodrome on Plough Lane (running from upper left to bottom right) with offices, hangars and passenger facilities. In the left foreground is part of the old military aerodrome. In the top right-hand corner of the picture are the many buildings that formed the original National Aircraft Factory, by this time in command of The Aircraft Disposal Company. The revamped aerodrome saw the razing of all these buildings and the severing of Plough Lane as the aerodrome encompassed this whole area, its new terminal area being built just off the picture at the upper left.

was popular without ever having had to be overtly popularised. And large numbers of people flocked to sample the excitement of 'aerial flight'.

The weekly magazine *Flight* reported on October 30th 1919 that:

> On Saturday, October 25, the Avro air fleet visited Brighton for the third successive week-end. The new aerodrome at West Blatchington Farm, which consists of about 50 acres, is being fenced round and hangars are being erected there. Tea was served on the ground and a band was present.
>
> A very large crowd collected on the aerodrome for each of the three days. Owing to the high wind the parachute descents had to be postponed, but Maj A G Taylor, AFC, put up a very fine exhibition of trick flying.
>
> The chief interest, however, centred in the appearance of the little Avro-Green Baby, which had been brought down from Hamble by Capt Hamerslcy, MC. The Baby played about in the air as usual, and delighted the crowd immensely. Another attraction was the display of the model aeroplane kites designed by an AID official at Hamble. These were made to perform most extraordinary feats in the air.
>
> Next week-end the Avros will visit Bournemouth...

If aircraft were expected to have but a short life in time of war (*see* Chapter 1), then public expectations in time of peace were almost equally pessimistic. In those days, Parliament did not enjoy the long recesses that are commonplace today and so it was still business as usual in the House of Commons on December 23rd that year when a curious exchange took place between the Coalition Unionist MP, C K Murchison, and Capt The Hon F E Guest, Chief Whip, Secretary of State for War. Murchison asked for a statement on 'the average life in flying hours under peace conditions of two-engined aeroplanes capable of carrying twenty to thirty passengers and single-engined aeroplanes carrying up to four passengers'. The question on durability was posed, remember, at a time when no commercial aircraft existed that could carry more than eight passengers (the Handley Page 'O' series). The answer he got was that:

> The period that has elapsed since civil flying under peace conditions commenced has been insufficient to allow such reliable data to be obtained as would enable a useful answer to be given to this question. The necessary data are being collected. It may, however, be observed in this connection that if the proper replacements, both of engine and aeroplane parts, are made during the periodical overhauls, there is no reason why any aeroplane should ever wear out, as after 200 hours' flying there will probably be very little of the original machine left.

The official belief, therefore, was that a one-hundred per cent spares holding would be essential to support every 200 hours of flying or, expressed another way, total amortisation of aircraft investment had to be budgeted for in that couple of hundred hours. For any organization holding stocks of spares, and dealing in those spares, the future seemed to suggest a singularly rosy investment opportunity!

One can imagine the City investor quietly making notes in his Georgian equivalent of a Filofax...

Chapter 5

Government Surplus Aeroplanes and their Disposal

CURIOUS members of the public peered at the advertisements that told of the war-surplus goods that they could buy. There were military uniforms, vehicles, boats and aeroplanes – just the sort of thing the average post-war Georgian man-about-Town renting a two-up and two-down terraced house in a South London suburb might wish to acquire in 1919 to add to the aspidistra and the window-box.

This was the summer of aircraft sales and the first of these came the day after the Hendon Air Meeting – harbinger of a series of auctions held by No.1 Aircraft Salvage Depôt at The Hyde, Hendon. It was here that a 110 hp Le Rhône-engined Avro made the highest price – £360 – while two FK.8 aircraft went for £260 each. A pair of BE.2e machines made £90 and £80 while half a dozen DH.6 went at anything from £100 to just £60 for a single-seater with an American Curtiss OX-5 engine.

David Marshall, later to found the business known today as Marshall's of Cambridge, bought a surplus Handley Page O/400 bomber for £5: it was never flown but some of its bits were used to build a sand yacht.

It should be remembered that aircraft and heavier-than-air flight were still comparatively new and the generation that would be born to accept flying as 'normal' had yet to follow on that which still recalled the invention as both pioneering and new-fangled. Consequently there were still many that viewed the manifestation of artificial flight as either miraculous or the work of the devil. A result of all this was that however cheap an aeroplane might be, it would only appeal as a desirable purchase to a very small minority of the population. And however many aeroplanes the country had to dispose of, that number was bound, by a huge percentage, to exceed even the wildest dreams of a home market. And while the man in the street might be certain he did not want to buy one for himself, he knew very well that *(a)* the things were expensive, and *(b)* he, as a taxpayer, had been forced to pay for them.

A news item was carried in the issue of *Flight* on May 1st:

> Now that civil aviation is definitely going to start, an opportunity occurs for those who wish to replenish their stock of spare parts on advantageous terms. The Aircraft Equipment Section of the MOM [Ministry of Munitions] Surplus Property Disposal Board has on hand a large assortment of material, components and fittings. It is impossible to give a complete list, but the following are a few of the items which are available in varying quantities: small bolts and nuts, strainers for brake controls, wire cables, wood screws, brass and iron, studs (various sizes), brass union connections, relief valves, petrol filters, copper and steel tubing, washers, rivets in all metals, joint pins, fork joints (steel), petrol tank fittings, Bowden controls and wires, brass cocks, hose pipe connections and clips, gimp pins for trimmings, accumulators, aluminium, duralumin and brass beadings, sheets, angles, etc., celluloid sheets for windows, acetylene lamps, electric switches, speaking tubes. Enquiries for any of these items should be sent to Room 544, Aircraft Equipment Section, Surplus Government Property Disposal Board, 544, Alexandra House, Kingsway, WC2.

The second RAF Tournament staged at Hendon on July 2nd 1921 fielded eight starters from a giant HP O/400 to a BAT Bantam. Winner, number 17, was Flg-Off J Oliver in this Sopwith Snipe. A few days later, on July 16th, Hendon hosted the one and only Oxford-Cambridge Air Race, three laps of a course totalling 129 miles. Each team comprised three SE.5A aircraft, with light blue or dark blue tails. All were loaned by The Aircraft Disposal Company to the Royal Aero Club for the event which Cambridge won: G-EAXT was one of the winning team. *[Croydon Airport Society Archive 854/03/4: Hillyer Collection via Albert E Smith]*

To many, the offer of aircraft parts (as distinct from a complete aeroplane) for so little money was irresistible. Propellers were turned into eccentric hat-stands, picture-frames and clock-cases, while steel tube was converted into utility bedsteads sprung with piano-wire cross-bracing. While, in a previous age, old wooden cartwheels represented the height of technology with which to enhance the appearance of your home, now gates, garages, public houses, restaurants and even private houses were embellished with a propeller screwed on the outside or perhaps polished and hung over the fireplace. As late as 1960 a back-street garage in Ryde, Isle of Wight, still displayed the tattered and delaminated remains of one of these First War propellers above its doors. Others were cut up to make ingenious items of domestic knick-knackery in the way that another age would see napkin rings lovingly turned from the teak handrails of HM ships that had been struck off charge, refitted or torpedoed.

Garden fences were renewed using brand new uncovered wings. Covered wings went for chicken runs, although it was found out too late that the dope poisoned pecking birds. Farmers eagerly snapped up trailer loads of them to enclose paddocks and fields since they presented a lower-cost means of fencing-in land than even the cheapest chestnut paling. As mentioned earlier, larger wire-braced fuselage trusses made excellent barn roofs and many an inter-wars farm building supported its roof on a couple of 'Brisfit' side frames.

If Prime Minister David Lloyd George's Coalition government had successfully tackled the challenge of organising a massive expansion of aircraft production in time of war (meaning convincing the British taxpayer that they must pay more money), then they now had to lead the run-down and virtual dismantling of the enterprise that government had built up. And it had to be carried out both quickly and accountably – but fundamentally accountably!

Anxious that the resource of flyable aircraft ought not to be squandered, a quango called the Civil Aerial Transport Committee had already made strong recommendations that every effort should be made to see that suitable aircraft were set aside to foster the establishment of airlines. On May 7th Lt-Col Moore-Brabazon asked the Under-Secretary of State to the Air Ministry whether he would be arranging with the Treasury that the Disposal Board carry out the recommendations of the Civil Aerial Transport Committee with regard to the selling of aeroplanes at a reduced price

Without Reserve.

G.  R.

Ministry of Munitions.

By Order of the Surplus Government Property Disposal Board, Mechanical Transport Section, 1, Grosvenor Place, S.W. 1.

At the

Royal Agricultural Hall,
Islington, London, N. 1,

GODDARD & SMITH

have been instructed to sell by Auction at the above Hall on

Friday next, July 18th,

at 11 a.m. precisely,

100 PEDAL BICYCLES
(One machine in each Lot)
including

Royal Enfield, New Hudson, Humber, Premier, Ariel-Coventry Cross, B.S.A., Alldays, Rudge-Whitworth, etc.

At 2 p.m. precisely,

MOTOR CYCLES (Some with Sidecars)
by

Triumph, Clyno, Douglas ($2\frac{3}{4}$ h.p. and 4 h.p.), B.S.A., Zenith Solos, etc., etc.
Clyno, New Imperial J.A.P. Combinations.

Lots on view Thursday, July 17th, between the hours of 10 and 5 o'clock.
Admission to the Hall and to the Auction by Catalogue only, price 1/- each, to be obtained from the Auctioneers:

GODDARD & SMITH,
at the Royal Agricultural Hall, Islington, N.1, and at their Head Offices, 196, Piccadilly, W.1.

[Flight 17 July 1919]

The Ministry of Munitions was charged with disposing of enormous quantities of the aftermath of the Great War. A sense of the enormity of the challenge can be gained from this notice from July 17th 1919 regarding an auction of bicycles and motorcycles. The sheer impossibility of ever clearing so vast a collection by methods like public auctions, not to mention the expense of storage, staffing and selling, shines through even today. Unemployment meant that few could afford the luxury of even a bicycle.

(quoting Appendix IV, paragraph 10, sub-section B of Parliamentary Debates) to substantial companies, with a view to helping commercial aeronautics from a national point of view? To this Maj-Gen Seely responded that 'The recommendation referred to is one which with other cognate questions is at present receiving the close attention of the Air Ministry'. Which suggested that nobody was too bothered for the moment.

While Government fiddled, things were nevertheless moving. At Waddon, the railway siding that had once brought in components and raw materials now brought in complete aircraft and assemblies for salvage.

A newspaper story in the *Daily Chronicle* of May 8th 1919 tells just what a treasure-trove was available to the public:

AEROPLANE BARGAIN SALE

The largest stock of aeroplanes in the world, under one roof, all ready for flight and all for sale, was inspected by a *Daily Chronicle* representative yesterday at Waddon Aircraft Factory, near Croydon.

This is one of several huge warehouses in which the Air Ministry is gathering its vast surplus stock of aeroplanes, engines, propellers and every variety of spare part, and assorting them for sale to the general public.

One immense shed contains 6,000 aeroplane engines, representing every power and make, and these continue to arrive at the rate of nearly 100 a day. They are grouped in four classes: A = new; B = used, but good as new; C = second-hand but serviceable; D = only fit for breaking up.

BY DIRECTION OF THE DISPOSAL BOARD.
Aircraft Disposal Department.

FOR SALE.

ENGINES.

TYPE.		H.P.	Type.	Cooling.	No. of Cyl.
Siddeley Deasy "Puma"	...	230	Vertical	Water	6
Sunbeam "Cossack" ...	...	320	,,	,,	12
Fiat A. 12 Bis.	...	300	,,	,,	6
Hispano Suiza (French)	...	200	Ve 90	,,	8
Hispano Suiza (Viper)	...	200	Vee	,,	8
Rolls-Royce "Eagle" ...	...	250	—	—	—
Marks I, II, III, IV, V and VI		300	Vee	Water	12
Mono	...	100	Rotary	Air	9

SHOCK ABSORBER CORD.

Black shock absorber elastic cord, new	3,550 feet.
,, and red shock absorber elastic cord, new	550 ,,
White ,, ,, ,, ,, ,, ...	667 yards.
,, and red ,, ,, ,, ,, ,, ...	4,500 feet.
Black ,, ,, ,, ,, ,, ,, ,, ...	668 ,,
,, ,, ,, ,, ,, ,, ,, ,, ...	500 ,,

HOSE.

Grey Hose, new 1 in. i/d ...	2,075 feet.	Grey Hose, new $\frac{3}{8}$ in. i/d 3-ply ...	250 feet.
,, ,, ,, $\frac{3}{8}$,, ...	554 ,,	,, ,, ,, $\frac{9}{16}$,, ...	459 ,,

RUBBER PADS.

F.E. 2 B. 7126-26	130	F.E. 2 B. 3895-35	318

PALMER WHEELS.

Palmer wheels, complete with tyres and tubes in various sizes.

AIRCRAFT GLUE.

Hide glue, best quality for aircraft, 85 cwts.

Tenders are requested for any or all of the above lots or singly in the case of engines, forms and all particulars may be obtained from :—
THE CONTROLLER,
Aircraft Disposal Department,
York House, Kingsway, W.C.

Closing date for Tenders, July 28th, 1919.

[Flight17 July 1919]

On the same date as the announcement of the bicycle auction, the Disposal Board's Aircraft department published a notice inviting tenders for a quantity of material including new aircraft engines. The cryptic note 'Tenders... for any or all...' again paints a picture of Civil Service unreality when confronted with a challenge of this magnitude.

> The would-be buyer can come here and take his pick... In another enormous shed are the aeroplanes themselves, nearly 1,000 in all, the bodies packed together as closely as possible, in such a way as to avoid all strain, and the wings of each in a rack nearby. Here, again, every up-to-date type is represented and you can come here, choose your machine, have it assembled, and try it from the large aerodrome which adjoins the factory.
>
> Smashed aeroplanes arrive in trainloads from France and every part of this country. Nothing of them is lost or wasted.

The story went on to relate how even the old fabric was recycled: first the dope was removed (details of this process are not recorded) after which the fabric 'fetches a good price from paper-makers where it is used in the manufacture of the highest-grade papers, especially that for banknotes'.

Waddon was by no means the only site where planned destruction now replaced construction. At Henlow brand new aircraft were being scrapped wholesale. Here labour was expended methodically stripping down every machine to its component parts. It was no great saving of the taxpayers' money for the aircraft were reduced to carefully-sorted piles of pieces. Turnbuckles, lengths of wire, pieces of metal, nuts and bolts – all were piled and identified but to what purpose? Very little of this processed material was reusable, let alone saleable. Far simpler would have been to salvage the engines and a few of the other valuable parts and burn the rest. Money would then have been saved.

Meanwhile, in *The Times,* a reader dropped one of those bombshells that, in another age, might have earned a place in the 'Disgusted of Tonbridge Wells' category. He told a graphic tale of destruction and waste of public funds that drew a fulsome editorial from Stanley Spooner in *Flight* on May 22nd. Under the heading *The Disposal of Obsolete Aircraft,* Spooner wrote:

> A correspondent of *The Times* has raised a considerable stir by a description of the methods adopted at Henlow of dealing with obsolete aeroplanes. He says that new machines of various types, delivered by the makers complete with the exception of engines, are taken in hand by gangs of mechanics and women workers, who, armed with hatchets and hammers, break them up. The pieces, except the metal work, which is sorted and stored, are mostly gathered into bags, taken away, and used as firewood. In the House of Commons Sir Samuel Hoare drew attention to the same sort of thing which, it is alleged, has been happening at Farnborough.
>
> As readers of *Flight* are fully aware, we have never hesitated, and never shall hesitate, to speak plainly where we conceive that there is wanton waste in Government departments, or any other abuse, for that matter. But in this case we really do not think the Air Ministry officials are so greatly to blame. It is unfortunately inevitable that there should be a colossal amount of waste in connection with any war, let alone a war of the magnitude in which we have lately been engaged, and from which we have so recently emerged. In fact, all war is waste, and the only thing to be done about it is to reduce that waste to the lowest possible dimensions. Now, in the case of the aeroplanes which are the subject of these charges, what was the Air Ministry to do in the matter of placing orders for them? It was engaged in the task of beating the Germans in the air at a time when improvement and progress were being recorded every day, with the consequent effect that the machine which was the last word to-day was utterly obsolete to-morrow. Obviously, it could not stand still and wait for the ultimate design – it had to carry on with what was best at a given moment, and thus to place contracts for machines which, when delivered, might be obsolete. That is what was inevitable, and what has actually happened.
>
> The next question that arises is that of what should be done with these surplus machines? Should they be retained in the Service; sold to private purchasers; or be broken up and the material used to the

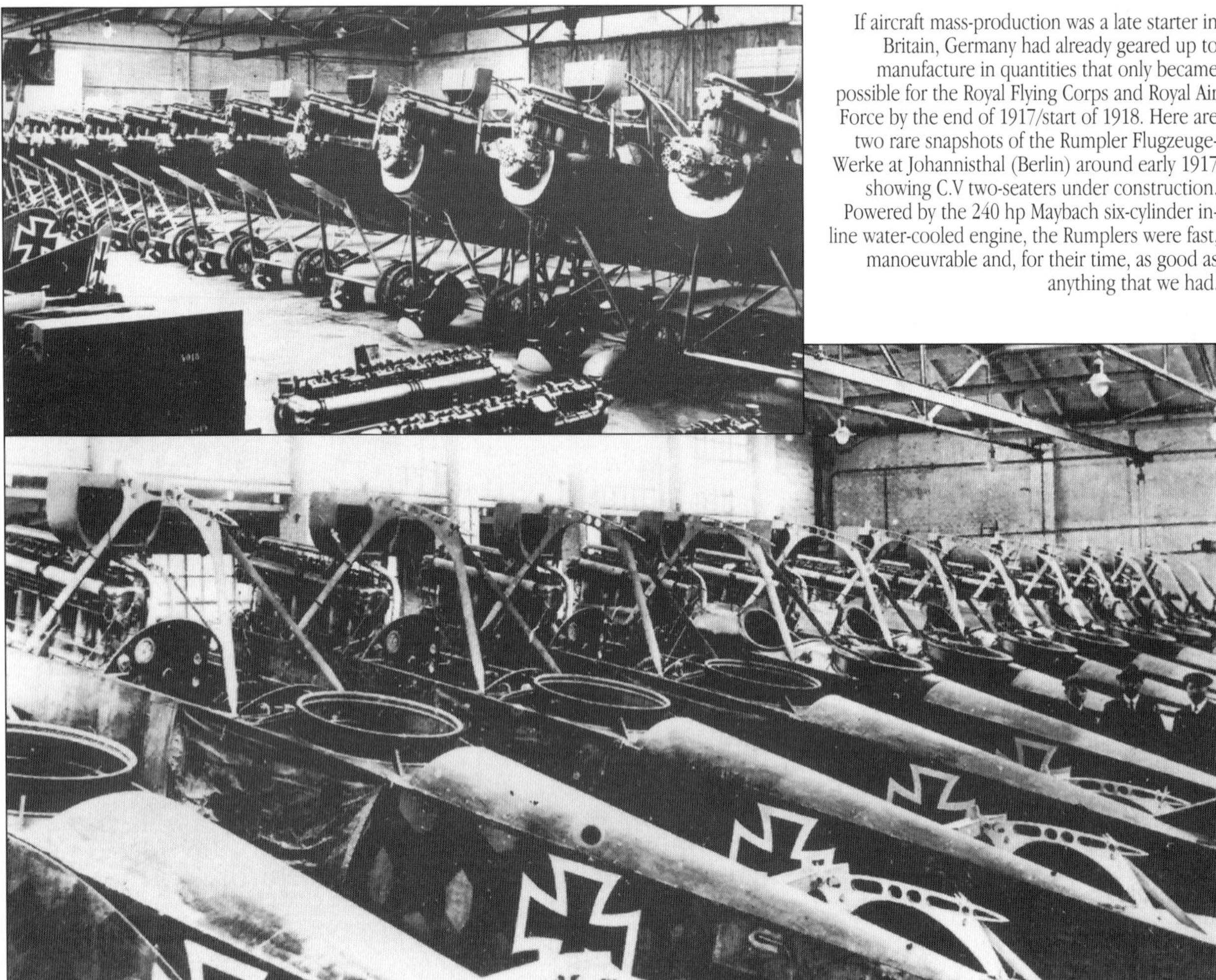

If aircraft mass-production was a late starter in Britain, Germany had already geared up to manufacture in quantities that only became possible for the Royal Flying Corps and Royal Air Force by the end of 1917/start of 1918. Here are two rare snapshots of the Rumpler Flugzeuge-Werke at Johannisthal (Berlin) around early 1917 showing C.V two-seaters under construction. Powered by the 240 hp Maybach six-cylinder in-line water-cooled engine, the Rumplers were fast, manoeuvrable and, for their time, as good as anything that we had.

best advantage? Obviously, it is no use retaining them in the Service. Their very obsolescence demonstrates that at once. The next alternative is to sell them for what they will fetch as complete machines. Here we come up against a difficulty. Many, if not most, are of types which were adopted because of their adaptability to war, and are practically useless for civilian flying – and they would hardly make useful school machines. Numbers have been sold, but it seems clear that there are far more for disposal than there is a market for, and we are thus driven back on the third alternative, which is to break them up and salve what material is worth saving. It seems to us the principal reason which has led up to the incurring so much post-War waste is that we had succeeded before the end of hostilities in achieving a rate of production which was actually in excess of our needs as they finally determined themselves. We had to strain every resource of production to render ourselves overwhelmingly strong in the air. An Air Ministry that had failed in its task would have stood condemned, but it did not fail and hence the sudden termination of a War which, up to its last phases looked like going on indefinitely, has necessarily left us with a vast accumulation of material on our hands, and we have to adopt apparently wasteful expedients for dealing with it. That seems to us to be the beginning and end of the matter. We do not say that the methods of the Air Ministry might not be improved in detail, but on the broad question of waste we are not inclined to take a harsh view.

The magazine obviously felt concern for the Public Purse over this whole matter for in the same issue it reported on what was really going on at Waddon as regards aircraft disposal. The tale is repeated here exactly as written although the original photographs have not survived in suitable form for good reproduction:

In spite of its uninspiring name, the Waddon Salvage Depôt is a most interesting place at the present time. Up to the time of the signing of the Armistice it was known officially as NAF. 1, or National Aircraft Factory No. 1, and was only just getting into its stride, producing aeroplanes. Now it is known as ASD. 3, and is being utilised as a centre for the disposal of surplus aircraft and material and the salvage of damaged and obsolete aeroplanes and parts.

It is such a short time since the cry on all sides was for more and more aeroplanes for the Royal Air Force that it is a little difficult to realise that one of the most acute problems facing the authorities at the present time is the disposal of its surplus machines. Down at Waddon can be seen rows and rows of aeroplanes and stacks of engines – not simply dumped down, but all carefully sorted and arranged so that they take up the minimum of room, yet leaving ample space for inspection. Great attention has been given to the question of ensuring that the machines do not deteriorate while being stored. In the case of the DH.9's seen in one photograph, the wheels are raised clear of the ground by wooden blocks, the weight of the fuselage is taken by the end of the longerons, and where one fuselage rests on another the point of contact is on a bulkhead, so that the framework cannot be distorted. This method is not suitable for all machines but in every case the principle is the same although the application may be slightly different. The wings are stored in separate racks in close proximity to the bodies, so that if anyone chooses a particular machine it can easily be got out in a very short space of time, and at the most only disturbing three machines. The same care is taken in the storing of propellers and spare wings.

In the case of the engines the process is a little different. They mostly arrive in cases and after being unpacked are mounted on a special stand, thoroughly cleaned and greased. Then they are graded as follows: 'A' brand new; 'B' used, but as good as new 'C' second-hand but serviceable; 'D' damaged or incomplete. They are then taken to the store where the various engines are grouped according to make and condition. One of our photos shows a corner of this store.

Alongside the factory is a large aerodrome, so that when a machine has been selected it can be assembled, tested and flown away.

So far we have dealt with the handling of complete machines and parts, but there is another side to the work at Waddon. It is a receiving depôt for a great deal of the 'junk' of the RAF – crashed and

Above: In many ways Germany had an easier task when it came to aircraft disposal. With no responsibility for recouping her taxpayers' investment, the conditions of the Peace Treaty left no alternative but disposal by destruction. This is the scene at Johannisthal early in 1919 as aircraft arrive in batches to be stripped of all reusable raw materials – including the valuable rubber tyres – and prepared for burning.

Right: A huge area of the famous and ancient aerodrome at Johannisthal became a wood dump and here, in the raw German winter, the most valuable commodity was firewood. Here men and boys were allowed to help themselves to this important by-product of defeat.

Looking rather dishevelled at some distant dispersal point, this Fokker Triplane displays a rather battered lower port wing as well as displaced aileron controls. Machines such as these were not even stripped of usable parts but generally burned where they stood at the war's end.

At the end of the War, a small number of German fighters found their respective ways, apparently unofficially, to other quarters mostly around north-eastern Europe. The majority, though, were quickly scrapped. One-time fighters, reconnaissance aircraft and bombers were simply hacked up where they stood. In this picture, taken at an unknown disposal site, several Pfalz D.XII aircraft are recognisable among others. The fuselage on the left shows clearly where the axe has cleaved it in two. In the main, apart from engines for scrap, the only items salvaged for re-cycling were tyres for Germany had an on-going and severe rubber shortage. Germany faced the same dilemma as we did in Britain, the only difference was that the German taxpayer was not in a position to object, and nor was the German government. Disposal in Germany meant wholesale destruction.

damaged aeroplanes and bits thereof – and it is the job of the factory to reduce this to 'produce.' When the train disgorges its load of broken wood and twisted metal it appears almost hopeless to turn such chaos into order, but the system has now been so developed that in a very short time the various classes of material are sorted out.

The fabric is carefully stripped and packed up to go to another factory, where the dope is recovered and then sent on to make high-class paper, the instruments, fittings, strainers, and wires, etc, are taken to the store, and the wood-work is utilised for making the racks and engine stands in the stores. The metal is sorted out and wherever fittings are recoverable they are taken off and sent to the store. As far as possible the steel parts are classified according to the material and the non-ferrous metals go to the foundry where they are melted down. The method of dealing with damaged radiators gives one an idea of the way in which the department goes to work. First, of all the radiator is placed in an oven and the solder is run oft; then the soft brass shell is melted down into ingots and the hard brass tubes, in their turn, go through a similar process; and all three classes of ingots are in great demand.

A visit to the factory leaves one outstanding impression – that a serious attempt is being made to turn all this surplus material to as good account as is possible and to obtain the utmost value from it. It is also extremely satisfactory to know that practically all the work is being done by discharged sailors and soldiers; many of whom have either lost a limb in the War or suffered some disablement. There is a certain amount of female labour employed, but, here again, preference is given to the widows and dependents of those who have given their lives for their country.

From what has been said it will be gathered that Waddon presents plenty of opportunities for those who are in the market for aircraft or materials; but, in the first place, enquiries should be directed to the Aircraft Disposal Board's offices in York House, Kingsway, where samples are on view of almost everything obtainable, from complete aeroplanes to bolts and nuts.

Waddon is, to all intents and purposes, a wholesale warehouse – and a wonderful place.

'Wonderful place' or not, the tales of unskilled and wasteful rampage with axes would not go away and the problem remained that none of the soft-soap stories (invariably in periodicals like *Flight* which the ordinary man on the street never saw) placated the potential problem of the taxpayers' reaction when news of this sort of tone eventually got out. No, even if the outcome was merely piles of rubbish that could then at a later date be disposed of, 'dismantling' sounded more businesslike than scrapping. 'Dismantling' had a vague air of applied skill of some even vaguer type. 'Scrapping' conjured up images of unkempt labourers and, somewhere, a horse and cart...

The accusations of wholesale wastage did not go away. No sooner was one dismissed than another reared up its ugly head. And now came fresh stories of brand-new aircraft being burned at Farnborough. Were these stories the mere rumours spread about by troublemakers? On March 7th 1919 Charles Kingsford-Smith, to become one of Australia's most famous flyers, wrote home to his family from No.5 (E) ARD Henlow. Kingsford-Smith, then aged 22, was about to be demobbed from the Royal Air Force having been one of 150 of his countrymen selected for the RFC in the winter of 1916. Blooded – and wounded – in the Great War, 'Smithy's' letters home

Johannisthal was the cradle of German aviation and was to Germany what Hendon was to Britain. At the end of the war it became a dumping ground for the German air force. Here at the beginning of 1919 a pile of scrap aircraft await the final ignominy. What is apparent is the poor external condition of these aircraft, some of which are new – evidence of the declining build quality as German industry ran out of quality material in the face of production demands.

form a part of his country's aviation history.[1] Here is an extract from that particular letter:

> [Cyril] Maddocks [then aged 28] is in charge of the Salvage section here, and he also superintends the breaking up of machines (perfectly good ones, too); and he can pull many strings. Result is we are getting three or four machines for about £50 each, and after paying freight to Australia, they will cost us somewhere about £100 each.

A little later on, the exuberant Kingsford-Smith was offered a job with a joy-riding operation back home in Australia by a fellow 'digger' who had 'pulled strings' with the Ministry's Aircraft Disposal Board and bought a number of Avro 504K aircraft for £200 apiece and shipped them to Australia having paid for them using Australian war-gratuity bonds.[2]

Matters of war surplus and salvage were now a paramount concern and the House of Commons was awash with Members' questions on military, naval and air force redundant arms. One debate, held on May 15th, revealed some interesting facts and also looks at potential solutions.

It all began when Lt-Col Sir Samuel Hoare asked the Under-Secretary of State to the Air Ministry whether he could form any estimate of the loss involved to the State by the destruction, at the Cove Camp, Farnborough, of a number of new aeroplanes never used and many not even unpacked; and whether he could not have found a market in neutral countries or amongst civilian purchasers for the sale of these brand new goods?

The Under-Secretary of State for Air at this time was Maj-Gen Seely. He responded, perhaps obliquely, but nevertheless very fully and at the sort of length that ought to make any questioner forget what he had asked:

> On the signing of the Armistice, the Air Council had some 20,000 aeroplanes and seaplanes on charge, and machines were being produced at the rate of 4,000 a month. The storage available, including hirings which had to be given up, was insufficient to enable these numbers to be stored under cover as well as the new machines of which the Air Council would have to take delivery.
>
> The Air Council had three alternatives: (1) To erect or hire buildings to store all serviceable machines, in the hopes that a market would be found or those not required by the Royal Air Force in peace. (2) To break up the least valuable machines, sending the useful portions to the Disposal Board and selling the remaining material as scrap. (3) To remove the instruments and engines, burn the machines and sell the metal remains as scrap.
>
> The first alternative would have been very costly and the market for the older machines before they became unserviceable in store did not justify such a course. The third would have required less expenditure of labour, but the disposal authorities of the Ministry of Munitions considered that a market might be found for the salved parts, and the second alternative was, therefore, adopted by the Air Council.
>
> The Air Council, in accordance with the policy they adopted, divided the machines into three classes (a) Standard machines for the Royal Air Force. (b) Machines obsolete for use in the Royal Air Force in peace or war, but suitable for civil aviation. (c) Machines obsolete for war purposes, and not suitable for civil flying.
>
> On March 31 there were 15,700 machines of the first class; of these large numbers are surplus to the requirements of the Royal Air Force, and are available for sale. On the same date there were approximately 1,000 of the second class, also available for sale to the public. There were 3,600 of the third class still awaiting reduction to produce.
>
> The Disposal Board of the Ministry of Munitions are responsible for selling machines of Class I and 2 not required by the Royal Air Force, but the Board have no large storage accommodation available, so that the machines or disposal usually remain in the Royal Air Force storage until a market is found for them by the Board.
>
> I am sending an officer to make sure that the policy of the Council is being efficiently carried out at Farnborough and Henlow, but I have no doubt that the policy adopted by the Air Council after the Armistice was sound, and involved the least possible cost to the State.

This drew a response from Lt-Col P B Malone (United, Tottenham South) who asked if any attempt had been made to find a market for those machines in foreign countries, adding as a sort of pungent afterthought the question whether he was aware that some of the machines which had been destroyed were brand-new machines straight from the manufacturers?

Seely shuffled nervously and then

1. Quoted from *Flying Matilda: early days in Australian aviation* by Norman Ellison, Angus & Robertson, Sydney, 1957, part two, page 247. Brisbane-born Charles Kingsford-Smith (1897-1935) had entered the £10,000-prize England-Australia race announced in 1919 but was eventually prevented from participating. Sixteen years later he set up an England-Australia record in a 120 mph Percival Gull and, in 1927, flew a converted Bristol Fighter as a pioneer airline pilot. With Charles Ulm he set up Australian National Airways. He lost his life under mysterious circumstances when his aircraft disappeared somewhere off the coast of Burma.

2. *Op.cit,* page 270-271.

Left: Graveyard of French aircraft at the end of the War. Most have been burned but amidst the metal frameworks and still recognisable is a Hanriot-Dupont HD1, probably a Belgian machine.

Below: The post-war disposal of French aircraft was a rudimentary chopping-up followed by chucking in a heap and then burning. This pile appears to be composed of Potez biplanes.

sidestepped with a deft response intended to halt further debate on the matter.

> I dealt with the question in the very long statement which I have read and I must apologise to the House for its length. The machines from which the engines are taken out and the rest disposed of by auction to the best bidder are machines which are not suitable for the Air Force and are not suitable for civilian flying. Some of these machines are quite new, but the science of flying progresses so quickly that many of them are now obsolete. It would be wrong to send our flying men in the Royal Air Force into the air on those machines and it would be equally wrong to release them for civil flying. If we could have foreseen seven or eight or ten months what we know now we would not have made them, but that is inevitable.

This earned a rejoinder from Lt-Cmdr J M Kenworthy (Liberal, Hull) who asked 'Have we come to the end of the obsolete machines, and what about the contracts?' Seely responded with the good news – and the bad. 'We have practically come to the end of the obsolete machines. The question of the closing of the contracts is a matter for the Minister of Munitions and not the Air Force.'

Another issue was running parallel to this, though – and because parliamentary memories were embarrassingly long, it concerned a blunder that was unlikely to be forgotten in a hurry. It all began several years earlier when, due to a chronic shortage of aircraft timber, an effort was made to find an alternative to spruce and ash – the two timbers most commonly used in aircraft construction. Somebody recommended cypress. Now this is an interesting timber, properly known as yellow cedar, Alaska cypress or, confusingly, Alaska cedar. It is prolific in North America and is a softwood known for its durability. And it looks almost exactly like spruce!

Government acted and at once ordered huge stocks of cypress to boost diminishing supplies of Scandinavian sitka spruce and Canadian spruce. No revision was made of strength calculations and only later after an aircraft with cypress wing spars suffered in-flight structural failure and fatally disintegrated, did somebody realize that their haste in direct substitution had been a terrible mistake. Cypress-built aircraft were hastily grounded – an embarrassing volte-face at a time when the industry was frantically trying to increase its aircraft output. Now the Coalition Unionist member for Macclesfield, J R Remer, asked the Secretary of State for War how many machines, manufactured and partly manufactured, had had to be discarded due having been built with 'an unsuitable wood for use on aeroplanes'.

The official reply was that no machines were discarded for this reason, 'but the substitution of other woods involved the supply of about 900 main planes, 100 main spars and 55 tail planes for machines on charge of the Royal Air Force'. Seely added that 'substitutions were also required for machines in the hands of contractors, and particulars of these are being sought for'.

Nine hundred wings sounds like a lot of discarding but because the words 'fuselage' and 'aircraft' were not used in this description, perhaps the slick-talkers thought they could get away with it. They didn't. Blood had to be sacrificed and heads caused to roll.

Recognising a sore spot when he found one, Remer pressed the Secretary of State for War for the names of his present advisers regarding 'the matter of the most suitable woods for use on aeroplanes'. He also demanded to know what were their pre-war occupations; and what practical experience of sawing and manufacturing timber they might possess. To this Seely responded: 'The Timber Committee of the Conjoint Board of Scientific Societies, in connection with the Royal Society, advises on the suitability of timber for aeroplanes. I will send my Hon friend a list of their names'. Sadly the records have not preserved any such list.

Getting rid of aeroplanes in some legitimate way preoccupied Government for much of the time but it fell to the Conservative member for Blackpool, Col W W Ashley, to hit on the idea of exporting the problem. He asked if anybody in a high place might consider offering some of the surplus aeroplanes now in the possession of the Air Ministry to the Overseas Dominions and Colonies with a view to their being used for postal and similar services.

A murmur of approval went through the House as the Under-Secretary of State to the Air Ministry passed the question to an assistant, J W Pratt (Liberal member for Linlithgow) who, getting to his feet, proclaimed in the formal and colourful language of his time: 'My Hon and gallant friend has asked me to reply. The question of the form in which assistance can be rendered to British Possessions overseas for the purposes referred to by my Hon and gallant friend is under consideration, and I hope to be able to announce a decision very shortly'.

To this Ashley proffered: 'Is the Hon gentleman aware that the Dominions would appreciate, not only the gift [of aeroplanes], but the spirit in which it was offered?' Pratt acquiesced and sat down. Now there was an idea worth looking into!

Earlier I made mention of that first and somewhat infamous auction of aeroplanes. It had been announced that on June 2nd no fewer than 15 complete machines would come under the hammer at a sale which Messrs Norbury-Smith and Company would hold for the Disposal Board at the No.1 Aircraft Salvage Depôt. At this rate, clearing thousands of aircraft was going to be a long job!

The sale, which took place at Hendon, aroused the public's curiosity, not the least because the popular newspapers gave plenty of coverage to its staging. As a result it attracted enormous interest and the store yard in which it was held was crowded with onlookers, observers and the curious, the majority of whom kept their hands firmly in their pockets. In the end, the event was described as a success although the prices obtained for the aeroplanes and associated aircraft material, as outlined earlier, cannot have been anywhere near what had been anticipated. The 400 lots (which actually included 16 complete aircraft) made just £3,155. It was reported that one lot of 700 hollow spruce struts, five feet long, only realised £5 – what would be known in the trade as a firewood-price.

As this auction was being prepared, the unflinching Colonel Ashley once more suggested disposal of aircraft to our unsuspecting Empire. He repeated his question about offering surplus aircraft to the Overseas Dominions and Colonies, asking Maj-Gen Seely outright if he would offer some of the surplus aeroplanes then in the possession of the Air Ministry, with a view to their being used for what had been described as postal and similar services?

Perpetuating the parliamentary practice of repeatedly asking the same question until such time as the recipient has been sufficiently worn down to produce an answer, the Under-Secretary of State for Air replied: 'This question is at this moment being considered. Perhaps [Col Ashley] will repeat his question next week. Since I drafted this answer a satisfactory conclusion has been arrived at by the Government and I hope to make a satisfactory announcement when the Hon member repeats his question'.

But Ashley was on a roll and quickly fired off another one. 'Will [these aircraft] be given as a free gift or will it be a purchase?' To which Seely responded: 'As a free gift to the Dominions, the Crown Colonies and to India.' At this, the Conservative Member for Chelsea, the venerable Lt-Col Sir Samuel Hoare, saw an opportunity to mention again the matter of scrap when he asked whether, in view of the high prices even then being realised for obsolete and old motor cycles and cars that were being sold by Government Departments, it would be desirable to offer some of the new aeroplanes, now being broken up by his Department, to the public by auction sale so as to test the market on this matter?

'The aeroplanes which are being reduced to produce are those which are obsolete for war purposes and unsuitable for civil aviation,' responded a battle-weary Seely. 'His Majesty's Government accordingly could not accept the responsibility of putting them on the market. The responsibility of the Air Ministry ends when they have decided what machines are surplus and which of them are obsolete for service use and unsuitable for civil aviation. Thereafter the question of disposal rests with the Disposal Board under the Ministry of Munitions.'

But Hoare was still not satisfied with this answer. 'Why could not the Right Hon gentleman put some of these on the market to see if there is a demand for them, and at the same time make it clear that any purchaser purchases them at his own risk?' It was, in truth, a fair comment, but Seely capped it satisfactorily. 'That is a matter for the Disposal Board of the Ministry of Munitions, and questions on that subject should be addressed to them.'

Riches to rags! The controversial aircraft builder J A Whitehead, left, poses with the mayor of Richmond in the summer of 1918 to mark the opening of his huge factory extension. Whitehead had just raised £1m on the Stock Exchange. Six months later aircraft orders were axed and the firm was wound up. Whitehead's family home later became Hanworth Air Park.

3501	Avro, 220 hp Le Rhône engine (Cambridge School of Flying) £360
4234	similar machine (Ogilvie and Partners) £360
6245	similar machine (Bournemouth Aviation Co.) £300
4340	similar machine (Capt Fanstone, RAF) £310
3505	similar machine (Bournemouth Aviation Co) £310
3510	similar machine (Capt Rutherford, RAF) £310
7384	Armstrong Whitworth, [FK.8] 160 hp Beardmore engine (Lt Howard, RAF) £260
D5150	similar machine (Capt Warren) £260
C7101	British Experimental, 2E. 90 hp RAF.IA engine (Aircraft Manufacturing Co) £80
A1298	similar machine (Lt Howard, RAF) £90
C2101	DH.6, RAF.IA engine (Aircraft Manufacturing Co) £95
C2943	similar machine. 80 hp Renault engine (Bournemouth Aviation Co) £100
C6503	similar machine, RAF.IA engine (Capt Fanstone, RAF) £85
C5220	similar machine, Curtis OX 5 engine (Mr Grahame-White) £95
C5224	similar machine, with ditto engine (less altimeter) (Mr Grahame-White) £80
C5231	similar machine (single-seater) (Mr Plumridge) £60

The full list of aircraft that were involved in the Hendon sale as taken from *Flight* (with sometimes inaccurate or at least untraceable serial numbers) together with purchasers' names and the prices realised.

At this, Lt-Col Moore-Brabazon joined in the debate by asking if any steps had been taken to dispose of some of the machines to neutral countries for trade purposes.

Rather petulantly, Seely replied: 'I have just announced the decision of the Government to make a free gift to the Dominions, Colonies and India of those required for certain specific purposes, but the disposal of the machines is a matter for the Disposal Board of the Ministry, and I shall be obliged if the [questioner] will address his questions to them, as they have all the facts at their disposal.'

And so the meanderings of Parliament rumbled on rather like one of those debilitating 'circular' bad dreams associated with fever where the same thing keeps happening over and over again. So it was when a week later the question of contracts for obsolescent aircraft was again raised by Lt-Col P B Malone. 'Will [you] state what contracts for obsolete or obsolescent aircraft remain uncancelled; and the date when it may be anticipated that these contracts will be concluded?' Answering for the Under-Secretary, the Rt Hon F G Kellaway assured him: 'All contracts for obsolete and obsolescent aircraft are now concluded'.

In the fullness of time, a large number of aircraft were presented to the Dominions. Wackett *[32]* relates that the first significant step towards setting up Australia's peacetime air force occurred in mid-1920:

> ...when the British Government, having great quantities of surplus war stock, offered Australia the gift of one hundred aircraft with a liberal allocation of ancillary equipment, such as motor transport, guns, cameras, bombs and spare parts of all sorts. The gift was gladly accepted and became the basic equipment to organize two flying stations and a stores depot, in addition to the original flying school. To control this embryo air force a headquarters was set up in Victoria Barracks, Melbourne, and I was transferred here as the first technical staff officer.

The early salvage sales and thoughtful gifts like this to our dominions overseas managed to get rid of some merchandise but even with this disposal technique, the large quantities of unsaleable parts could not be cleared and much that was old, obsolete or damaged was still unceremoniously burned. But this still left the problem of the huge numbers of completed or near-complete new machines and their engines, all of which were 'accountable' and under the hawk-eyed scrutiny of those out for a good political truncheon and the opportunity to wield it.

The Government itself had no mechanism for actually merchandising all this material either to the public or to other interested countries. The overriding concern was that this inventory represented goods paid for by the taxpayer in time of war and if the lot was simply destroyed it could result in the posing of embarrassing questions. What was really wanted was a way of converting the stuff into stock that was saleable to earn some return for the Exchequer.

In a curious move, Government now decided to hold a public bazaar to appeal to those of the public looking for bargains amongst the surplus aircraft equipment available. Around the middle of June a show of sample aircraft and accessories was set up near the main entrance of the Agricultural Hall. The actual goods, in bulk, were to be acquired from the Aircraft Salvage Factories at Hendon in North London and Waddon in Surrey, and members of the public wanting to go and see for themselves were invited to apply for a permit to view from the Controller, Aircraft Disposal Department, Kingsway.

This unique retail store opened to a still-curious public and offered everything from old uniforms and furniture through to vehicles and motorcycles (which sold easily), aircraft – in fact just about everything.

It should be remembered that at this time many factories were still powered by steam while others used steam engines to drive electricity generators. That July a press item appeared that the people in the disposal business were able to add to their well-thumbed portfolio of ideas.

> **UTILISATION OF SURPLUS WAR MATERIAL.**
> **AERO ENGINES FOR COMMERCIAL PURPOSES**
>
> Considerable attention is now being directed to the subject of working up much of the surplus war material, at present being disposed of by the Ministry of Munitions, into commercial propositions. It is interesting to note in this connection that a very successful test has just been carried out as to the utility of aeroplane engines for commercial purposes. A 200 hp eight-cylinder aero engine was installed in a London factory as a stand-by power unit, and the space occupied was approximately 8 feet long by 5 feet wide by 5 feet high, the total weight not exceeding 800 lbs, exclusive of radiators.
>
> The water cooling was effected by running the water through the ordinary cast-iron radiator as used in factories for warming the air in the shops. Coal gas was used, and the general running was found to be quite satisfactory, the noise being almost negligible compared with that of the other machines in the shop.
>
> It is estimated that the total output of this engine at a speed which may be reasonably supposed to give the engine a life of satisfactory duration should be about 75 hp.
>
> The Management of the factory concerned expressed themselves satisfied with the running of the engine, and it would undoubtedly appear that such units constitute easily adaptable and convenient stand-bys for such purposes.

The scene at Hamburg in 1919 where many hundreds of German fighters, reconnaissance aircraft and bombers were destroyed. Behind the burning pyre of fuselages lie rows of others awaiting the same fate. To the far left many hundreds of wings are heaped up on the grass. The original print of this picture reveals dismantled aircraft receding into the far distance. All have had their tyres removed.

Unfortunately this un-named factory appears to have been an isolated instance of aero-power and there was no subsequent rush across Industry to follow suit. Even so, the MOM was not short of ideas, even if some of them were not very good ones. A magazine was started. Named perhaps a little unimaginatively *Surplus,* it was the official organ of the Surplus Government Property Disposal Board of the Ministry of Munitions and was illustrated with a number of photographs showing a few of the articles and things to be sold. *Flight* reported on July 17th that: 'Those who are on the look-out for materials of all sorts will, doubtless, find this little magazine very interesting. It is published on the 1st and 15th of each month, and is sold at all bookstalls and newsagents at 3d.'

One could say that the budding aviator's every need might be addressed through the surplus market. Besides aeroplanes and flying clothing there were other and more tangible properties as *Flight* reported on June 19th:

> In the important sales of Government property now being held in various parts of the country, the Disposal Board of the Ministry of Munitions have arranged to include several aerodromes that are not permanently required for Government purposes. Of these, two are situated at Goldhanger and Stow Manes in Essex, two in Suffolk at Burgh Castle and Covehithe, one at Lilbourne, on the borders of Northants and Warwickshire, and the others are at Ramsey (Hunts), Telscombe (Suffolk) and Edzell (Kincardine). In some cases the buildings, with the land on which they stand, might be acquired without the aerodromes, and by means of their admirable situation be made suitable for factories, hospitals, convalescent homes, training centres, etc. The various buildings are of brick, corrugated iron, and timber, with water supply and electric light installed, and could readily be adapted for any of the purposes mentioned. There are also permanent roads. Intending purchasers may obtain further particulars by applying to the Disposal Board, D.B.1a.3, Room 135, Charing Cross Buildings, Villiers Street, WC2.

Aeroplanes and aerodromes were only part of the story. In April of 1919, for example, *The Daily Graphic* newspaper reported that:

> Thirty fighting tanks are included among a variety of goods which are being sold by direction of the Disposal Board of the ministry of Munitions. The tanks, which are at present lying at the training center, Wool, Dorset, will be disposed of by tender.

As regards the aircraft side of things, matters appeared to take an upward turn that August. An Australian gentleman by the name of S W Copley, who was said to be well known in insurance and financial circles, became the biggest private owner of aeroplanes when, for reasons best known to himself (and never subsequently disclosed) he bought 260 new Avro aircraft from the Aircraft Disposal Board. It was reported, somewhat erroneously as it turned out, that this comprised the whole surplus stock of the type that the Board held. It was also said that the largest number of aircraft sold to a single purchaser previously was about 100.

That, though, was not the only 'good' news, for another big deal was reported in which the United Aircraft Engineering Corporation of New York, through its London agents, the Canadian and General Trust, Ltd, had bought from the Aircraft Disposal Board 700 aircraft engines as well as a large number of complete aircraft. These were reported to be for export to Canada and the United States, 'to develop the commercial use of aircraft in both countries'.

In the end, though, the Americans proved to be a little more astute than imagined and this and other US deals were effectively blocked by the American Courts following an application for an injunction by the then already powerful Wright Corporation. This is described in Chapter 7.

Clever accounting for the benefit of public scrutiny offered the news that by July 12th 1919 the sum realised by disposal sales of surplus Government property had already exceeded £141,000,000. It wasn't immediately made clear that this figure included sales amounting to £32,800,000 that were completed after the date of the Armistice and prior to the setting-up of the Disposal Board of the Ministry of Munitions. It also included £76,000,000 for sales on trading account and £65,000,000 for other surplus stores.

The grand exhibition of tools and other miscellaneous stores arranged by the Disposal Board of the Ministry of Munitions at the Agricultural Hall, Islington, was forced to seek a new home that August through a conflict of space-booking. As a consequence it moved to Earls' Court where it re-opened that October. At the same time the headquarters of the Aircraft Disposal Department, Ministry of Munitions, shifted from York House, Kingsway, to Earl's Court Exhibition's Welcome Club, where it promoted the availability of its huge stocks of aeroplanes, aeroplane engines and equipment.

Meanwhile Hendon had become if not the final resting place then certainly the surplus dump for a large number of machines, chiefly SE.5 fighters. It was reported that this store was being added to on a daily basis 'whilst those disposed of balance more or less the new-comers'. It was one of these aircraft, an SE.5A serial

German aircraft dismantled at the end of the War and awaiting disposal in a storage hangar. The aircraft are, from the left, Rumpler, three Pfalz D.II, and four Halberstadt CV aircraft. The wings stacked up in the background are all finished in random lozenge camouflage.

number F9022, that became the first of Jack Savage's 'skywriters'. The aircraft, later registered as G-EATE, was bought by Handley Page Ltd at an auction staged by the Disposal Board at Hendon in February 1920. It was sold on the following November (1921) to Maj John Clifford 'Jack' Savage who converted it to the prototype sky-writing aircraft for his expanding business which would be based for years to come at Hendon and was to become the only major civilian operator of the type.

Summer turned to autumn yet still Parliament was pre-occupied with aircraft surplus and Seely faced questions from Alfred T Davies that October 27th. The Coalition Unionist member for Lincoln sought confirmation that large numbers of aeroplanes had been destroyed by burning in the occupied districts of France and Belgium, whether aeroplanes of the newest type had still been delivered under contracts until the summer of that year, and whether the Canadian Government, adopting a different policy, had disposed of similar aircraft with commercial advantage? No doubt feeling as if his circular dream was in full repetition, Seely explained:

> Instructions have been given: (a) that any aircraft declared obsolete for all purposes (ie, Air Force and civil) shall be reduced to produce, and the produce handed to the Disposal Board; and (b) that any aircraft totally wrecked and beyond repair shall be reduced to produce, and the wreckage burned after removal of all parts of value. The number of crashed aircraft burnt after the removal of the valuable parts under (b) has been 28. In addition, since July 1, 1919, the residue of 259 crashed and 359 deteriorated or obsolete machines has been burnt after the valuable parts had been removed. The answer to the second part is in the affirmative. I have no official knowledge of the matter referred to in the third part of my Hon friend's question, but I think he has in mind a transaction carried out by the representative of the Ministry of Munitions in Canada on behalf of His Majesty's Government. If I am correct, I would refer him to the Minister of Munitions.

There was some progress and places such as the Number 2 Northern Aircraft Depôt was being prepared for closure. That November Parliament was told that since October, when repair work came to an end, the staff had been employed in clearing up and concentrating stores for disposal. As a result, the labour strength was only 894 people, this being 33 per cent less than it had been at the end of September. This was to be further reduced to a care and

SURPLUS
GOVERNMENT
PROPERTY FOR SALE

By Direction of the Disposal Board, Ministry of Munitions.

Army Huts
Building Material
Timber
Machine Tools
Engineers' Stores
Motor Lorries
Motor Cars
Bicycles
Electrical Machinery and Fittings
Furniture
Army Boots
Factories
Hardware
Textiles
Dock Equipment
Chemicals
Iron and Steel
Food Stuffs
Medical Appliances
Factory Clothing
Army Horses
Aeroplanes
Engines
Railway Material
Agricultural Machinery
Oil and Colour Trade Sundries, &c.

For detailed list of the above and all other surplus Government property for Sale, apply for

Price 3d. SURPLUS Price 3d.

(The Official Organ of the Disposal Board).
Published on the 1st and 15th of every month.

No. 4 NOW ON SALE.

Obtainable of all Newsagents, Bookstalls, &c., or from the Director of Publicity, Surplus Government Property Disposal Board, Armament Buildings, Whitehall Place, London, S.W.

[Flight]

The fortnightly magazine *Surplus,* although published for the public bookstalls by the Disposal Board, must have been seen as an effete gesture. However, the publication must equally have been unique in offering just about everything from Army horses, dock equipment, chemicals and aeroplanes to the acquisitive magazine-buying Clapham omnibus-rider.

maintenance party by mid-December.

Despite all this outward indication of action to clear surplus, the problem was still getting worse. At Bradford, Blackburn Aircraft was typical of the many companies up and down the land building aircraft to Air Ministry order. After the end of the war, the last of Blackburn's completed production were passed by the AID Inspection, collected by road – and carried away to be burned.

But even this somewhat draconian disposal technique still left the problem of the endless numbers of completed or near-complete machines and their engines stored up and down the country. Then there was the government's responsibility to the taxpayer, for nobody was allowed to forget that it was the man in the street that had paid for this lot. And sooner or later somebody would ask yet more leading questions in the House of Commons, if not the correspondence pages of *The Times.*

If Britain had no proper system for disposing of its own war surplus aircraft, then the situation in Germany was even worse. There were two reasons for this: first there was no accurate information on the quantities of armaments that Germany had for surrender, and second was the irrefutable fact that the Germans were devious in the extreme. The images that we have of war machines being broken up and scrapped only show the tip of an iceberg the full size of which, one suspects, nobody ever knew.

I did say that the Germans were devious. Thinking hard about it – and choosing my words with infinite care – there is no question that they lied, were deceitful and were obstructive when it came to the execution of the conditions of the Peace Treaty.

The conditions of the Peace Treaty were thrashed out in Versailles and it took almost a year of negotiations before the details, debated and discussed *ad nauseam,* finally emerged as an action document. The conditions of the Treaty demanded that the Germans hand over all their paraphernalia of war for supervised disposal, either by sale or acquisition, or for scrap. There was plenty of evidence of individuals sabotaging goods so that they could not be used again. One of the things we were keen on having were Zeppelins to augment our own airship fleet, and these were subject of special dealings that are outside the scope of this present work. Suffice it to say that there were instances where punctured gas-bags allowed airships to settle in their hangars so sustaining irreparable damage.

It was, however, the sheer size of the task that really compounded the wits of the occupying Allies. Just as with Britain, Germany was a large country with a large and dispersed aircraft manufacturing industry. Even the accurate counting of aircraft was impossible. The former enemy were understandably disinclined to co-operate and employed any manner of ruses to hinder any progress. On December 16th 1919, a questioner in the House of Commons had queried the total number of guns and aircraft that had been handed over and how these numbers tallied with the numbers totally declared. The answer given was that the figures were 5,000 guns, 25,000

At the end of the War Germany had plenty of unwanted aircraft and engines. To avoid surrender some were assigned to other duties. Here, in 1919, an engine and its propeller are being used to draw a railway train. Coal was in short supply so the experiment was justified. Propeller-driven cars had been tried in this country, notably by propeller-designer and manufacturer Dashwood Lang who, in 1919, climbed the test hill at Brooklands in a car powered by a Gnôme rotary and achieved in excess of 50 mph. Hydroplanes and motor boats had been air-propeller-powered and there was a serious proposal that river and canal barges should be driven in this manner.

machine guns, 3,000 trench mortars – and 1,700 aeroplanes. And these quantities were 'the numbers laid down' in accordance with the terms of the Armistice.

It quickly became apparent that this answer and the figures given bore little relationship to the actual totals and, what was more, there was little agreement as to what those 'actual totals' might have been. The whole saga occupied most of 1920 and nobody knows how thoroughly the task was discharged.

The matter was clouded by the decision by Germany, revealed to a surprised British government, that internal commercial flying was to be 'resumed' on January 7th 1920 having been delayed for some weeks due to an extreme shortage of fuel. Because civilian flying had not been mentioned in the Peace Treaty, there was little that could be done about this development, except to note that the possibility was that possibly many German warplanes were to be painted brighter colours and given extra seats.

In truth, this didn't happen because the German aircraft industry wisely started off with a clean sheet of paper and geared up for commercial aircraft production instantly. The effect of this was to blur the main tenets of the Peace Treaty, namely the location of one-time warplanes (not helped by the non-co-operation of the German authorities), the counting of these aircraft – and their destruction. Historians would later unite in lamenting that no representative collection of these aircraft was kept. Even the giant Friedrichshafen G.IV bomber, parked engineless on the grass of London's St James's Park to the awe of thousands of curious spectators over that Easter, was eventually taken away and wasted.

Speaking in the House on April 15th, 1920, the Secretary of State for War (Winston Churchill) revealed that more than 12,000 war planes were still in the possession of the Germans. The following week Colonel C Lowther (Independent, Lancashire Lonsdale) asked the Prime Minister whether any date has been specified for their surrender; and, if so, what date and how many?

Prime Minister David Lloyd George deputed Churchill to reply and clearly the information he had was incomplete.

'The points raised are already answered, so far as I am in a position to answer them, by the statement which I made [last week]. I am not in a position to add anything further.'

Lowther was not happy with this and challenged as to what excuse was being offered by the German Government for the non-delivery of over 12,000 aircraft. Noel Pemberton-Billing, displaying feigned incredulity, reinforced Lowther's position with rhetoric. 'Is it a fact that there are still 12,000 war planes in Germany?' he postured.

Churchill said that it was and added an assurance that 'the aerial material is being handed over and the question of its destination is in the hands of the Allied Council'. This drew a prompt return from Lowther who suggested that, regarding this 'paraphernalia of war', there must be little else so easy to hand over as war planes. Churchill could only reply with 'They are being handed over and their destruction is now being taken in hand' to which the Conservative Unionist Member for Acton, Sir Harry Britain, piped up with the näive response 'Why do you want to

The British Army Aircraft Workshops at Farnborough was originally known as the Army Balloon Factory, later the Royal Aircraft Factory. This was the 'approved' source of most military aircraft until time of War when aircraft had to be sourced not just from here but from 'the Trade' as independent makers were called.

Among the many aircraft manufacturing contractors was the great factory of Frederick Sage at Peterborough. Highly skilled at shopfitting, they quickly gave of their all in defence of the Realm. From constructing aircraft as sub-contractors, in 1917 Sage began designing its own original machines. Here in the erecting shop is the Sage No.4A Seaplane, N116, and other machines under construction.

destroy them?' Somebody probably promptly sat upon him.

All this really did was underscore how little understanding of the real problem both Lowther and Churchill actually had. It was not helped by a general parliamentary ignorance of matters concerning the Peace Treaty.

Churchill was able to confirm, for the benefit of Sir Harry, that the German aeroplanes would be surplus to all possible British requirements, and consequently it had been decided that, except for some machines reserved for exhibition purposes, they would all be reduced to produce and the material sold.

The man in charge of the Inter-Allied Commission of the Air Control was an Air Commodore by the name of Masterman and he delivered a report at a special Ambassadors' Conference in Paris, in which he emphasized the necessity for immediate Allied action to force Germany to execute the Clauses of the Peace Treaty dealing with the suppression of military aircraft in Germany. He went on to press the urgency.

Masterman's report, leaked before its reading, clearly raised doubts as to whether Britain should trust her late enemy in regard to the 12,000 aeroplanes which, as part of the Treaty, should already have been handed over. This raised more parliamentary questions and Mr Churchill was forced to explain that Masterman's job fell short of having to regulate or monitor the enforcement of the Air Clauses of the Peace Treaty. The man with this task was the senior French military tactician Marshal Ferdinand Foch who had been deputed by the Allies to supervise the Military and Air Clauses of the Treaty. Foch's responsibility was to refer to the Council of Ambassadors as he saw fit while Masterman, an officer of the Royal Air Force, and merely sent weekly reports to the Air Ministry on the progress of his work under the Inter-Allied Commission. It was a move to devalue the importance of Masterman's doubts, yet Churchill chose to overlook the plain fact that Masterman had been invited to present his personal reading of the situation to the Conference.

So what was going to happen with these 12,000 German aeroplanes that Churchill assured everybody would safely arrive in this country? Rather exasperated, Churchill gently explained that they would not be coming to Britain and the intent was that they should be broken down on the spot and reduced to produce and disposed of in the best possible manner.

Pemberton-Billing, ever controversial, leapt to his feet and asked Churchill if he was 'aware of the enormous commercial value to Great Britain of these large bomb-carrying aeroplanes' adding the hope that he would offer them to those desiring to introduce a commercial service in this country.

Churchill parried the question without demur, suggesting that Pemberton-Billing should communicate with the Disposal Board of the Ministry of Munitions.

And there the matter rested, more or less, all through May with only occasional cross-bench bleats about the tardiness of the Germans. In the background, the more literate MPs were adding up German aeroplane totals and discovering alarming anomalies.

The matter erupted again on June 15th 1920 when Winston Churchill was asked to state the number of airships and aeroplanes in German hands at the end of hostilities, and how many or what proportion of these had been handed over or destroyed under Allied supervision. The answer given was that 'approximately' 16 airships and 18,500 aeroplanes represented the strength of the former enemy and that up to May 29th that year no airships or aeroplanes had been handed over to the Allies, but 700 aircraft and 3,000 engines had been destroyed.

Churchill added: 'I would remind [the House] that Germany was under no obligation to destroy aircraft material until the ratification of the Peace Treaty [this did not take place until January 10th 1920 – AO-H]. For various... reasons – the state of confusion owing to the revolution, etc – the actual work of destruction was not commenced until May 3rd [1920]'.

So often we forget that it is people that built aeroplanes. Fortunately this was the era when group photographs of factory workers were popular and so some of these forgotten faces can be remembered. From the Sage archives comes this picture of one group of workers with their foreman seated at the front. Standing either side are believed to be Eric Cecil Gordon England (left) and Clifford Wilfrid Tinson.

Frederick Sage built a number of Short 184 seaplanes during the War. Handling the machines where there wasn't a convenient slipway meant lifting the aircraft out of the water. Here a jetty steam crane raises an unmarked example. Note the early form of stepless float, the wing-tip stabilisers and the tail float. The summer of 1917 saw the one and only Sage Type 4a (N116) seen below on its slipway. Although adopted as a training seaplane, the Armistice intervened before contracts could be placed. Associating with seaplanes invariably called for getting wet feet. Here (bottom) the Sage is seen on test at Felixstowe in 1918. While numbers of Shorts were allocated for post-War disposal, Sage's useful trainer never had the chance to prove its worth – and be rendered surplus.

This drew a sharp rejoinder from Noel Pemberton-Billing who pointed out that Germany was building more aircraft that they had destroyed since the end of the war. 'They are manufacturing three aeroplanes to every one that is being built in this country!' Churchill countered that the reverse was true and that we had built 300 aircraft since the end of the war and Germany just 60. He did not explain that the majority of those 300 were uncancellable war contracts thus adding early credence to the belief that there's lies, dam' lies and statistics, to which could be added 'political obfuscation'.

The unaccountability of the whole question became further confused soon afterwards when Prime Minister Bonar Law told the House (on July 1st 1920) that 'up to June 19th... nineteen seaplanes had been handed over to the Allies and 2,846 aeroplanes destroyed under Allied supervision'.

Germany's aircraft disposal problem was also something of a free-for-all and there were pickings to be had for those that asked. In the same month that Britain (under the Imperial Gift scheme discussed earlier in this Chapter) gave the Union of South Africa 112 aircraft and four airships worth £1,750,000, Italy claimed her share of the German air force and, compliant with the terms of the Peace Treaty, selected two Zeppelins, 100 aircraft and 300 motors. Loaded on 50 railway wagons, these were to be delivered by the Germans before the end of July 1920. And a few months later, Japan was due to receive her share of the loot, namely 50 aircraft 'including some of the most modern type', for which the Japanese government voted the sum of ¥500,000 for the construction of hangars at the military aerodromes of Tokorozaiva and Kagamigahara to accommodate the new acquisitions. Two airships sheds at Juterbog, Berlin, were also to be dismantled and re-erected by German engineers on Japanese soil.

It must have been painfully obvious to those in charge that the Allied task of accounting for German war planes was like trying to count smoke. On July 13th 1920 a despatch from Friedrichshafen said that the Allied destruction commission had visited 22 sites where aircraft material was produced notably the Manzell aeroplane works at Seemoos, the Maybach works at Friedrichshafen, and the Mercédès works at Unterturckheim where material had been destroyed. The following week Zeppelin L.64 was successfully flown from Ahlorn to Pulham to join L.71 already surrendered.

How any of the foregoing information might be reconciled with the Prime Minister's written answer to a further MPs question that 'up to July 31st (1920) 128 aeroplanes and seaplanes had been surrendered, 813 aeroplanes and seaplanes destroyed, one airship surrendered and another destroyed' is anybody's guess. Similarly it is hard to be sanguine about the message from Berlin on September 17th (1920) that the delivery of aircraft to the Allies in accordance with the Versailles

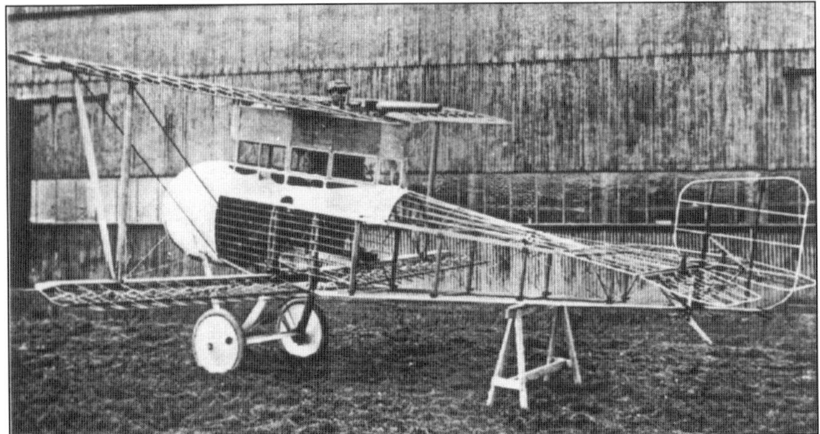

Strangest of all the aircraft to emanate from Peterborough was the Sage Type 2 Scout designed in the spring of 1916 (left). Designed by Clifford Tinson, it was an attempt to make an effective fighter with a wide field of fire before the age of the interrupter gear. The fuselage centre section was an enclosed cabin for the pilot and his observer who could stand up through the hole in the top wing. With a close-cowled 100 hp Gnôme Monosoupape and a span marginally over 22 feet, the Type 2 first flew on August 10th 1916 (bottom) and flew extremely well. However on September 20th the rudder-post failed and the aircraft was destroyed in the resultant crash landing. By this time, interrupter gear was available and the Type 2 was abandoned. Sage gave up aircraft work at the end of the War.

Peace Treaty had been completed.

The final anomalous news broke later in the year when a report sent to Paris from Berlin claimed that up until November 3rd 1920, the Inter-Allied Aeronautic Commission had taken possession of 28,000 aero engines, a figure 12,000 in excess of the number the Germans had faithfully owned up to. At the same time some 18,000 aircraft had been confiscated on top of those delivered, in accordance with the Armistice terms, to other nations such as Italy and Japan. These figures should have matched those given out to Parliament in April when Mr Churchill revealed that the Air Ministry 'estimated' there to be 15,248 aeroplanes. And this was before the revelation, made by the Ministry of Defence on April 29th, that Germany had placed her 'entire stock' of available aircraft – namely 400 aeroplanes and 820 engines – at the disposal of the Entente!

One cannot truly blame the Germans for dishonesty in such matters in time of defeat, but it does mean that nobody today has the slightest idea how many aeroplanes had to be disposed of: they probably had no idea and, unquestionably, neither had we!

The year 1920 tended to be one of disillusionment on more fronts than one. If the sum total of our efforts at emasculating the Luftwaffe was unquantifiable, rather worse news was to come, especially for the American tax-payer.

In February 1920 details of conclusions set out in the final report of the Aviation Sub-Committee of the American House of Representatives gave what *Flight* termed a 'cold douche' to the wonderful stories prevalent in 1918 of how American aircraft crowded the air in the War area and brought the enemy to heel. The report stated that the War Department had spent £210,000,000 for aviation during the 19 months of America's participation in the War, with the result that only 213 American-made planes, all of the DH.4 observation type, reached France. The total number of aircraft with the Americans at the time of the Armistice was 740, including 527 bought from the Allies, and the report emphasised that no American-built combat, pursuit, or bombing plane reached the front, despite the huge expenditure.

The Report, extending to 50,000 words, charged the Secretary of State for War, a Mr Baker, and various high officers in charge of the aviation branches with the failure of the United States to be a factor in the air and with wasting many millions of dollars. It was also revealed that the fatalities among American flyers were five times greater proportionately than those of any other Power and this fact was attributed to inferior machines and insufficient training.

What with the revelations from America and the events unfolding in Germany, nearer home our own war-surplus problems represented a thorny problem that showed no signs of going away. All the effort that had been expended through 1919 had not even scratched the surface of the predicament. In fact the activities of the Disposal Board had been undertaken at excessive cost. Run like a government department and rich in staff, it had operated with overheads that were unsuitable for close scrutiny.

What was wanted was a separate and commercially-run undertaking where the customary business brief would imbue the operation with that one feature denied any Government department – cost-efficiency.

The answer lay in the formation of a parasitic business that on the one hand would satisfy the most ardent critic of military arms disposal methods, while on the other it would actually produce a return on the investment. It would help the Government Exchequer by avoiding questions (if not downright assertions) of profligacy with taxpayers' money.

But there was to be a darker side to the coin for, in providing a solution to the immediate problem, it would create a legacy that was to have serious if not profound repercussions for the entire aviation business. More importantly, it would impinge on the whole aircraft industry, for many years to come.

The mechanism for disposal was to come from within the aircraft industry itself although it should not have taken a marketing genius to anticipate that whatever solution was found to the problem it was bound to have repercussions. The extraordinary thing is that nobody had the common sense to foresee what any such strategy would lead to in the long term. But you did not have to be a master chess-player to work out the inevitable outcome of each move. Certainly not so soon after the Great Aircraft Fabric Fiasco!

Chapter 6

The Great Aircraft Fabric Fiasco of 1919

IN the world of Government Surplus, most of the parameters that define the sale of 'normal' consumer goods are chucked out of the window. Today, with the experience of two World War aftermath disposal to refer back to, the pattern of these sales is easy to identify. The principal ingredients are enormous stocks (meaning vast numbers of individual items), goods with narrow and often specialist appeal – and consequent unrealistic prices.

After the Second World War, many stores concentrated on selling goods of this type and one in particular will be remembered in London's Tottenham Court Road where Spitfire, Lancaster, Mosquito, Hurricane and, later, Gloster Meteor parts could be bought for a song right up into the 1970s. Undercarriage and flap-operating hydraulic jacks, as an example, varied in cost from 7s 6d to 45s! Their real cost was considerably more.

From this one can readily appreciate that often it is the sheer volume of surplus goods that must be shifted which creates the problems in marketing. As 1919 advanced, Britain found itself becoming a gigantic department-store of redundant equipment. First there was all the finished and unfinished aircraft that had been in production when the Armistice was signed. Then there were all the aircraft brought back from the conflict itself. Some flew back home, others came back by surface transport. Then there were the tons of spares parts ranging from wings and engines through to washers and split pins. The product was in glut! And there were only just a few people who might take the family shopping for a Sopwith Snipe – even at bargain price.

Selling cheaply – today we tend to refer to such events as 'clearance sales' – causes instability in the market. We all know that, yet it seems nobody was willing to learn.

Curiously, though, there was already a precedent. The scene had been set rather earlier on and in a somewhat unlikely quarter. The villain of the piece in this instance was none other than cloth – Irish linen aircraft fabric to be precise. It formed the leading topic of conversation across that first peace-time Easter, generated several newspaper cartoons and some vitriolic letters to the popular press. Admittedly cloth was more saleable and to a wider

Across the history of aviation, many a malicious shed and numerous marauding telephone poles have succeeded in bringing down unsuspecting aircraft. Here a nearly new Avro 504K, D2059, one of a batch of 150 built in 1918 by the shop-fitting business Frederick Sage & Co of Peterborough, falls victim to such an attack. Of particular interest is the high quality of the fabric finish, especially on the wings. *[Graham Simons]*

Women fabric-workers in the Manor Park Works of Whitehead Aircraft Co Ltd of Kingston. John Alexander Whitehead secured contracts to built Maurice Farman Shorthorns and Sopwith Pups (which he persisted in calling the 'Whitehead Fighting Scout') as well as DH.9 and 9A aircraft. The youthful Whitehead was not one of the most popular men in the business. When his company raised £1m for expansion in 1918, he (and his shareholders) could not imagine that the War's end was mere months away – and that his now-vast factory would be without work. Despite his protestations that the Government owed him nearly £½-million, in October 1919 his firm was wound up with liabilities of £85,000 against assets of barely £15,000 and he was declared a bankrupt.

audience than were old RAF fighters. Looking back on it now, it all seems rather silly, yet it almost toppled heads in very high places. Here's the outline of the story.

The Great Fabric Fiasco began quietly enough yet in the short space of a few months it had generated not so much ripples as a huge bow wave that swept a great deal before it. The tale is worth recounting for in many ways it turned out to be a prophetic one. It also demonstrates how to do things the wrong way – but we have to remember that politicians and enthusiasts have been practising that for a very long while.

First, though, what do we know about aircraft fabric. Well, in those days, as for many decades after, aircraft were covered in linen of the highest quality. Linen is made from flax and Ireland has made a name for itself as the place where this is converted into thread that can be woven into this special high-strength cloth.

So important was Ireland and its linen during the Great War that in 1918 Westminster imposed severe penalties should the product of any Irish spindles fall short of target. This was a rather obtuse manner with which to enforce a fervent hope that Ireland would supply no other country but Britain with its valuable product. The press reported the matter in the terms that would be clearly understood by those concerned:

> An Order of the Ministry of Munitions, dated May 17th, prohibits persons owning or controlling scutch mills in Ireland from scutching flax straw after July 1st, 1918, without the licence of the Director-General of Aircraft Production. Licences will be issued on his behalf by the Administrator of the Flax Supplies Committee, Whitehall Buildings, Ann Street, Belfast. The terms of the Order are as follows:
> (1) No person owning or controlling any scutch mill in Ireland wherein flax straw is scutched for any person other than the owner or controller thereof shall, without a licence issued by or on behalf of the Controller of the Supplies Department of Aircraft Production. scutch or cause to be scutched at any time after the first day of July, 1918, any flax straw.
> (2) Any person failing to comply with any provision hereof, or with any condition of any licence issued hereunder, shall be guilty of an offence against the Defence of the Realm Regulations.

The Board of Agriculture ran a flax production division which provided free seed to growers and, from July 1918, offered aid through the Flax Companies (Financial Assistance) Act. This is why, by the end of the war, aircraft fabric production touched seven million yards a month.

As an interesting aside on the matter of aircraft cloth, the Germans suffered an acute shortage of quality fabric during the First World War. Irish linen supplies, available to them until the trade was restricted by war, were quickly exhausted as were imports of cotton, so leaving factories with no suitable yarn for weaving, and manufacturers without cloth for covering. Germany did not possess an indigenous cloth industry of any size and all cotton and flax had to be imported. Many were the experiments carried out by the Germans in producing alternative cloths from a wide variety of substances extending from grass to animal hair, but the one that seems to have triumphed was the common-or-garden thistle. Here's a paragraph from *Flight:*

> Before the Armistice was signed, German aeroplane manufacturers were not finding it easy to get supplies of aeroplane fabrics, and it is stated that on some of the machines used towards the end of hostilities the wing coverings were made of thistle fibre, which is described as being only approximately half the strength of linen. It is also stated that, owing to the shortage of rubber in Germany, the only part of the aeroplane made of this material were the tyres, and these were of reclaimed rubber. Necessity truly is the mother of invention.

Britain, on the other hand, was not just well off for linen: it had enough on the shelf to cover ten thousand aeroplanes!

The story began with a brief report, again in *Flight* (March 20th 1919) and slipped in almost as a filler, that the Government had committed itself to 40,000,000 yards of aeroplane cloth. It said:

> With the cost of linen soaring at its present price, few traders care to commit themselves to a speculative purchase. It will probably be found necessary to let it loose in the market by

> degrees as at present to cover cost nothing much under 7s per yard retail would be of any use.

The dirty-stuff hit the fan on March 28th when Lt-Col Cecil L'Estrange Malone, (Independent for Leyton East), having read this news item, raised a question in Parliament. He enquired of the Under-Secretary of State to the Air Ministry how many yards of linen were then in the possession of the Aircraft Disposal Department. The Deputy Minister of Munitions (who was also The Under Secretary) was Frederick G Kellaway. He answered very precisely. 'The total stocks of linen in the possession of the Ministry of Munitions and available for disposal' he told the House, 'is 31,970,725 yards.'

Well, so it wasn't forty million after all, but it was still sufficient cloth to stretch not quite three-quarters of the way around the globe. However, the news made the selfsame Lt-Col Malone think. He came back with further questions. What, for instance was the price paid per yard for the cloth and who were the exact suppliers? What arrangements were being made for its disposal?

Mr Kellaway, replied very cautiously that linen had been purchased from no fewer than 137 contractors and the price per yard varied with the cost of the flax. 'At the time of the Armistice the price ranged from 1s 8d for spaced fabric to 3s 0½d for solid fabrics.' he answered, no doubt in the assumption that everybody knew the difference between 'solid' and 'spaced' fabric. He added that a considerable quantity of linen was being disposed of in this country in small lots by public tender and some was to be sold abroad.

Given a subject upon which to erect a debate, no self-respecting MP can resist the temptation to trowel as deep into the matter as he can and Kellaway's answers fuelled more questions. Soon the House of Commons found itself embroiled in a sort of Cloth War.

'How many millions of yards of linen are now being treated as scrapped by the authorities?' thundered Malone, to which Kellaway responded that none of it was being so treated.

'Then how many millions of yards were over-ordered?'

'The probable surplus is something like 40,000,000 yards.'

We were back to that familiar round figure again! Which is more than 90 percent of the world's circumference.

'And what price is being obtained for it?' Clearly the Lt-Col was not going to let his cloth be cut from around him.

One may only imagine the braying of the opposition that greeted Mr Kellaway's reply that, while he could not give exact figures offhand, contractors had offered a shilling per yard. Some measure of uproar followed. The Cloth War was now developing into a good-sized scandal story. Perhaps one should have been thankful that 'tabloid journalism' had not been invented at that time otherwise there would have been even more of a hullabaloo.

By Easter-time, the news of 40 million yards of aircraft linen had percolated into the ears of the public. *Flight* now commented that:

> ...surely there should be little difficulty in getting rid of it in reasonable quantities, having regard to its very high quality, at reasonable rates, more than enough to cover the average contract rates of 1s 8d to 3s 1d per yard at which the country has acquired it.

The Government was now on the brink of going into the drapery business and selling dress-lengths to people up and down the land. Aware that the general public was unlikely to buy cloth in sufficient bulk, the Government selected an arbitrary span of 80 yards that would be the minimum length it would supply to individual customers. The labour costs involved in handling, administration and packing and postage were probably overlooked in the calculations. It was probably just good fortune that spared this plan from ever reaching fruition because there was to be a dramatic turn of events – about as dramatic as a battle over a jumbo-sized roll of cloth can get.

The linen stocks business turned from amusing farce into a potentially hard economic disaster by mid-summer when it was suddenly discovered that the government had unexpectedly done a deal – apparently without being quite aware of it – and flogged the entire lot for a round price of £4,000,000 and considered it had done well out of it. Judging by all that had gone before, it certainly was a good deal – on the face of it.

What happened next was an awesome portent to what would so soon be planned as the inevitable fate of the aircraft industry. The market was flooded with low-cost linen of the highest quality. It goes without saying that since the best linen is still, as then, Irish and that all the material was of Irish manufacture.

Now the industry faced a threat to its traditional markets from the person or organisation that had done this huge deal. The market, claimed the Irish, would be awash with cheap linen. It wasn't quite a case of washing dirty linen in public, but more the airing of very clean linen before the corporate Bank Manager. It was becoming a magnificent storm in a cup that appeared to grow in size and importance by the day.

The giant Avro works at Newton Heath underwent systematic expansion between 1916 and 1918 and by the Armistice it was said to cover in excess of 35 acres. How much of that was covered space is undisclosed but judging from the size of this fabric-shop, it was certainly on the big side. Wings racked vertically in the foreground have been fabric-covered, sewn, doped and taped. Fuselages behind await treatment by the nimble-fingered ladies who invariably staffed these departments.

Another picture of Avro's workshops from the time of the Great War. This is the dope shop attached to the fabric-shop where cellulose dope was applied to the raw linen cloth to tighten it, render it air and water-tight and to provide a surface that could be camouflage painted. These dope shops had to be well-ventilated and it was discovered early on that drinking milk helped negate the effects of breathing the heavy fumes. Free milk was provided on medical grounds.

It didn't require a degree in economics to see that selling cloth like this was little different from selling anything else that was government surplus. Aeroplanes for the masses would be next.

History very quickly repeated itself when, that same July, the textile business again became a Government prerogative. Almost immediately after the 40 million yards of linen deal was finalised, another little transaction for 12 million yards of rubberised balloon cloth went through. *Flight* reported that:

> A Manchester man is this time the 'acquirer' for round about a million sterling, and in the view of those who ought to know, this sale by the Cotton Textile Department of the Ministry of Munitions is an advantageous one. Of quite a different character is this balloon fabric to the aeroplane cloth. It is much more saleable as, being of finer texture, it is well suited for the manufacture of men's shirts, ladies' underwear, etc.

Once somebody has found a flaw in the system, others will seek to capitalise on that failing. It's what keeps Parliament going and Lobby Correspondents in beer money. At the height of the cloth flop, another threatened to rise. This time it was the President of the Board of Trade – a man prosaically called Hope (James F Hope) – that bore the brunt of a question from the Floor on April 13th. It was a simple question, but with the sort of attached sub-questions guaranteed to bring a man of the Rt Hon Hope's stature to the brink of breakdown. How many standards of silver spruce purchased for aircraft production have been sold since the Armistice, asked J R Remer, Coalition Unionist Member for Macclesfield. That wasn't all, for he also wanted to know the dates of the sales, the names of the firms to whom they were sold – and the prices realised in each case!

Now you begin to see why a career in Government only appeals to hereditary masochists with thick skins. Anyway, he gallantly responded that 3,145 standards of silver spruce had been disposed of to 60 firms at prices varying from £30 to £100 a standard according to quality and condition of the timber. This had cost the taxpayer up to £170 a standard to buy.

Hopes that wood would wane as a topic proved forlorn for the following week Brig-Gen Page-Croft, Nationalist Party Member for Bournemouth chose a related material – plywood! He asked the Parliamentary Secretary to the Ministry of Munitions if it was true that a large quantity of the stuff had recently been sold for £160,000 and if so whether public tenders were invited or other means used to obtain offers. There was also the matter of an alleged 2½ percent commission that had been paid on the deal.

Once again it was James Hope that answered. He was able to confirm that aircraft plywood had been sold for £117,000 but public tenders had not been invited because 'a legal doubt existed as to whether certain firms had a prior right under arrangements with the Aircraft Production Department'. He explained that it was normal practice in the timber trade to operate through a broker and while a very good price had been obtained, it was still necessary for the Government to 'toe the line' and effect the deal through a commissioned broker whose job it was to guarantee the sale and make payment.

Remer must have kept his ear to the ground or may have had a 'mole' in the trade for he was back with more wood problems on December 6th 1920. He asked Winston Churchill whether he was aware that, the Timber Supply Department of the Board of Trade had just sold all its surplus aircraft ash at 5s 6d per cubic foot sawn into planks, yet was now involved in negotiations to buy English ash trees unsawn at 7s 6d a cubic foot. He wanted to know why. It was an endless wrangle and would continue until all the surplus material was somewhere – anywhere – out of sight and out of mind.

And so the affairs of Parliament rattled along with a myriad of questions on surplus goods; questions about bicycles, tanks, old uniforms, whether officers' swords were confiscatable – and so on and so on.

After more than a year of peace, the disposal of aeroplanes had begun at a slow pace. Admittedly quite a few had gone but the numbers that remained were enormous and there was the fear that unless something drastic was done about the stockpile they would deteriorate and become unsaleable – and that would create yet more trouble for the Exchequer.

I have already said that, like many solutions both before and since, the answer came not from some faceless Government-appointed committee of chinless wonders with Public School backgrounds and no sensible ability in the real world, but from within the aircraft industry itself.

What happened next led to the creation of an extremely successful and profitable enterprise whose very prosperity nearly killed off the industry that had fathered it. Although it lasted for eleven years and despite changing its rôle several times during its existence, the impact of this operation on British aviation was to be of far-reaching importance.

To make a metaphor cocktail, the cloth business was only the tip of the iceberg...

Chapter 7

The Creation of the Aircraft Disposal Company

THE War had been over for a year, civilian flying had begun, and the first airlines were bravely flying intrepid passengers across the waters of the English Channel to far-off Paris, Amsterdam and Brussels. During this period of flux, the nation had experienced a series of auctions of surplus material overseen by the Government-controlled Disposal Board from its expensive and over-staffed offices in Kingsway. Despite this, it was clear to see that all it had really succeeded in achieving was no more than scratching the surface of the surplus problem. This volume of sales-drive, like the awful reality of trench warfare, lacked the solace of any imaginable conclusion.

In fact it was reliably forecast that, at the then rate of disposal, it would turn out to be a never-ending task since the obsolescent goods would become quite obsolete and therefore impossible to sell and incapable of disposal long before the various 'sell-by' dates came up.

As 1919 turned into 1920 there was an increasing feeling of desperation in high places as the burden of surplus disposal became ever more irksome, pressing – and expensive. Government departments, however many staff they employed, were not experienced at foot-in-the-door salesmanship for war surplus of any kind, let alone aeroplanes.

Deep underneath all the outward trappings of projected efficiency, it was obvious that the Aircraft Disposal Board was not particularly good at its job. In fact selling aeroplanes seemed quite beyond its abilities, certainly in any useful quantity. 'Each aeroplane sold,' thundered one observer, 'costs the taxpayer almost as much as the aeroplane's worth!' In other words, the operation had simply ceased to be economical in its present form.

Somebody, surely, must have longed for one of those accidental fires that potentially bankrupt companies were known to suffer... Perhaps, they probably dreamed, they could stage a 'pre-Fire' sale! Only the need to remain accountable to the Public Purse, however, kept the match-striking urge at bay!

The vast piles of aircraft and equipment, now concentrated on Aintree, Hendon and Waddon, took on the air of immovable objects that, in military terms, ought to be moved, saluted – or simply painted white. The white paint seemed the more attainable fate.

There was another doubt that was causing concern to a minority of very senior people 'in the know' and that harked back to those earlier questions in the Commons regarding suitable timbers for aircraft construction. It was an ill-concealed secret that as the War had progressed, the quality of timber used in aircraft production had been allowed to vary. Besides the cypress or yellow cedar scandal (which had been satisfactorily resolved, it seemed), spruce of less than 'A1' quality had gradually been allowed into the construction chain. And now aircraft made of uncertain materials were being converted for taking the public on joy-rides!

If anything really went wrong while an ex-military aircraft was being used in such a manner, who would have to assume the ultimate responsibility? Might not the Government itself have damaging blame heaped upon it? The bunch of advisers in high places who knew about these things

Outside the great hangars of The Aircraft Disposal Company stood the vast expanse of the old Waddon aerodrome. From here every aircraft overhauled in the factory was thoroughly tested before going to its new owner. Here preparations are in hand for the test-flight of a newly-overhauled DH.9 powered by an equally-restored 240 hp Siddeley Puma engine.

Hewlett & Blondeau Ltd of Clapham, London, built a number of BE.2c aircraft in 1916. The RFC markings of this era included the use of the small-roundels design seen next to the aircraft serial number, 8416. The engine is the 70 hp Renault characterised here by the long exhaust pipes either side of the fuselage as distinct from the more common form that directed the gases up and over the top wing. The airframe cost £1,072 10s and the engine £522 10s. It is this motor that, upgraded to 80 hp, formed the basis of the Aircraft Disposal Company's Airdisco and Cirrus engines.

were whispering; hushed tones concealed the fear of discovery.

Perhaps it was in a gesture of alarm and desperation that, following yet another question in Parliament, it was made known that the Government would be prepared to dispose of the entire stock to any competent company or syndicate that would be capable of regulating the resale of the material in a safe and satisfactory manner. In short, the sale of the aircraft ought to be much more conditional on civilian airworthiness standards than was possible with the random auction sale currently employed. Ordinary people buying ex-military aircraft were probably in no position to undertake a thorough structural vetting before beginning to fly them and facing consequences that were unthinkable.

There was one man who understood all of these aspects while also harbouring an idea that a dedicated commercial undertaking might better achieve what a Government office clearly could not. That man was pioneer aviator and bomber-builder Frederick Handley Page.

Many a businessman in post-Second World War Britain was to make his fortune in dealing with war surplus. It was an established way of profiting (or, occasionally, profiteering) from the spoils of victory. The problem was that, in 1920, such an operation had never been undertaken before. Accordingly there were no guidelines, no precedent and nothing to learn from.

It had all begun very soon after the end of hostilities when a small group of entrepreneurial businessmen led by Handley Page began to wonder what would happen once the war effort was over and Britain's aerial might was wound down.

The disorganised manner in which the Ministry of Munitions' Aircraft Disposal Board operated and the outcome of its first public auctions of aircraft and parts served as the catalyst for their idea. It wouldn't be the last time that Post-War Man has seen short-term benefits through dealing in war surplus! The difference was that this was to be a first!

Frederick Handley Page and his team, having studied the problem, believed that this would be a unique chance to access a worldwide market with the Government's unwanted merchandise. They saw no downside to a venture that would earn money relatively easily. The only urgency was to step in quickly before too many more aircraft and associated goods were 'wasted'.

Page's simple solution to the surplus aircraft problem was to create a new and separate private commercial organisation to acquire from the Government all of this material as might be saleable in exchange for one quick no-hassle price – and then use their combined aircraft engineering and business skills to turn the resource into cash, part of which would be returnable to the Government through a percentage of profits.

It certainly seemed straightforward enough and had anybody suggested that, for

ADC took over huge quantities of the Bristol F.2B Fighter and these were reworked and sold all over the world for both civil and military duties. They had 275 hp Rolls-Royce Falcon III or 300 hp Hispano Suiza engines. Here is a view of the F.2B workshop showing wings being worked on in the foreground while countless fuselages stand in the background. By the end of 1923, twenty-two of F S Barnwell's 'Brisfits' were on the British civil register. It is said that the demonstration aircraft were sold at £800 apiece.

Above: One can gain an impression of the huge area of the factory premises occupied by The Aircraft Disposal Company from this company aerial photograph taken of its buildings soon after they were taken over by the firm. Outside on the grass can be seen two aircraft prepared for flight, one an SE.5A and the other appears to be a DH.9.

Below: In the final assembly shop, a fully-overhauled Puma-engined DH.9 is having its rigging verified prior to its test-flight. A mechanic inspects the engine magnetos while two others are tramelling with a tape-measure – checking that the diagonal from propeller hub to the outboard lower forward interplane strut is the same on each side. This is a necessary verification to prove that the aircraft has been 'square rigged'.

The original caption to the ADC photograph reads 'A Corner of the Aeroplane Store'. This type of phraseology, subsequently taken up by estate agents everywhere, was usually used by people who were trying to make their premises look larger than they really were. Usually we find that the view shown in the picture was all that there was to see. In the case of ADC, however, we know that this was not the case and the caption was actually hyperbole-free! This one picture reveals at least 80 brand new fuselages representing a huge chunk of a batch of 300 Avro 504K aircraft built at Hendon by the Grahame-White Aviation Co Ltd at the very end of the war.

Below: The same stack of 504K fuselages but this time further along and forming the backdrop to an engine inspection room. Dismantled engines lie on the bench as two men, centre left, check over a crankshaft. The bench, centre foreground, displays a set of bracing wires.

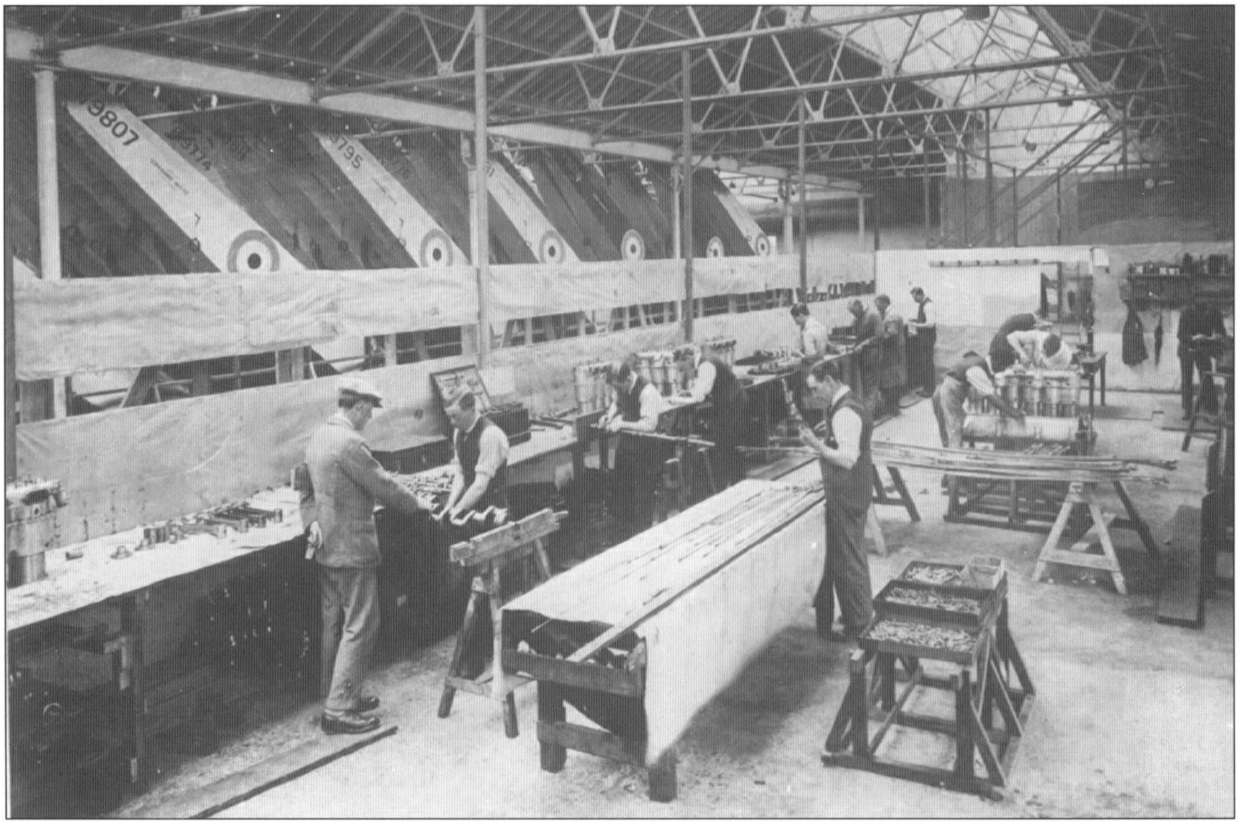

example, the operation would return to haunt and practically inhibit growth in the aircraft industry over the years ahead they would surely have been greeted with derision.

The upshot was to be by far and away the most important aviation business to be created out of the War. Its purpose was to succeed to the Aircraft Disposal Department of the Government's Ministry of Munitions' Disposal Board and possibly Handley Page thought that the nearer the name of the new business was to that official handle, the more kudos the business might present to the commercial world. The new company was duly named The Aircraft Disposal Company Ltd.

Before looking at the formation of this, though, it is worth looking into Handley Page's other post-war activities. It is generally overlooked today that Handley Page already had a toe in the 'surplus aircraft' business besides his own O/400 bombers in Handley Page Transport Ltd. And for this we have to go back to the summer of 1919 which, as already outlined, was a grim year for the British aircraft industry. Order-cancellation brought many makers to their knees, some closed for ever, while others were victims of magisterial indifference in high places.

The scandalous circumstances surrounding the financial collapse of the Norman Thompson Flight Company, makers of flying boats who were based at Middleton-on-Sea, Sussex, has been commendably recorded by Goodall *[10]*. When the company went into voluntary liquidation on July 12th 1919, Frederick Handley Page made his first soirée into the world of government-surplus. In a deal financed by his family he acquired the whole business from the liquidators the same month. The actual price is unknown but it cannot have been anywhere near what the business was truly worth.

Page set up an operating business called the Flying Boat Company Ltd with the intention of running passenger flights on the South Coast using surplus NT.2B flying boats but this seems to have come to nothing. Nine months later, the Norman Thompson/Flying Boat Company business would be absorbed by Page's new creation – The Aircraft Disposal Company Limited.

Registered on March 4th 1920 as a private company with a mere £600 in share capital, The Aircraft Disposal Company Limited was described in its Articles of Association as 'manufacturers of and dealers in aircraft, spare parts, etc'. Funding an operation such as the target task of acquiring the properties of the Aircraft Disposal Board required access to funds which were way in excess of those available from within the Page circle. External funding was thus crucial to the fulfilment of the new company's goal.

Industrial and business finance was then, as now, the province of City investment companies. One of these was an organisation called The Imperial & Foreign Corporation. Like all financial facilitators, it did not exist specifically to have an interest in aviation. In fact it was more involved in shipping and the manufacturing industries.

Imperial & Foreign Corporation possessed an impressive management team headed by Lord Balfour of Burleigh, KT, (Alexander Hugh Bruce) as chairman. Other members of the board of directors included Sir Ian Heathcoat-Amory (Bart), Sir John Sutherland Harmood-Banner, MP, G Benenson, Hon A H S Cripps, H Guedalla (managing director) and John Herbert Dudley Ryder, the Earl of Harrowby, who was also a partner in the exclusive Coutts Bank.

Through family connections, Handley Page had access to Lord Balfour. He was a singularly useful contact in the financial world and it was to him that the young Page went with his grandiose scheme for acquiring all Britain's war-surplus aircraft and selling them on at a profit.

Whatever discussions went on behind the closed doors of the IF&C, Handley Page must have convinced Balfour and his Board that he was not just the man for the job but, given the wherewithal, he could turn the Nation's adversity into profit. He got the go-ahead to make an offer of a million pounds.

It was thus in the name of this esteemed Corporation that Handley Page tested the official waters of the Government's Disposal Board. Prime Minister David Lloyd George's reaction, like those of the Ministry of Munitions, must have been ecstatic! Here was some dam'-fool aircraft man prepared to rid him of a problem that kept him awake at night. What's more he'd pay for the privilege!

Given the green light, it was at this point that Handley Page immediately registered the trading name of his new business – The Aircraft Disposal Company Ltd – which was obviously intended to trade in the shadow of the old Disposal Board. The business was positioned as a new division of Handley Page Limited with the clear aim of not just satisfying its backers and the Chancellor, but putting money into the Page coffers.

Two weeks after its registration, on March 18th, the newly-formed board of the

The Avro 548 was a two-passenger conversion of the 504. Here is the third example built, G-EALF, which was first seen at the Hendon Air Show on July 20th 1920. The newly-formed Aircraft Disposal Company saw this as a golden opportunity to civilianise some of their existing stock of Avros and so made a number of similar conversions. Of the ten machines so produced, however, only the first (G-EAYD) looked like Avro's own conversion. ADC's subsequent conversions included the first Avro 548A which was a 548 fitted with a Halford-converted Airdisco engine. That was G-EBKN which survived until the end of 1932.

company formally appointed Handley Page Ltd as its sole agent. It was by far the biggest aviation deal of the age.

The purchase money was raised the day after formation (March 5th) by an issue of debentures to the value of £1,080,000 charged on the company's properties. This was financed by the Imperial & Foreign Corporation. Besides being a well-respected City company director, Lord Balfour also happened to be Parliamentary Secretary to the Board of Trade. It was in this capacity that, back in July 1916, he had been appointed chairman of the committee set up to enquire into the whole subject of trade after the war. He thus had some knowledge of the composite problem of surplus disposal and sales management. One might consider him to have been a unique ally to the Page enterprise.

On March 15th 1920, the newly-formed Aircraft Disposal Company purchased the entire stock of the Aircraft Disposal Board from the Ministry of Munitions. Besides the 10,000 aircraft there were also 35,000 engines, between 500 and 1,000 tons of ball-bearings, 350,000 sparking plugs, 100,000 magnetos and huge stores of sundry bits and pieces ranging from nuts and bolts upwards. The book value of the entire stock was given as £5,700,000 for which The Aircraft Disposal Company Ltd had paid £1,000,000. The arrangement was that the company had to take everything offered and half of the profits on sales would be paid to the government.

So who were the characters behind this coterie that had planned and executed this monumental and far-reaching aircraft-industry coup? Not surprisingly, it was led by Frederick Handley Page himself (with his company acting as technical adviser and sole selling agent) and his brother Theodore Page. The others included Lord Reading's brother Godfrey Isaac (director of Marconi and a long-standing family friend). The intention was to offer on the world market fully reconditioned aircraft that would be in perfect, newly manufactured and tested condition. These could be provided either to civilian standard (*ie* unarmed) or to full military specification for foreign service use. This, they believed, would benefit the name and reputation of British aviation.

Flight for March 18th 1920 announced the deal in its extensive editorial under the heading 'The Great Aircraft Deal'. Editor Stanley Spooner, in concluding that it was a very good deal all round, would probably rue his implied aura of *bonhomie* before the year was out:

> The great deal whereby the whole of the surplus machines, engines and aeronautical stores on charge to the Ministry of Munitions has been disposed of to a commercial company for a cash payment of £1,000,000 and 50 per cent of future profits, must be pronounced a good thing from every point of view. At first sight it might be thought that the sale of stores, which have cost the taxpayer some thing more than £1,000,000 for so comparatively small a sum is against public policy, and that the only people who are likely to reap real benefit are those associated with the purchasing side of the bargain. It is not so in fact. It must be remembered, in the first place, that the £1,000,000 down is only a first instalment of the purchase price, and that a further great sum may well accrue to the funds of the State when sales have been completed. Further, all the machines and stores which are the subject of the deal are fast becoming obsolete and depreciating in value every day, apart altogether from the natural deterioration they must suffer through being held in stores or piled in dumps as they are at present. Again, by disposing of them the Ministry should be able to dispense with a very large number of people who are at present employed in looking after these stores, and a substantial saving to the Exchequer should result from this. On the whole, and regarded purely from the point of view of economy, the deal is, we think, a very good one for the taxpayer. The Disposal Board has not been conspicuously successful in its efforts to

Pilot training in the Royal Flying Corps and later Royal Air Force was revolutionised by a new type of aircraft – the Avro 504K. The design, however, was pre-war and, when introduced at the Aerial Derby of September 1913, it was by a long chalk the most advanced aircraft on the field. The first 'light' aircraft to have a high-lift wing-section, the original 504 was in every respect a sensational machine. This one, numbered 785, was one of the first production machines built to the first wartime order of 44 machines. The engine was the 80 hp Gnôme. A staggering 8,340 machines were produced of various types and when the war ended, more than 3,000 were either in store or awaiting delivery. The vast majority of these ended up on the surplus market and provided income for The Aircraft Disposal Company for many a year.

REDUNDANT ENGINES MADE LIKE NEW AGAIN

The Aircraft Disposal Company's attitude towards aircraft engines was thoroughly practical for the goal was to provide engines that were not second-hand in any respect, but fully-overhauled and zero-houred. The huge number of engines the company had were accordingly graded very carefully, dismantled and meticulously checked and inspected before being built up with the same skills that went into the manufacture of the original engine. In fact, so methodical and expert was this engine facility that it quickly gained a reputation for a product that was second to none. The company's advertisements proudly proclaimed the successes achieved by aircraft that were fitted with engines that had passed through its workshops. In the top picture here we see a huge assortment of engines stored. The first row in the foreground shows, at ground level, Hispano Suiza 300 hp engines, each supported on a neat wooden stand. The upper level reveals eight-cylinder Renault Vee engines all lined up. The second aisle shows Siddeley Puma engines racked up in the same way. At the end of the row, far right, is the small gas-engine-powered lifting crane that could lift up a selected engine for working on. The other aisles of engines cannot be identified from the picture but the store seems to hold at least eighty engines per aisle – and seven aisles are visible. Right, above, can be seen an engine lifted off the stack and about to be lowered onto a wheeled trolley. Right, lower, is a view of part of the engine servicing shop. Here engines are being dismantled down to their smallest component parts.

Left: A view of the engine inspection shop. In the foreground is a Puma crankcase and behind it are sets of cylinder barrels complete with their heads and inlet manifolds. On the bench, crankcase upper halves, gaskets, water-jacket seals and a myriad of other parts are laid out on the benches. Despite all this activity, the workshop gives the impression of being spacious, light and airy. It was, however, a cold place to work in the winter.

One of the success stories of the First World War was the American Liberty engine, designed, built and put into production in a remarkably short space of time to supplement the supply of engines available to Britain from other sources. Many of these excellent engines were at sea when the war ended, so large numbers still entered the country long after they were no longer needed. Here in one of the ADC workshops, we see (left) part of the workshop devoted to the stripping, inspection and rebuilding of Liberty engines. What is clear from these pictures is the enormous resource of manpower needed for these many operations.

Right: A view of the precision inspection shop where used engines were examined for excess wear. Ever part that went into building a fully-serviced ADC engine, regardless of type, had to pass these stringent tests as falling within design tolerances. The engineer, right foreground, works on a solid steel surface table where he is checking a crankshaft.

Left: Finished engines had to be test-run and the area used for this was the former unloading platforms of the by-now-disused railway branch line. With the old track bed in the foreground, we see engines mounted in test cells. Approximately ten are in this picture. Engines were test-run for many hours before being passed for sale or installation in an airframe. Local residents complained of the noise from this part of the factory, for the engines were often run at full power far into the night.

Right: Fully-overhauled engines are displayed in the Aircraft Disposal Company's neat and tidy sales showroom. Intending customers could visit here and select the engines that they wanted to buy. Each engine was on show complete with its documents by way of log-book and certificate from its test-running. This was, at the time, a unique operation. All around the room on shelves are fully-serviced engine components to give the customer an indication of the degree of servicing and inspection that went into each job. It was this application to detail and obvious pride in the standard of their workmanship that gradually elevated ADC from being a glorified scrap-merchant into being accepted, somewhat grudgingly by some, as a legitimate supplier of aircraft and components.

sell machines and engines singly or in small numbers, and it has done quite the wisest thing in selling the whole lot to what amounts to a new Board run as a private commercial company.

Apart from the economic side of the matter it must be excellent in its effect on the British industry The result of the scientific commercial disposal will be that the 10,000 odd machines and the 35,000 engines involved will be that British machines and engines will be distributed all over the world, and, as one of the objects of the company will be to satisfy its purchasers, every machine and every engine will be sold, not merely as a speculation, but with the idea of giving good service in the conditions under which it is to be employed. That is to say, every unit will be a potential advertisement of the excellence of British aircraft and engines. It is almost impossible to realise how much potential good lies in the proper disposal of this huge number of aircraft and engines. It may well mean the creation of a new industry built upon what we are only too greatly afraid must be called the ruins of the old.

There is another aspect of the matter which ought not to be lost to sight. At present the industry is oppressed by the spectre of these machines and engines awaiting disposal on any sort of terms the Disposal Board could get. Many felt that it was useless to try to secure orders for aircraft while these huge stocks remained on hand, to be suddenly thrown on the market at knock-out prices. That menace now disappears, because we may be very sure that the company which has secured them is not likely to sell them at any but a fair commercial price, lower it may be than the same machines or engines could be bought from private constructors. So far as we are able to see there is no single criticism which is called for. The deal, on all counts, is to be applauded.

In the same edition of *Flight* as that leader was a factual news report which helped put some flesh on the bones of this quite remarkable deal:

Elsewhere [in that edition] we deal with the sale of all surplus aircraft by the Government. The following official announcement was issued by the Air Ministry on Monday [March 15th 1920]:-

'All the aircraft in England have been sold to the Imperial and Foreign Corporation, Ltd. The purchasers have the right to form a company for the disposal of this material subject to the approval of the Ministry of Munitions.'

The following was issued by the Ministry of Munitions:-

'The entire stock of surplus aeroplanes and seaplanes, aeronautical engines, accessories and spares in Great Britain has been sold by the Disposal Board, Ministry of Munitions, for £1,000,000. In addition to the price paid, the purchasers are to hand over to the Government 50 per cent of the profits they may make on reselling. The purchasers have also assumed responsibility for the cost of storage, insurance, and other similar charges.'

The syndicate interested is known as the Aircraft Disposal Co Ltd, and they issued the following announcement-

'The sale by the Government of all its surplus aircraft material, engines, spares and accessories was completed at the end of last week. We did not purchase direct from the Government, but we have now taken over the whole of the benefits and liabilities of the purchasers. The company, which comprises widespread British interests, has been specially formed to carry on the whole of the work previously undertaken by the Ministry of Munitions in disposing of the surplus stocks of heavier-than-air machines and equipment. Offices have been taken in Kingsway, and as rapidly as possible the organisation will remove there from the present Disposal Board Offices. The whole of the storage organisation and the management of the large aircraft depots all over the country will pass into our control. The Disposal Board since the Armistice have sold large numbers of machines, but their potential sales have been very much handicapped by their limitation to selling machines as they stand. Many of the machines for disposal are quite new, but in order to ensure that every machine, engine, accessory and spare is in perfect condition, detailed inspection will take place before delivery, and certificates of airworthiness will be given for all machines sold.

'Handley Page, Ltd. (the well-known aircraft manufacturers) are members of the syndicate, and we shall have the full advantage of their experience in aircraft matters, as they' will act as our technical advisers and be our sole agents for the disposal of the material.'

The following week, March 25th, Stanley Spooner returned to the subject (even repeating the same story headline)

Nearly 1,800 examples of the BE.2 series were built, predominantly BE.2c models. This Royal Aircraft Factory design, in which Geoffrey de Havilland had a hand, began with the pre-war BE.2 of 1912. Powered by a 70 hp Renault, this was the forerunner of the British light aeroplane and was the first practical and successful Farnborough design. This particular example, No.206, first flew on September 5th 1912 and was used extensively in trials with an oleo-damped undercarriage. In December 1914 it flew to France to join No.6 Sqdn. After a busy and productive life it was still flying with 15 Sqdn at Dover in November 1915. Its successors would provide an extensive, if very dated, shelf-line for The Aircraft Disposal Company six years later.

The Aircraft Disposal Company had a number of DH.10 aircraft on its books, although this example was one of those that remained in service. Confusingly there were several different DH.10 designs, the prototype being a pusher with propellers operating in wing trailing-edge cut-outs. Other variations including the positioning of the engines. This unidentified example served with 216 Sqdn after the war and is pictured here at Abu Sueir in Heliopolis during 1921.

and proceeded to relate further details surrounding the deal. It seems that perhaps he was not alone in being blind to the implications of cheap aeroplanes on a world market.

> In connection with the great deal whereby the whole of the Government stocks of surplus machines, engines and spares have passed into private hands for disposal, Messrs Handley Page — who are closely associated with the deal — have issued a statement as to their objects and policy regarding the matter. It states that at the conclusion of the Armistice in November, 1918, the company turned its attention to the development of civil aviation. Subsequently there came the decision to drastically cut down the Royal Air Force, involving the handing over for disposal of increasing numbers of machines at ever-decreasing prices. The consequence of this was that it became impossible to manufacture machines at market prices which might at any moment be materially reduced. This, the statement points out, threatened the very existence of the aircraft industry. The one solution of the difficulty thus created was to take over from the Government the whole of its surplus stock of aircraft, together with all material surplus to requirements. The statement continues: 'The financial syndicate which has supplied the capital necessary for the purchase is the Aircraft Disposal Co, Ltd, but we have been appointed sole managing and selling agents, and as we are the largest subscribers to the Syndicate, the financial success of the arrangement should materially benefit the shareholders of Handley Page, Ltd. With proper commercial organisation the sale of the material should prove many times more lucrative than it would have been under the control of a Government Department, and as the Government will receive a half share of the profits, in addition to the usual taxes, the total yield to the Exchequer should be considerably higher than as if the business had remained in Government hands."
>
> It is just as well that such a statement should have been made, because it clears up any ambiguity in the terms upon which we commented last week. Now that these terms have been thus confirmed, we are more than ever of opinion that the Government has done wisely in thus transferring the task of disposing of the huge accumulation of aircraft and engines on its hands to a private enterprise. We agree entirely with the view expressed in the Handley Page statement, that the sale of this material will prove many times more lucrative than it would have been under the control of the Government Department.' Therefore, the country, as well as the Syndicate, is to be congratulated upon the fact that in at least one direction the Government has done the right thing in liquidating its war liabilities.

Full details of the shear size of the acquisition was contained elsewhere in the same issue. Once again the piece was entitled 'The Great Aircraft Deal' as if to underline that it was so momentous an event that no other words might be found to describe it. Repeating some of the aspects already commented upon in the leader article, the piece tells us:

> Some further details are now available regarding the deal by which the whole

BRITISH

AIRCRAFT

120 h.p. "AIRDISCO" ENGINE.

ECONOMY.

RELIABILITY.

AMPLE POWER

LOW PRICE.

120 H.P. "AIRD SCO" ENGINE.

A RELIABLE STATIONARY TRAINING ENGINE.

BRIEF SPECIFICATION:

Type	No. of Cylinders.	Cooling.	Nominal H.P.
V.90°	8	AIR	120
Normal H.P.	**Maximum H.P.**	**Total Dry Weight.**	**Dry Weight per H.P.**
128	140	452 lbs.	3.53

Simple in Construction. Efficient and Reliable in Service. Without the a tendant troubles of a Water Cooling System. Passed by the Air Ministry as Airworthy.

We have a Competent Designing Staff; Highly Skilled Mechanics; an Approved Inspection Department and a Well-equipped Factory, all of which ensure First-class Work being carried out to our clients' requirements.

AIRCRAFT DISPOSAL COMPANY, LTD.

REGENT HOUSE,

Telephone · Regent 6240.

89, KINGSWAY, LONDON, W.C.2.

Te egrams: "Airdisco, London."

The Aeroplane October 1st 1924

BRITISH

AIRCRAFT

UTILITY PLUS RELIABILITY.

A D.H.9 FITTED WITH "PUMA" ENGINE.

The machine shown in the above illustration has been supplied by us to our clients The Northern Air Lines.

Similar machines can also be supplied with float undercarriage.

We have a competent designing s'aff, highly skilled mechanics, an approved inspection department, and a well-equipped factory, all of which enable first-class work to be carried out to our clients' requirements.

Spares available in large quantities for most types of machines and engines.

AIRCRAFT DISPOSAL COMPANY, LTD.

REGENT HOUSF,

89, KINGSWAY, LONDON, W.C.2.

Telephone: Regent 6240.

Te'egrams: "Airdisco, London."

The Aeroplane

Sopwith Pups date from the early part of 1916 and this example, N5180, was the first of a 20-strong batch built for the RNAS by the Sopwith factory at Kingston and most of which were deployed with Nos.3 and 8 (Naval) Squadrons. The engine is the 80 hp Le Rhône which cost £620 while the airframe, less instruments and armament, cost £710 18s. At the end of the War, of the 1,770 examples built, more than 1,200 were still on charge and many of these were sold on to foreign military clients by The Aircraft Disposal Company.

of the Aircraft Disposal Department has passed from public control into private hands, a statement setting forth the position having been issued on March 19th by Messrs Handley Page, Ltd. This statement says:-

'Immediately on the cessation of hostilities at the end of 1918 we turned our attention to the development of aviation for commercial purposes. An order was accepted and executed for the manufacture of passenger-carrying machines for a foreign Government and similar machines were manufactured in addition at our own expense for use on Continental Air Services and by air-transport companies which we had established in India, South Africa and elsewhere. Bombing machines were also purchased by us at full war prices and adapted for passenger carrying.

'Then came the Government decision for the drastic reduction of the Royal Air Force which involved the handing over for disposal of increasing quantities of machines at ever-decreasing prices. This made it prohibitive to manufacture aircraft and unwise to purchase surplus machines at market prices which might at any moment be radically reduced.

'This state of affairs threatened the very existence of the aviation industry, and the one solution to the difficulty was to take over from the Government the whole of its surplus stock of aircraft, together with all material which they might find in the future to be surplus to their requirements. With influential financial assistance this arrangement has been successfully negotiated, but it is only fair to state that in its inception and execution the task has been mainly the work of Handley Page, Ltd.

'The financial syndicate which has supplied the capital necessary for the purchase is the Aircraft Disposal Company, Ltd., but we have been appointed the sole managing and selling agents, and as we are also the largest subscribers to the syndicate the financial success of the arrangement should materially benefit the shareholders of Handley Page, Ltd. With proper commercial organisation the sale of the material should prove many times more lucrative than it would have been under the control of a Government Department, and as the Government will receive a half-share of the profits in addition to the usual taxes the total yield to the Exchequer should be considerably larger than if the business had remained in Government hands.

'Although the undertaking of this agency means much additional work we shall still pursue our normal business as aeronautical engineers, and the individuality and constitution of Handley Page, Ltd, will remain unchanged. It is the policy of the syndicate, moreover, that their stocks shall be disposed of equitably and impartially in the interests of all British aircraft firms.

'We propose to stabilise the aircraft market by issuing a price list fixed and definite for all purchasers, and on these prices a rebate will be given to all British aircraft manufacturers and British merchant firms dealing in aircraft. A further fixed rebate will also be given to those aircraft firms who desire to purchase back any of the machines of their own design originally supplied by them to the Government.

'Owing to the existence of these stocks, the aircraft industry has to face a period when little manufacturing will be required, but the modifying and renovating of the Government aircraft means much work for the industry. We hope that British firms will participate in this by contracting to the syndicate if possible for all this work and co-operate with us in establishing beyond question the supremacy of British aircraft in the world's markets

'The use of aircraft during the War demonstrated the possibility of aviation, but the world has still to be educated in its use as an everyday mode of transport. Owing to the large supply of machines

at low prices, the opportunity to do this and firmly to establish aerial transport on a commercial basis has now come; and with wise organisation and sound finance the aircraft industry may look forward to a period of great prosperity.'
The 10,000 machines taken over include Vickers-Vimy, DH.10, DH.9, DH.9A, DH.6, Sopwith Pup, Camel, Dolphin and Snipe; the Avro 504K; Bristol Fighter;. Martinsyde, the Government-designed machines SES, FE.2B, BE.2E, and a few Handley Page O/400 two-engine aeroplanes fitted with Rolls-Royce or Liberty engines. In addition there are large and small flying-boats of the F, H, and NT types. The 35,000 engines include Rolls-Royce Eagles and Falcons; Napier Lions; Siddeley Pumas Wolseley Vipers and Adders; French 200 and 300 hp Hispano-Suiza's; Curtiss; Renault; RAF; Fiat; Anzani; ABC; Le Rhone; Clerget; BR 2; Monosoupape, etc, as well as an immense quantity of engine and aeroplane spares, hangars, etc. The greater part of this stock is absolutely new and has never been used. A very large number of the machines and engines have been delivered quite recently direct to the depots from the makers.
Before any of the machines are despatched by Handley Page, Ltd., they will be subjected to a very thorough inspection by their experts so as to ensure every machine, engine or part sold being in perfect working condition.

This text suggests that Handley Page was aware of the likely consequences of The Aircraft Disposal Company's potential damaging effect on the rest of Britain's aircraft industry, yet chose to proceed anyway.

The Great Linen Scandal of the previous year was still fresh in the minds of many people, yet the full import of the Handley Page idea and its potential for destablising the whole aircraft industry seems to have escaped everybody. One might have assumed that the Government would be running scared at the thought of starting another public disagreement situation. In fact the aeroplane fabric story probably played a significant part in the decision to form the Aircraft Disposal Company in the first place. The Government was under pressure not just to get rid of aeroplanes, engines and parts but, of equal importance, to rid itself of the growing abuse it was facing regarding one of London's Royal Parks and its untidy spares depot.

The House of Commons, however, never takes anything lying down and MPs have since time immemorial relished any subject that gets them quoted as 'having asked a question'. The disposal of aeroplanes was thus a golden opportunity that was grasped by the Conservative member for Midlothian, Lt-Col Sir John A Hope during Prime Minister's Question Time on March 21st 1920 who asked whether, in view of the recent decision to sell all surplus aeroplanes to a private company for a fixed sum and half profits on resale, it was the intention of the Government to dispose of all other surplus war stores on a similar principle, and so terminate the cost of the Ministry of Munitions at an early date?

He was answered by the Under Secretary to the Minister of Munitions, Frederick G Kellaway, who told the House: 'The conditions of the sale referred to were exceptional in that there is not, for surplus aeroplanes, either the demand or the established market value which obtain in respect of most of the other commodities

Every aircraft or aircraft part that entered the Aircraft Disposal Company's premises was stripped down, carefully examined, and then restored to new and certifiable conditions. Above can be seen the workshop where wings and tail surfaces were overhauled. In the background, distant right of the picture, is part of the final erection shop where components were assembled into aircraft that were, to all intents and purposes, brand new. Components that were found used or damaged were either repaired or scrapped. Another store was given over to propellers, left. Here many hundreds of propellers for different types of aircraft and engines were stored or racked. In the foreground are piled up salvaged propellers complete with hubs as removed from aircraft. The others are all brand new and never used.

The Martinsyde F.4 was one aircraft of which The Aircraft Disposal Company had large numbers and it was the eventual acquisition of the rights to the name and the design, obtained when the Woking-based Martinsyde firm finally went into liquidation, that enabled ADC to experiment with its own varieties of the machine. While many F.4 aircraft were disposed of early on in the company's existence, by the time it was able to develop its own variants, the design was not just obsolescent but quite obsolete. While the Avros and the DH designs soldiered on, the Martinsydes were soon forgotten – a sad end to a once-famous family of good, solid and reliable aircraft. G-EAWE, formerly H7780, was used briefly as a Handley Page hack and demonstrator until it was sold to Poland on January 29th 1921. *[Richard T Riding]*

Below: An amazing scene revealed in the Aircraft Disposal Company's workshop probably 1920-21. In the foreground is an assortment of Airco machines including DH.4 H5898. The thoroughness of the 'overhaul' on each machine is shown by the amount of new plywood skinning on some fuselages. In the middle distance is a batch of DH.6 machines prepared for the Spanish air force including M-MHDO, M-MHEF and M-MHEA standing behind an unidentifiable 'Brisfit'. In the background, row upon row of Avro 504K fuselages stand dismantled on their noses. Among the many identifiable on the original photograph is a Sunbeam-built example H2055 and a 'real' A V Roe-built one – H2550. Across the width of the building and forming a front to back partition is a rack containing a large number of pairs of mainplanes stacked vertically, roots lowermost. *[Mike Hooks.]*

Above: Another part of the ADC storage area displays closely-stacked fuselages, their axles supported on short stands to preserve the tyres. On the left are Armstrong-Whitworth FK-8 aircraft including C8633, while to the right are DH.9 fuselages including Airco-built H9195 and Alliance-built H5776. An interesting machine here is H8174, shown in lists as 'reserved allocations but not used'. *[Mike Hooks].*

Below: Fuselages under overhaul in the ADC workshops. Just as with all other parts, these were completely stripped down to their smallest component parts and methodically restored to as-new condition. Note the areas of new plywood being used on these DH.6 fuselages. The size of the workshop is impressive and in the distance, far left, are countless rows of fuselages awaiting work.

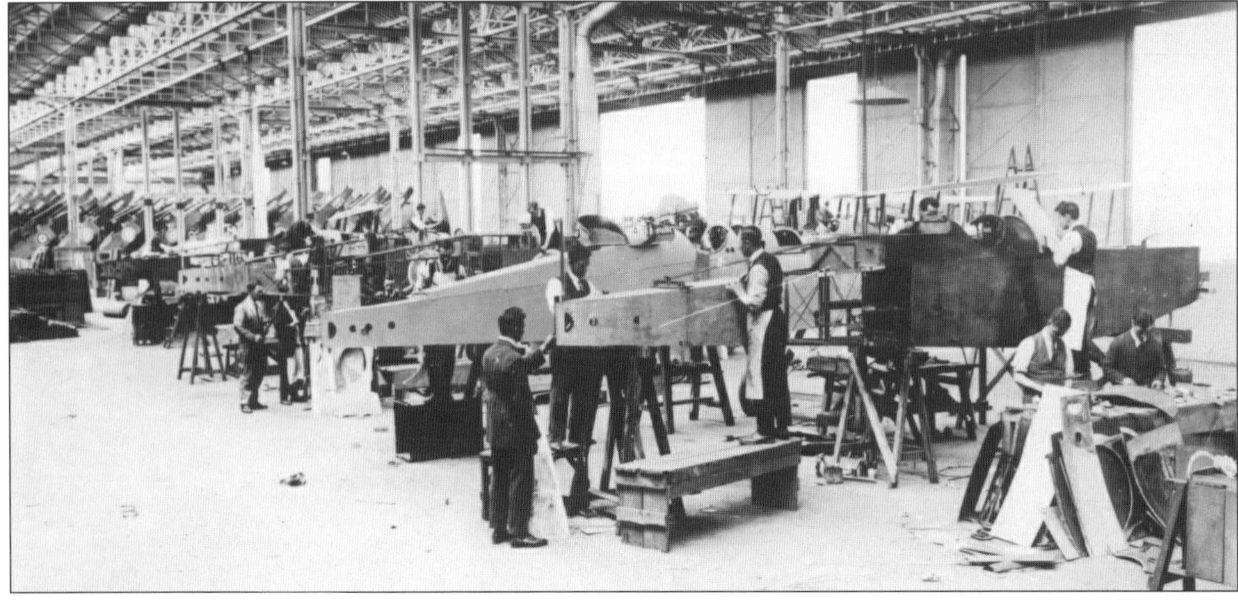

which the Ministry has to sell. It would not be in the interests of the Exchequer to apply generally to stores to which these conditions do not apply the methods and terms of disposal adopted in the sale in question.'

This drew an immediate response from the ever-outspoken Noel Pemberton-Billing (Independent member for Hertford East) who queried: 'Can [you] say whether the question of half profits is to be based on the difference of price paid for the aeroplanes and the price at which they were sold, or the price of sale less the expenses of this private firm? If so, what steps does he propose to take to overlook the expenses of the firm?' to which John Hope added: 'Does the hon gentleman consider that half profits will amount to more than the £27,000,000 that the Ministry of Munitions is costing the country each year?'

Kellaway was quick with his reply, advising that he thought it would be a very unfair test to take the whole expenses of the Ministry and apply it to one single question. 'I may say that the Disposal Board will have the books and contracts before them.'

Pemberton-Billing, however, decided he wanted an answer. 'Will the company be allowed their expenses from the prices paid before there is any further payment to the Government?' Kellaway was forced to repeat that the answer was yes and, as to expenses, the Disposal Board would have the accounts for scrutiny.

Life in Parliament is never straightforward and if you explain something regarding one aspect of a subject (here meaning aircraft as part of the whole disposal of munitions question) then somebody will fail to understand. That person was none other than the worthy Sir John who asked: 'For what purpose does the Ministry now exist except for the sale of surplus stores?'

Kellaway responded that the total assets of the Disposal Board represented goods worth a staggering £180,000,000. Aircraft, by comparison, had only really made up a small part of that fearful total. And, at present, receipts from sales of surplus stood at between £4m and £5m per week. Many of these goods were more saleable to the ordinary public than aeroplanes. The Disposal Board thus had a long career ahead of it, even though it was rid of flying machines.

The next relevant parliamentary exchange came on the morning of April 5th 1920 when the Labour member for Mansfield, William Carter asked the Under-Secretary of State to the Air Ministry whether all the Government's surplus aircraft material had now been sold to the Aircraft Disposal Company, what was the price paid by the buying companies; whether there was a valuation of the material before it was sold and, if so, what was the estimated value?

The Financial Secretary to the Ministry of Munitions was James Hope and it was he who replied:

> All the Government surplus aircraft has been sold... No valuation in the ordinary sense of the term is possible, as the items involved have no definite ascertainable market value. The total stock of aircraft, which has already become or will become surplus, is sufficient to meet several times over the potential world-demand for the next few years.

Well, there it was in black and white, so to speak. Official government-uttered confirmation that the world demand for aircraft was now to be filled with our obsolete war-planes. Looked at another way, the aircraft industry could now stand down for a couple of years and do some laurel-resting...

Handley Page himself said of the deal:

> A fixed rebate will be given to those aircraft firms who desire to buy back any machines of their own design. Owing to the existence of these stocks, the aircraft industry has to face a period when little manufacturing will be required, but modifying and renovating Government aircraft means much work for the industry. We hope that British firms will participate by contracting to the syndicate all this work and co-operate with us in establishing beyond question the supremacy of British aircraft in the world's markets.

It was a rather high-handed statement and predictably it upset some in the industry. Others, much later, would view it as the first indication of a characteristic of Frederick Handley Page that tended to ride roughshod over others in the furtherance of his business activities. There are some that might attribute the final demise of his company half a century later to the obstinacy that developed from this trait.

An immediate problem was the storage and cataloguing of all this material and even a building the size of the one-time National Aircraft Factory called for considerable forethought as to the most efficient use of

Martinsyde F.4A G-EAQH is pictured here at Brooklands where the Woking-based company assembled and test-flew its machines. This particular two-seater did little flying before being scrapped at the end of 1920. *[via Richard T Riding]*

space. As goods came in by both road and rail, finished aircraft were stripped and stacked carefully to maximise space.

The start of The Aircraft Disposal Company's business effectively put the brake on the hitherto *ad hoc* disposal of parts to the public for pence. In less than a year this free-for-all had barely impacted on the vast quantity of material that now became the property of the ADC.

While it was a godsend to the National economy and the taxpayer in particular, the activities down at Waddon did not necessarily rate highly in the popularity stakes with aircraft and engine manufacturers. Despite being offered 'a fixed rebate' should firms choose to 'buy back any machines of their own design', the market was now awash with aircraft, albeit fully re-conditioned and airworthy. The 'real' aircraft industry, meanwhile, was left to face a period when there would be little or no demand for new machines. Seldom have so many things been stacked against an industry: the aftermath of the War, the terrible 'flu epidemic, the economic recession, the uncertainty over the future of the Royal Air Force – and now The Aircraft Disposal Company!

For half a decade to come, airworthy aircraft would be collected from places such as the Aintree, Castle Bromwich or Heaton Chapel depots and transported to Croydon for re-manufacture and then delivered, usually by air, to anywhere in the world by a team of pilots under the command of chief pilot, Capt Herbert Howard Perry. The other company pilots comprised Capt Reginald Herbert 'Rex' Stocken (*b.* London June 11th 1893), and Maurice Walter Piercey who is remembered for his fine flying of the Wee Bee and the ANEC in the 1924 Lympne Light Aircraft competitions. Occasionally there was so much test-flying and delivery flying to be completed that extra pilots had to be drafted in to assist.

As we have seen, in the days before the formation of The Aircraft Disposal Company Ltd, there had been some fairly significant dealings in unwanted aircraft that followed immediately on the Armistice. Once after the war ended, A V Roe & Company proposed that it would re-purchase all of the Avro 504K aircraft held in stock by the Disposal Board. This offer had been turned down on the grounds that the Disposal Board had no idea how many saleable aircraft it was responsible for.

Number 1 Aircraft Salvage Depot had been at Hendon and here it had begun the enormous task of selling off surplus machines begun. All this had, of course, come to an end with the formation of ADC. Now A V Roe tried once more to acquire its own-brand surplus machines under the fixed rebate scheme. The offer was once more rejected and now ADC found itself in conflict with the manufacturer which took out an injunction to prevent ADC from selling any aeroplanes or goods as Avro products unless of A V Roe's own manufacture. This was a curious case that established an unexpected point of Law that A V Roe may not have foreseen.

Mr Justice Peterson, in the Chancery Division, made the point on July 29th 1920 that the Aircraft Disposal Company Ltd should not sell or offer for sale any aeroplanes or similar goods, not being of A V Roe's own manufacture, as Avro goods, so upholding the earlier interim injunction. It was the actual wording that was to undermine the case as far as Roe was concerned, for it was revealed that during the war 'Avro' aircraft had been constructed (to Government order) by other companies and then presented as 'Avro' aircraft. The esteemed judge found that, 'contrary to its undertaking, the Ministry of Munitions had sold machines which were not manufactured by the plaintiffs under the name of 'Avro' to the defendants (Aircraft Disposal Company) and the defendants were selling them to the public'.

A very simple case had suddenly become highly complex and his Lordship stated his opinion that 'nobody was entitled to sell them [as 'Avro' aircraft] and the interim injunction ought to be continued, but so as not to prevent [the] defendants from selling Avro 504K as "Avro type"'.

Interesting to relate is the fact that among the early exponents of joy-riding using surplus Avro 504K aircraft was A V Roe and Company itself: in the first peacetime summer, the company carried more than 30,000 passengers as it toured the seaside resorts. A V Roe and Company thus had the distinction of forming probably the first 'barnstorming circus', a mantle for which others, such as Alan Cobham, gained considerable credit and acclaim in the years to come.

During 1919 and the early part of 1920, the Dominions were each presented with an Imperial Gift of aircraft which included the Avro 504K. Australia received 48 of them, Canada 63, 18 went to India and 21 to New Zealand although at that time she had no Air Force. At least 14 went to South Africa.

G-EATD (D4267) was an ADC Martinsyde which raced for the company in the 1922 Aerial Derby held at Waddon on August 7th: pilot Capt R H Stocken was forced to retire in this 200 mile two-lap race around London. It is believed to have been sold abroad later and its marks cancelled. *[via Richard T Riding.]*

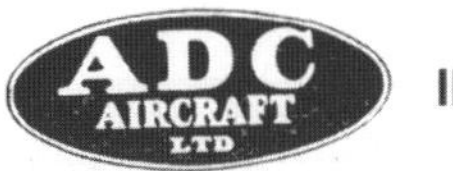

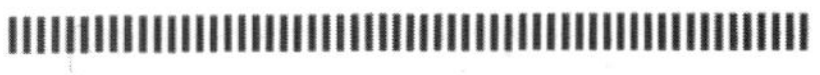

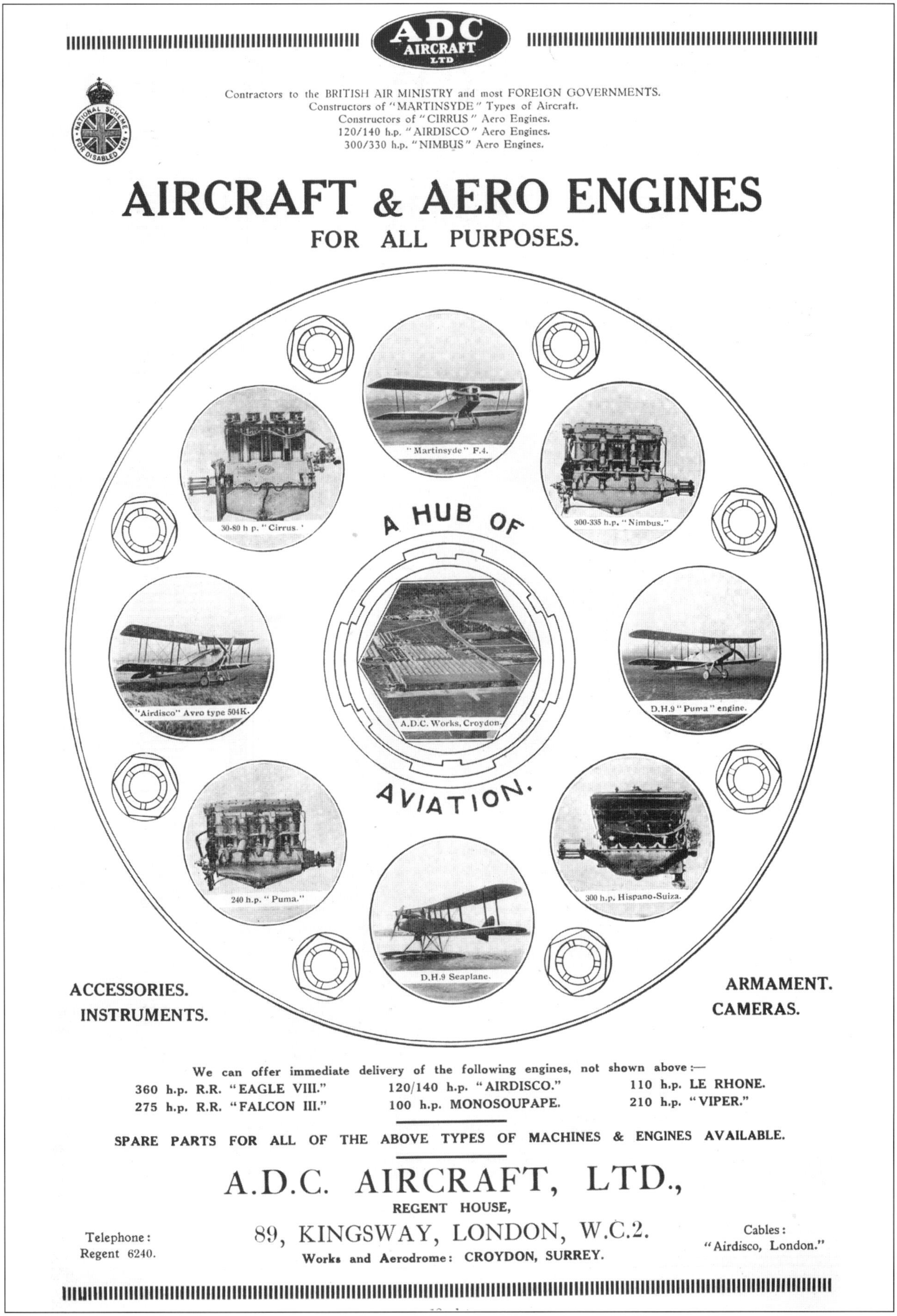
ADC AIRCRAFT LTD
NATIONAL SCHEME FOR DISABLED MEN
Contractors to the BRITISH AIR MINISTRY and most FOREIGN GOVERNMENTS.
Constructors of "MARTINSYDE" Types of Aircraft.
Constructors of "CIRRUS" Aero Engines.
120/140 h.p. "AIRDISCO" Aero Engines.
300/330 h.p. "NIMBUS" Aero Engines.
AIRCRAFT & AERO ENGINES
FOR ALL PURPOSES.
A HUB OF AVIATION.
"Martinsyde" F.4.
30-80 h.p. "Cirrus."
300-335 h.p. "Nimbus."
"Airdisco" Avro type 504K.
A.D.C. Works, Croydon.
D.H.9 "Puma" engine.
240 h.p. "Puma."
300 h.p. Hispano-Suiza.
D.H.9 Seaplane.
ACCESSORIES.
INSTRUMENTS.
ARMAMENT.
CAMERAS.
We can offer immediate delivery of the following engines, not shown above:—
360 h.p. R.R. "EAGLE VIII."
275 h.p. R.R. "FALCON III."
120/140 h.p. "AIRDISCO."
100 h.p. MONOSOUPAPE.
110 h.p. LE RHONE.
210 h.p. "VIPER."
SPARE PARTS FOR ALL OF THE ABOVE TYPES OF MACHINES & ENGINES AVAILABLE.
A.D.C. AIRCRAFT, LTD.,
REGENT HOUSE,
89, KINGSWAY, LONDON, W.C.2.
Works and Aerodrome: CROYDON, SURREY.
Telephone: Regent 6240.
Cables: "Airdisco, London."

Janes AWA 1925

The 1920 Olympia Aero Show was the first since 1913 and everybody did their utmost to present a good and united front. In the Annexe there was mounted a 'Historical Exhibit' of aircraft loaned by the Aircraft Disposal Company. Displayed in full war paint (for the occasion), they included an Avro 504K, Armstrong-Whitworth FK.8 with a 160 hp Beardmore engine, a Norman Thompson Flying Boat 2B with 210 hp Wolseley Viper engine, DH.I0A Liberty-engined bomber, DH.4, DH.9, SE.5A, Martinsyde F.4 Buzzard (D4309), Porte/Felixstowe F.3 flying boat (N4007), Bristol Fighter, FE.2b, Sopwith Snipe, Handley Page O/400 heavy bomber, and Vickers Vimy. Additionally there was an arena given over to engines and parts. In all it was a huge and impressive display.

The year 1920 was one of a general slackening in trade as one of Britain's all-too frequent market recessions forced a restraining influence on business. Besides the war and its terrible waste of life, Britain had suffered badly in the worldwide influenza epidemic of 1918-19. An estimate quarter of a million people had died. It was not just our own war wounds that had to be healed as the second decade of the twentieth century ebbed away.

When, later that same year, the Cambridge School of Flying closed down and its property was auctioned off, an Avro 504K in perfect condition made just £50. Worse still, three DH.6 trainers went for £2 5s, £3 10s, and £6 10s respectively, and a 50 hp Gnôme engine fetched 35s, two propellers made 7s 6d each and a new acetylene welding plant complete with generator (an acetylene-gas generator, presumably) made £7 10s.

The Aircraft Disposal Company Ltd had been allowed unique privilege. During the War, London's Regent's Park had been set aside as an emergency landing ground and was also a major spares depot. Aircraft parts were delivered here from sub-contract manufacturers where they were stockpiled against despatch to those companies involved in manufacture and assembly.

At the end of the war, by far the largest depot of the Ministry of Munitions' Aircraft Disposal Board was that located at the Regent's Park site in a major area now represented by the Zoological Gardens and the immediate acreage of park South of there.

This operation was another cause of friction in Parliament and, as early as May 1919, a question from the Liberal member for Limehouse, Sir William Pearce who asked the Under-Secretary of State to the Air Ministry Maj-Gen Seely to state how many people were then employed 'in the Air Force buildings, Regent's Park; what is the nature of the work; and when this portion of the park will be vacated by them'. Seely, adept at fielding the awkward ones, replied that the number of RAF personnel at Regent's Park totalled 2,332.

'They are engaged on the receipt, salvage, storage, and issue of aeroplane engines and their spares. Standard stocks are gradually being transferred to Ruislip, and it is hoped to complete this process by September 30th. The buildings and stocks not required to be retained will be handed over to the Aircraft Disposal Department of the Ministry of Munitions, the period of whose retention of them will, I understand, depend upon the time required for the disposal of the stocks transferred'.

Not surprisingly, the people of London were far from happy having one of the Royal Parks still used in this manner in time of peace. When in March 1920 The Aircraft Disposal Company was formed it was allowed to take control over this whole mess of rather ramshackle buildings and outdoor storage. While it had its own reconditioning and erecting hangar at the old NAF building in Waddon, it only took aircraft components as it needed them from Regent's Park.

The company's tenure of the Royal park, initially viewed by the Treasury (and leased as such) as just long enough to clear out the material, showed no early signs of coming to an end. As late as September 7th 1922, *The Morning Post* published a letter querying why, almost four years after the cessation of hostilities, the public was still denied access to a major part of the Park due to the activities of a private company.

Colonel Maurice Ormonde Darby ran both the ADC's London office at Regent House, 89 Kingsway, WC2 and the Regent's Park depot. Explaining that the company had already evacuated about a third of the area it originally occupied, Colonel Darby suggested:

> It is a question of expense to the taxpayer. It would cost from £50,000 to £60,000 to move at the present time and a large part of the cost would have to be borne by the Government.

He added that if they were left alone to move material as it was sold, they could be out within a year 'at practically no cost to the taxpayer'. The value of stock (now mostly engines, engine spares and electrical equipment) was put at £800,000. Colonel Darby also suggested that it would require 55,000 lorry loads to clear the stock. Nobody thought to query that rather wild estimate which would entail more than 150 lorry-loads a day, seven days a week, to meet that one-year deadline.

At all events, it was not until the end of 1923 that the site was fully vacated and the material moved down to Waddon adjoining Croydon Airport where Maj John R Grant was in charge of reconditioning.

The Aircraft Disposal Company, already being known colloquially by the acronym ADC or Airdisco (which latter name was registered as its telegraphic address), consolidated at Croydon's Waddon site under its joint managing directors, Lt-Col Maurice Ormonde Darby, and Lt--Col J Barrett-Lennard. Sales manager was B Cassam and works superintendent Ernest Stephen Olney.

Wisely the new business realised that the first task was to dispose of the oldest and, potentially, most useless aircraft first. Early advertisements promoted the two-seat pusher FE.2B fitted with a 160 hp Beardmore engine. The advertisement copy read:

> This type is in many ways to be recommended as a reliable cross-country machine. It is easy to handle in the air, and lands at slow speeds... As a test of its efficiency, it may he mentioned that this aeroplane remained in the list of service fighting machines longer than any other type... A distinct feature is the excellent view afforded the pilot. His seat is in front of planes and engine, and he has unrestricted vision... An eminently suitable machine for long distance trips where reliability rather than speed is desired.

The selling price quoted was £500.

It would be wrong to say that the Aircraft Disposal Company had everything its own way, for during its first year of operation it suffered a major set-back when a huge deal brokered by Handley Page himself was blocked by the might of the American Courts. Almost as soon as the initial transaction had been completed with the Ministry of Munitions' Disposal Board, Page had sailed for the United States where he quickly organised a distribution site for surplus British aircraft. On his return he had in his pocket orders for 2,365 aeroplanes and a massive 34,000 engines.

Proceedings to stop this influx of British war-time goods were at once initiated by the Wright Aeronautical Company on behalf of the entire American aviation industry. American manufacturers, they stated, did not wish to stifle fair competition but at the same time they did not want the American

Rack upon rack of tiny and rather meaningless components makes for a boring picture yet this view of one area of a parts store conveys immediately the enormous undertaking that was ADC. These racks of components had largely come from the Regent's Park storage depot giving an impression of the logistics involved in shifting such a volume of bits. Far right is a rack of cylinder heads and manifolds while on the end of the rack in the foreground somebody has chalked the words 'starting handles' – a reminder that these commodities were once part of the flying scene.

market flooded with aeroplanes and engines, parts of which were obsolete and of war-time design and production.

In granting an injunction at the beginning of December 1920 restraining both The Aircraft Disposal Company and Messrs Handley Page from importing this surplus material, American industry was spared a taste of the problems that were only just beginning to bite over here.

Despite this snub from America, the company prospered and as it found its feet, it recognised that its unique position in the marketplace made it an ideal organisation to sell any type of aircraft, in other words to become a second-hand dealer or broker. In the summer of 1923 ADC advertised 'commercial types' for delivery including DH.18, Westland Limousine, Vickers Viking, and Vickers Vulcan. It does seem, though, that handling other people's aircraft sales was only a short-lived exercise for by the start of the following year the Aircraft Disposal Company had embarked on a whole new approach to its core business and second-hand sales were no longer offered.

John Kenneth Lane, who later became assistant designer, managing director and later chairman of the company that designed the Robinson Redwing biplane, remembers joining the Aircraft Disposal Company at its Waddon factory in that year. He was to work on the redesign of the Martinsyde F.4 as the ADC. 1, with John Kenworthy. Writing in the *Journal* of the Croydon Airport Society (No. 1, 1981) he recalled that:

> There were hundreds and thousands of aircraft parts stored in the huge factory including wings, fuselages, tail planes and engine parts – they were the result of cancelled contracts at the end of the Great War. It was our task to build complete aircraft using what parts we could.
> I remember one contract we obtained from the Polish Government for a number of aircraft using Martinsyde wings and fuselages with Armstrong Siddeley engines. They were sold to a very tight specification and it was hoped that the Poles would not be too critical. This, however, was wishful thinking and the Polish inspectors insisted on the specification being kept to the letter. After a struggle we managed to satisfy all the conditions of weight and speed, etc, but the climb which had to be 10,000 feet in twelve minutes seemed almost impossible to achieve. Our test pilot was certainly good, but just could not make it. Finally someone suggested that a freelance pilot, Frank Courtney, be invited to have a go. Frank was remarkable; he had very poor eyesight, wearing thick pebble spectacles, but he had a feel for aircraft that was quite exceptional. At the first attempt he achieved the desired result, the curve on his barograph looking as though. it had been drawn with a pair of compasses.

This type of work, assembling aircraft for foreign air forces, continued for a number of years. But to return to the immediate post-war year, what was the state of affairs in the aircraft industry?

Chapter 8

British Aviation: an Industry in Crisis

AS the penumbra of war lifted from Europe, many countries began experiencing a minor economic boom accompanied by a general market buoyancy, especially in aviation. This even included, to a certain extent, Germany despite the Fatherland being crippled with war debts. Now the first flying clubs came into being while in Germany and elsewhere the new sport of gliding was taking a firm hold. Unfortunately this economic confidence in aviation did not extend to Britain and what small market there was seems to have been influenced by the ready availability of Airdisco's competitively-priced newly-manufactured machines.

The Nieuport & General Aircraft Company Ltd (formed in November 1916 for the purpose of manufacturing Nieuport designs in England) had availed itself of the Aircraft Disposal Board's offer to buy back its own aircraft (the Royal Flying Corps had had a number of largely obsolete Nieuports on strength) at a fixed rate in the curious and mistaken belief that they would be able to sell their fighters to a peacetime market which had yet to be created. The company no doubt thought that this move would protect its own image as well as the barely nascent market: it was wrong. The Cricklewood works were closed down and the Receiver moved in during September 1920. A large quantity of aircraft and parts disappeared, believed burned, on the factory site.

More successful was Bristol Aeroplane Company which bought back from the ADB four of its M.1C fighter monoplanes for civilianisation for which they were successful in finding a market (G-EASR, G-EAVP and M-AFAA for Spain while the remaining example was sold to America). Ideal as communications or racing aircraft, acquisition of these machines represented a safe and pure commercial venture for the company.

The cancellation of all military aircraft contracts forced either the closure of some companies or their dramatic reduction in size prior to diversification. There were some businesses that had gone over completely to war work and abandoned their core products. On the other hand there were some that had been set up expressly to benefit from the huge contracts that the Ministry of Munitions had issued during the war. These latter were particularly vulnerable when the contractual 'golden egg' failed to hatch.

Of the casualties in this category, perhaps the least missed was the flamboyant Whitehead Aircraft of Feltham. With both mistaken ideals and lack of prudence, the business of John Alexander Whitehead had started with the 1914-18 war and flourished with contracts for Maurice

SE.5A F862 was one of the many hundreds of examples of this fighter built during 1918. Constructed by Wolseley Motors Ltd of Birmingham, it was test flown by Lt A H Curtis at Castle Bromwich apparently in 1919 but this date may be in error. Other contractors for this type of aircraft included Martinsyde at Brooklands and Woking most of whose production went straight into store for ultimate disposal.

One of the principle fighters of the Great War was the SE.5A designed by Henry Phillip Folland with the assistance of John Kenworthy and Frank Widenham Goodden. At the end of the war, 5,205 had been built of which some 1,407 were in store. This example, D7000, was the last of a batch of 150 built by Wolseley Motors Ltd in Birmingham during 1917. Many of these aircraft ended up at Waddon for disposal.

Farman Shorthorns followed by the Sopwith Pup (which he persisted in describing as the Whitehead Fighting Scout), DH.9s and DH.9As.

Whitehead expanded his business at the family home Hanworth Park House and built a larger factory on what would later be known as Hanworth Air Park. He also extended his other factories, notably at Kingston, and floated a £1-million stock issue in 1918. Once the war was over, things changed dramatically and soon he was appealing to the Government for money so he could survive. Despite protestations that the government owed him nearly £1/2m, his pleas fell on deaf ears and in July 1919 the business went into voluntary liquidation with liabilities of £85,000 and assets of barely £15,000.

If Whitehead was least missed, then the tragedy of The Grahame-White Company was scandalous. Claude Grahame-White (1879-1959) was a pioneer and patriot as well as an ace flyer. It was he who coined the phrase 'Wake up England': he flew his Farman across the country in 1912 with electric light-bulbs illuminating these words under his wings. During the war he was a leading aircraft-producer and owned Hendon Aerodrome that he had himself established in the pioneering days. At the Armistice his very large orders were instantly axed, stopping all work in progress. He was owed considerable sums by the authorities not the least being rent for his own aerodrome that had been forcibly commandeered.

A combination of a static market for civil aircraft (he produced two potentially useful airliners but they were too expensive for the purses of the unsubsidised early airlines) and official procrastination cost him his rightful rewards and he unwisely diversified into his other love – motor-cars. He lost his airfield and his money (although many years later he was adequately recompensed) but above all he stopped making aircraft.

Some casualties of the post-war slump were quick: on the Isle of Wight the aircraft division of long-established boat-builders J Samuel White ceased production of aircraft on January 21st, 1919, and finally closed down on July 28th that year. White had begun shipbuilding on the Isle of Thanet at the time of the Armada. Around 1800 the business moved to Cowes and became renowned for the building of fast ships. It was natural that the business should turn to seaplanes and, through the influence of Howard T Wright who joined the company in 1912, White had its No 1 Seaplane, designed and built in six weeks, on show at the 1913 Olympia Aero Show.

A succession of 'Navyplanes' followed, inventions such as a rack-and-pinion wing-folding system and floats were patented and, as the First World War progressed, White became a major manufacturer, sub-contractor and military aircraft supplier. Short seaplanes were built under licence, the DH.9A was equipped with a White flotation gear and retractable undercarriage for amphibious use – and so on.

From being a major player to having no work took just a few months as J Samuel White's military orders were cancelled. White went back to ship-building.

The matter of the Norman Thompson Flight Company has already been alluded to in the previous Chapter. Suffice to say that from being a major provider of flying boats to penury was, for this important maker, a mere matter of months. Norman Thompson had secured a deal with Curtiss in America for the supply of engines to boost our own insufficient output. A quantity contract was in position when the Armistice came and all orders for finished aircraft were cancelled. Curtiss would not agree to closing its contract deliveries to Norman Thompson who naturally contacted the Government for assistance. Total indifference to the problems of his company forced liquidation and demonstrated yet another example of how very short corporate memories really are. An attitude of 'you're invaluable – just so long as we need you: once you've outlived your usefulness, then we don't owe you, and we don't know you' existed and affected both the maimed troops back from the battles and the suppliers of the materials of war.

In the belief that there was a peacetime market to be tapped, the Austin Motor Company tried to produce the first post-war light aeroplane. This machine was the Whippet, a delightful aeroplane designed in 1918 by John Kenworthy that had everything going for it. However, it was priced in economic terms at a time when reconditioned one-time RAF machines could be bought for half the price. Austin tried hard before succumbing to the pressure of reality. It vowed never again to build aeroplanes and went back to cars.

Not just airframe makers but the engine-providers suffered as well. The aircraft engine divisions of Peter Brotherhood and Gustavus Green were quickly closed. The biggest and most famous name to fade, however, was Sunbeam. This company made good aircraft engines but it recognised that its forte was in meeting military requirements and the prospect of launching itself into the uncertainties of the open market of peacetime filled it with trepidation. The management shrewdly foresaw the onset of the economic downturn just in time – and the business quickly reverted to car and car-engine making. They knew no Government largesse existed for anybody.

But the post-war slump had other victims to pull down. Take the case of the Alliance Aeroplane Co Ltd which had its offices at 45 East Castle Street, London W1 and a factory at Cambridge Road, Hammersmith, West London. It shows how quickly profitability could turn to penury. At the beginning of 1917, the impressment management at Hendon Aerodrome decided to rid itself of as much of the non-Service activity on the field as it could. One of the casualties of the resulting 'squeeze-out' was the Ruffy, Arnell and Baumann School of Flying Co Ltd. Actually this business welcomed the opportunity to set up its own airfield on land it had acquired at the grandly-titled if spatially-challenging London Aviation Ground (better known as Acton aerodrome) at Noel Road, Acton.[1] The Italian Felix Ruffy and the Swiss-born brothers Aimé and Edouard Baumann lost no time in building hangars on the new field for their Caudron trainers.

Flying commenced and all went well until July 1918 when the Air Council shut down the school for 'inadequate training'. That many illustrious flyers of the time (including Albert Ball, the first British ace pilot who was posthumously awarded the Victoria Cross) had trained with the business either at Hendon or at Acton cut no ice. The school closed. This coincided with the need for furniture-makers Waring & Gillow to expand its aircraft production facilities. Ruffy-Baumann's business was acquired at once for the sum of £1500 (which presumably included the land and buildings), their hangars given over to aircraft production and a new 200 ft by 153 ft assembly factory erected.

To consolidate the new business, Samuel Waring (later Sir Samuel) of Waring & Gillow created a new business – Alliance Aeroplane Co Ltd. The manufacture of DH.9 aircraft began at Acton aerodrome while the Hammersmith works, hitherto engaged in Sopwith production, was engaged in making parts for the new Handley Page V/1500 bomber. The end of the war stopped all this in its tracks, but Alliance decided to stay in the aviation business, hiring J A Peters to design civil aeroplanes.

A couple of run-of-the-mill trainers appeared (one being a machine first designed by Ruffy-Baumann which was now styled the Alliance P.1) followed by the ill-fated Napier Lion-engined 53-foot span two-seater called the P.2 Seabird. This aircraft, K.160/G-EAGL, flew non-stop from Acton to Madrid in July 1919. A second example, G-EAOX, was built for the projected trans-Atlantic competition. Grand notions that this would be developed into an eleven-passenger airliner were dashed when, on November 13th, 1919, the machine set off from Hounslow to fly to Australia, but crashed just six-and-a-half miles away at Surbiton killing its Australian pilot and co-pilot and attracting considerable adverse publicity concerning the aircraft's airworthiness. The cause might have been something to do with the unfortunate fact that the crew sat inside the fuselage with only an oblique view of the world outside.

Samuel Waring, who also set up The British Aerial Transport Company, now entered financial difficulties. The business had lost all its military contracts and the production on which company hopes had been pinned disappeared. The Aircraft Disposal Company had yet to be formed, but the sales of cheap aeroplanes undercut the price at which he could build them. His company profits plummeted. On top of that, Frederick Koolhoven and a number of other key staff left BAT, rendering that business no longer viable.

On December 31st 1919, Alliance ceased business and was officially wound up by March 1920 – just weeks before the formation of ADC. Waring sold off the aerodrome land at Acton for housing, keeping the one-time aircraft factory until 1921 for the manufacture of gramophones.

Meanwhile at Peterborough, the business of Frederick Sage & Company Ltd, massively expanded to cope with war production, now struggled to keep its rapidly-reduced work-force occupied. The aviation department of Sage had as its chief designer the brilliant young Clifford Wilfrid Tinson who had been Frank Barnwell's capable right-hand man at the British & Colonial Aeroplane Company (later re-named Bristol). He had then joined Admiralty Air Department before coming to Sage in 1916 where he worked under Eric Cecil Gordon England.

Now in 1921 Sage was forced to close down. Tinson, the man who had designed the first metal wings for Blériot's monoplane and Gordon England's GE3 biplane in the absence of Frank Barnwell, then went to A V Roe as chief draughtsman 1921-22 before going back to what was by then the Bristol Aeroplane Co Ltd in 1923 as senior draughtsman.

1. Little is recorded about the formation of Acton Aerodrome and that which does exist is confusing and incorrect. In 1909, an Acton-based man by the name of Ambrose Grattan Power designed a heavily-braced monoplane (the Power Monoplane) the construction of which he entrusted to an engineering firm named R Lascelles & Co of 13 Greek Street, London. This firm also made internal combustion engines and one of its motors was to drive Power's aeroplane. Lascelles' creation proved to be incapable of flight when tests began at the Lascelles own test field which they named London Aviation Ground and which was managed by a company called London Aviation Ground Ltd formed in June 1910 by E R Beney and R Lascelles. Gratton Power then agreed to purchase from the same firm an 'Ornis' monoplane that E Robert Beney, director of Lascelles, exhibited at the 2nd Olympia Aero Show of March 1910. The price was £450 and it was described as 'guaranteed to fly' – which proved an unfortunate exaggeration! Mr Power, who had taken the machine to the larger Brooklands aerodrome, sued Beney for the return of his money and won the case. The early aviator Lt-Col Louis Noel (who qualified for his RAeC Certificate No.116 on a Farman at Brooklands on August 17th, 1911) also attempted flight at Acton in 1910 with Robert Beney's aeroplane. The 'Ornis' was styled after the Blériot Monoplane and had a span of 28 feet, a chord of 6 feet and a wing area of 170 sq.ft. The overall length was 28 feet, and the machine had an all-up weight of 450 lbs, 150 lbs of which was allocated for the 4-cylinder 'semi-radial' Lascelles engine. This, priced at £150, had a bore of 100mm, a stroke of 120mm and developed 35 hp driving a Weiss propeller. The later history of Acton is well-documented and the company London Aviation Ground Ltd should not be confused with London Aerodrome Ltd, the business formed in February 1910 by the proprietors of the Hendon Flying Grounds. A curious aside is that this same Ambrose Gratton Power was also a knowledgeable person in the world of church organs and was a frequent contributor to the musical press of the time. He was to gain his Aero Club Certificate No.498 on June 2nd 1913 on a Grahame-White Biplane at Hendon.

The curiously-named but greatly admired Sopwith 1½-Strutter (so named because of the unconventional splayed parallel centre-section struts) distinguished itself in combat. Lt Louis Arbon Strange (1891-1966) modified this example to try out a machine-gun mounting of his own design. Such individual and unofficial modifications to one of His Majesty's aircraft were frowned upon – but if they worked (as this one seems to have done) they were 'blind-eyed' by the higher brass. The engine here is the 130 hp Clerget 9BC. Large numbers of these aircraft ended up at Waddon for disposal..

Almost lost amongst this spate of post-war company casualties was the British business of Deperdussin. In Britain, the British Deperdussin Aeroplane Company Ltd operated as contractors for the Ministry. Formed by Lorenzo Santoni (who later founded the Italian Savoia firm) together with Dutchman Frederick Koolhoven, the managing director was John Cyril Porte who made his name with pioneer flying-boats and who, it is reputed, took up flying to cure his tuberculosis (which was finally to claim him on October 22nd 1919). Porte had also put money into the business.

Now as a consequence of the termination of its contracts, British Deperdussin found itself unable to continue. Again a flaccid market was being fully exploited by ADC. A Receiver was appointed to British Deperdussin and the business failed in 1923.

Most of these casualties were directly due to the cancellation of war work. Now that the 1920s had settled in, though, the success of Airdisco increasingly threatened the livelihoods of many in the factories whose former products were now being sold off so successfully around the world. The conventional aircraft industry could not compete on the same terms.

The first really serious British casualty among dedicated, long-standing businesses in the peacetime regime was Martinsyde, one of the oldest and largest aircraft manufacturers in Britain and one which consistently built good, if rather solid-looking, aircraft to the design of George Harris Handasyde.

Among its many creations was a robust single-seat fighter that was known as the F.3. Built at Brooklands during the autumn of 1917, the F.3 was powered by a 230 hp Rolls-Royce motor which, in contemporary official reports, was referred to as a 'Falcon Experimental' *[22]*. This originally drove a four-bladed Lang propeller, later a two-blader. Almost from the beginning, Martinsyde had suggested the more powerful 240 hp water-cooled V-8 Lorraine de Dietrich as a suitable alternative.

The Martinsyde F.3 was unusual in that its two-part fuselage was robustly built around solid longerons of hickory with spruce intercostals. Its first flight took place mid-September and early in October the aircraft went to Martlesham Heath where it received glowing reports from those test pilots that flew it.

Although ordered into immediate production using the 275 hp Falcon III, the authorities had overlooked the prior and overriding demands of the huge production run of the Bristol F.2B Fighter which took almost every Falcon Derby could make. This created a succession of production problems and delays with the overall result that only six F.3s were completed early in 1918.

A new version known as the F.4, later to be officially named the 'Buzzard', was also designed having lower wings of a narrower chord and with the cockpit moved aft in order to improve the view downwards. This model was to be powered by the 300hp Hispano-Suiza 8Fb engine. Immediately this was ordered into full production and, by the time the war had ended, some fifty-two had been delivered although the Armistice came before they could actually see service. The remainder was cancelled.

Martinsyde quickly realigned itself and become a public company early in 1919. Now, suffering acutely through the cancellation of war-time contracts, the Woking-based firm produced a number of competent aircraft of sufficient variety to suggest that a civilian market could be fostered. While a few aircraft sales, supported by heavy advertising, bore witness to this confidence, it could not be seen as fostering any hope of long-term prosperity.

By the Spring of 1920 things were grim. Still hoping to stay in aviation, they submitted a machine for the Air Ministry's commercial aircraft trials held at Martlesham Heath. After engine-failure, they were forced to withdraw. Then the same problem, this time a failed oil pump, caused Martinsyde's Semiquaver (which had set a new world speed record with a staggering 161.434 mph at Martlesham on March 21st 1920) to drop out of the Gordon Bennet race in France that September, and things got worse.

Wisely, then, Martinsyde diversified into farm carts and motorcycles (some 2,000

Martinsyde-Newman machines were made between 1920 and 1923).

On Saturday September 25th 1920, fire – quite accidental in origin – destroyed much of the factory, consuming 127 completed wings, as well as many fuselages and other parts to a total value of between £20,000 and £30,000. Despite adequate insurance coverage, money and goodwill proved poor tools with which to mount any offensive against a slack market awash with cheap aircraft from Croydon.

The final blow came when the Treasury at last caught up with War Payments and unfairly imposed a heavy Excess Profit Duty. The company's bankers felt forced to appoint a Receiver in November to protect their assets with priority over any Revenue demands. Martinsyde dragged on, selling a few aeroplanes where it could. Meanwhile, Airdisco was able to offer the same, or substantially similar, machines Government surplus, at a lower cost.

The Martinsyde affair dragged on: the business was not finally wound up until February 1924 upon which the remaining aircraft stock, manufacturing rights (but not the Woking factory), goodwill and components were acquired by the ever-grasping Airdisco which cared not one jot about the part it had played in the demise of one of the oldest aircraft businesses, that of Helmut Paul Martin and George Harris Handasyde first set up on June 1st, 1906.

Meanwhile Handley Page himself could barely make ends meet. Far from the anticipated wealth that had accompanied his business plans, he was in trouble having overstretched himself through the premature and consequently unsuccessful promotion of air transport services in the Colonies and South America. With the value of the company's Ordinary £1 shares down to just one shilling, a sum of £400,000 due to Aircraft Disposal Company could not be paid. This money was commission on sales that HP had accrued as selling agents under the terms of its agreement with ADC. A similar sum was due to the Bank of Scotland. Now ADC shareholders accused Handley Page of having spent their money on failed business enterprises while, according to Handley Page, the cash had had to be spent in order to keep Handley Page Limited afloat.

Far from being a sympathetic sibling prepared to help out its ailing parent, Airdisco promptly turned and, in a wrath of monumental filial disloyalty, threatened to liquidate Handley Page Limited! It was a delicate scenario for all parties since Airdisco had obligations under its contract with the Government which it now could not honour.

The Bank of Scotland proved to be the genial uncle in this conflict, arranging for Frederick Handley Page to remain as managing director so long as both the Bank and the Aircraft Disposal Company were each allowed to nominate two new directors to the Handley Page board *[2]*. These included Lt-Col John Barrett-Lennard to serve as chairman for six years. The company secretary was Maurice O Tribe.

The deal preserved Handley Page's position at the cost of £179,000 due to him personally by way of royalties for his slotted-wing patents which he voluntarily handed over.[2]

At the Handley Page Company's annual general meeting on June 23rd 1922, chairman Barrett-Lennard revealed to shareholders that the financial impasse had caused great concern to both organisations and as a direct consequence, the Aircraft Disposal Company had rescinded the arrangement whereby HP acted as its selling agent.

Matters for Handley Page Limited were bad and the heavy bank borrowings added to its problems. Its liabilities (interest on bank loans), administration and the protection of its patents meant that £50,000 a year had to be found in order to keep the firm afloat. Frederick Handley Page himself announced he had written off a further £176,000 that his company owed him in order to try to cover debts. His brother Theodore resigned as director of the Aircraft Disposal Company and, in return for not annihilating its founders, the company sought – and got – the right to nominate the management of Handley Page Ltd.

For Handley Page it was a bitter pill to swallow. His 'grand coup' in setting up The Aircraft Disposal Company had seriously backfired after little more than a year and he was no longer in charge of selling aircraft for the business. And to make matters worse, ADC's new blood had infiltrated his own management board!

Almost annihilated by his own creation, Handley Page moved into car-manufacture, building the Bean family tourer and, later, the Campbell Sports Saloon with its noisy Anzani engine. Early prospects of good profits were short-lived and the motor business resulted in yet another financial loss for the business. Part of the factory was now sub-let to a coach-builders. Another tenant was a one-time Cricklewood Lane barrow-boy by the name of Frank Smith *[2]*. He had the idea of making potato crisps in 1920 – and quickly became both a household name and a millionaire!

Meanwhile at Rochester, Short Brothers was only able to avert disaster by switching over to the manufacture of light-weight aluminium bodies for the newly-introduced fully-enclosed double-deck omnibuses being operated by the London General Omnibus Company and Thomas Tilling Ltd.

To the list of Airdisco-inspired failures one is tempted to add the name of Sopwith which was forced into liquidation very soon after the end of the War. However, while Airdisco's business did nothing to help the survival of Sopwith, that company's demise was the direct result of the scandalous way in which the British Government rewarded one of the most significant makers of fighter aircraft which played a major part in defeating the enemy.

Like Martinsyde, Sopwith's problems were in the main due to crippling Treasury claims for Excess Profit Duty during the time of the war. (The unfairness of this assessment lay in its rejection of all company capital outlay in the expanding of premises and equipment to meet the ever-increasing demands of production.) On top of this, the company was denied the opportunity to offset subsequent heavy trading losses, so in 1920 the company went into voluntary liquidation, the Sopwith business and all assets being transferred to a new company led by Harry George Hawker (who was to lose his life on July 12th 1921) and Thomas Octave Murdock Sopwith.

Sopwith, a wise, honest and experienced businessman and (as everybody who knew him agreed) a gentleman, knew that by folding his company when he did and then reforming it under a different name he could secure his business creditors in full: to his great credit, this he did to the last penny by the end of 1922. Airdisco's part in this collapse was thus perhaps uncharacteristically passive.

It is easy to forget the plight of the engine manufacturers before this litany of aircraft makers' woes. They, too, were up against the wall. This became clear at the 1920 Olympia Aero Show where there was an all-pervading aura of uncertainty.

2. The Bank's decision to allow Handley Page to remain at the head of his company was not quite as unrealistic or unlikely as it might at first appear. Page's patents were being taken up by manufacturers all over the world and the Bank clearly valued the royalties potential in excess of the monies outstanding. In fact by the time the patents expired in 1938, the master patents for his wing slot had earned royalties in excess of £750,000.

Not quite in the same league as the Sopwith Pup and the SE.5A, de Havilland's rather strange-looking DH.5 was a contender for the RFC's fighter requirement. Designed in 1916 with production starting the following year, some 550 or so examples were built at a cost of £874 each plus £771 10s for their 110 hp Le Rhône engines. The curious 'pre-crashed' appearance of the machine gave rise to an unfounded criticism that this machine was tricky to fly: it was not although above 10,000 feet it was easily out-performed by other British – and German – fighters. Which is probably why this example, A9363, built by the Darracq Motor Engineering Company, was shot down possibly by Manfred von Richtofen in November 1917. It is believed that some 67 examples were declared surplus for disposal at the end of the War.

Although they displayed at Olympia makers such as Beardmore, Gwynne, and Sunbeam (who had the largest engine on exhibition, the Sikh, for which an output of 800/900 hp was hoped) were balking at the cost of engine development.

Competing against every manufacturer, whether aeroplane or engine, was the Aircraft Disposal Co, with prices below any equivalent item the British aircraft industry could produce, including sparking plugs, instruments, magnetos, and carburettors, all available by the hundred thousand. It was a most significant pointer to the need for caution.

In the fullness of time the engine business was to have a slightly better long-term outcome as a result of Geoffrey de Havilland's 1924 conviction that there was a potential market for light planes equivalent to that for private cars. The story of his single-handed campaign that lead to the Aircraft Disposal Company building the world's first practical light aircraft motor is told in the following Chapter.

This, though, is somewhat ahead of our story, so we must return to the early 1920s and, as well as the manufacturing side of the aviation business, take a look at the other aspects of aviation. What about pilots? Writing of the problems of the fledgling airline industry at Croydon, Penrose *[24; p.131]* relates that there was a coterie of airline and free-lance pilots of whom most were still only in their mid-twenties.

By any standard, says Penrose, pay was modest, even to eking a precarious livelihood by flying new machines at a ridiculously low figure while waiting for a job in the aircraft industry to turn up which would offer a more definite prospect. For production testing a Disposal machine the fee was £1. To deliver it to Brussels gained £8, but the pilot had to pay his own expenses, netting a mere £3 for the two-hour flight and overnight sea-going return.

It had been an attempt to induce some spark of ignition into the aircraft industry that the government staged a three-day Air Conference in the Council Chamber of the Guildhall. Its aim was to familiarise the business community with the potentialities of aviation for commercial purposes. Opened by Winston Churchill on October 12th 1920, it was full of good intent and was well-received, especially when the announcement was made that 'the Government intends to assist aviation by every means in its power'. The fact that the promise proved as insubstantial as a butterfly's wings in a wind-tunnel would only be established in time.

For the moment, though, it was a promise to be lauded. For many of the delegates, the highlight of the event came on the second morning when a small fleet of motor-buses transferred everybody to London Bridge station to catch a special train to Waddon. They were escorted during the entire journey by the large rigid airships R.32 and R.33 which kept pace easily with the train. When they disembarked at Waddon, the airships hovered around like some sort of aerial pre-historic predatory whales while more buses were boarded for the journey into the airport when once more the airships gave escort.

The party toured the aerodrome, took time to sample the skies through the courtesy of several operators with spare aircraft, had lunch – and got back to the Guildhall in time for another lecture. They did not go near the Aircraft Disposal Company's vast hangars nor, strangely, was the enterprise listed in the conspectus of Croydon's operators and their hangars, a copy of which was presented to each of the visitors.

While the conference was nothing if not filled with excitement and great ideas, time would condemn it since it largely preached to the converted and was therefore something of a futile exercise. A month earlier the Air Ministry had staged its competitions to find a suitable commercial aircraft. That, too, had been something of a farce.

Now with the fresh hope of stimulating interest in civil aviation, the Government held another Air Conference in February 1922, also at the Guildhall but this time without the airships. On this visit, unlike its predecessor, the group would get the chance to see the 'other aspect' of Croydon Aerodrome. Penrose *[op.cit]* takes up the story:

> It was preceded by a visit to Croydon on a perfect day of blue sky and bright sunshine, with every type of airliner on display. Arriving by special train from Victoria, the visitors passed through the Aircraft Disposal Company's building, with its stacks of aeroplanes tipped on their noses to save space, and were met by Sir Frederick Sykes, who explained that this area would eventually house airliners, and the temporary buildings by Plough Lane would be replaced by permanent offices and works. Flights and demonstrations followed, but in fact only served to accentuate that no real progress had been made with civil aircraft since the previous Conference. However, a pleasant party was had by all…

Aircraft were being sold, though, in quite large numbers from ADC. The business of supplying what had been top-line Royal Air Force machines to foreign air forces around the world showed little sign of diminishing in the immediate future. There was always activity at the Waddon site and several new or reconditioned aircraft left every day. Again, Penrose *[op.cit]* takes up the story:

> Of the several companies selling reconditioned machines, Handley Page with his Aircraft Disposal Co was having the greatest success, thanks to the

administration of Colonel Darby at the London Office and Major Grant who supervised reconditioning at Waddon adjoining Croydon. Two years' trading had established a splendid reputation for thorough overhaul of airframes and engines, and the company was selling at a good profit, half of which was of direct national benefit, for it was returned to the Treasury. There were many satisfied customers and numerous repeat orders.

The sheer variety of aircraft available from Waddon virtually guaranteed that the Aircraft Disposal Company could meet almost any needs, military or civilian, from anywhere in the world. The caveat that each machine was 'thoroughly checked and reconstructed' was not just a necessary sales adjunct so much as an essential prerequisite. While AID inspectors never openly adjusted their requirements, there is no doubt that as the demands for production increased pressure was brought on the Department to relax some of its demands.

The matter of replacing top-quality aircraft spruce with cypress has already been mentioned. For areas of longerons subjected to high stress, especially compression, it was normal practice to reinforce with a suitable hardwood such as ash: Martinsyde actually used hickory for fuselage components – an ideal timber but, at that time, extremely expensive and in short supply. As the war progressed, a national shortage of ash naturally led to other hardwood being investigated, the most obvious being oak. This had all the required qualities except that it was difficult to glue using the casein adhesives of the time and was twice the weight of spruce.

Part of Airdisco's 'remanufacturing' process was therefore to check for overall quality of manufacture and, in particular, the use of suitable materials. Oak engine-bearers were acceptable so long as unplated brass or steel woodscrews were not used in it for the acid in the oak produced corrosion.

It was inevitable that a good proportion of the aircraft acquired by the company in its deal with the Ministry of Munitions' Aircraft Disposal Board would be impossible to sell on in any form. Foreign governments and air forces, desperate as they were for low-cost aircraft with which to equip their fledging services and airlines, were nonetheless selective. There was only so far that one could go in making somebody else's unwanted cast-offs seem attractive to a buyer.

The upshot was that of the many aircraft that filled the storage spaces at Waddon, only comparatively few would take to the air. Those that did were, in the main, new and undelivered examples of the more useful designs that the mixed bag of customers might find attractive. Large numbers of Bristol F.2B Fighters went to the Belgian Air Force as did DH.4, DH.9 and Avro 504K machines. Even the big flying-boats such as the Felixstowe F-3 found a market along with a few Parnall Panthers.

It was a good measure of the status and reputation of the Martinsyde Company at Woking and Brooklands that its products were snapped up quickly. A large number of F.4 machines went to Portugal while the Latvian Air Force chose the Martinsyde ADC.1 variety as developed and produced at Waddon.

Large stocks of unwanted components for the DH.2, obsolete by the end of the war, were destroyed on site or reduced to produce while the DH.6, stored in equally large numbers, proved impossible to sell. The DH.4, on the other hand, was well sold to the Belgian Air Force with a regular ferry-flight run from Croydon as the aircraft were delivered to their new owners.

One machine that did poorly on the post-war market was the SE.5A. It had been thought that the type would find a ready market and a batch of eight was immediately prepared for the home market, the first of which was G-EAXQ. No sales came, though, and eventually the whole eight, and a quantity of others, were broken up. Another machine that was difficult to sell was the Sopwith Pup – desirable in time of war, but too small and costly to operate to find a viable peacetime use.

The big success story for Waddon, though, was the emergency in Spain. The Riff rising in Spanish Morocco came in 1921. It was led by Ab-del-Krim and was, for Spain, a very serious matter. Spain thus became one of the first countries with a real need to expand her air force. The Spanish war office turned to Britain and France for help and placed orders for machines. Orders were placed for Bristol Fighters, DH.4 and DH.9A aircraft and the suppliers were the Bristol Aeroplane Company Ltd, de Havilland Aircraft Company Ltd, and The Aircraft Disposal Company Ltd.

Urgency surrounded the whole matter and the prices quoted – and accepted – were for delivery to Madrid and it was found better to build and fly in Britain and deliver by air, than to dismantle, crate, transport, re-erect and test-fly again.

The air route to Spain was from Bristol

Pictured at Aboukir, Egypt, Lt C L Wills poses by the propeller of his 200 hp Hispano-Suiza-engined SE.5A with a friend (and dog). The machine was operated in 1919 by 'X' Sqdn AW.2 Wing. Many examples of this famous fighter ended up for disposal at Waddon.

to Croydon, Croydon to Lympne for Customs, across the Channel by Folkestone-Gris Nez (circling above the ground station to allow the aeroplane to be recognised so that its safe arrival over France could be telephoned to Lympne), Le Bourgêt (Customs), Tours (military aerodrome), Merignac-Bordeaux (Customs), Lasarte-San Sebastian (Spanish Customs), across the Pyrenees to Burgos, thence across the Guadarŕama Mountains to Cuatro Vientos aerodrome, Madrid. All of these flights, incidentally, were carried out under Spanish civil registrations and bearing the letter 'M' as indicative of their country of ownership – Spain. They were only given military markings once they had been taken over by the authorities in Madrid.

For those first few years of operation aircraft sales were The Aircraft Disposal Company's staple income source. This lasted for as long as its by-definition obsolescent stock could find a buyer.

The airframes and aircraft were thus the revenue-earners and it is said that the company had a variable-pricing policy that allowed for leeway in satisfying a sales enquiry. On the other hand, it was found that engines were not so robust as salesware. Many never ran again, being merely dismantled to salvage the valuable copper from their water-jackets and manifolds.

The Aircraft Disposal Company had been operating for four successful years and it began gradually to change its rôle in the aircraft business. Gradually it began to put something back into the industry that it had almost annihilated. *The Aeroplane* was able to report on November 19th:

NEW AIRCRAFT DISPOSAL CO PRODUCTS

The design department of the Aircraft Disposal Company have recently evolved two exceedingly interesting productions.

The first of these is a clever modification of an old engine and is called the 130 h.p. A.D.C.-Renault. A standard 80 h.p. Renault engine has been taken and by various means which will be described in an early issue of *THE AEROPLANE* has been made to develop 136 h.p. and has just completed a ten-hour type-test under Air Ministry supervision. It has been installed in an Avro and has enabled the climb to 10,000 feet to be accomplished in half the time that has been possible with any rotary engine. It is now being installed in the D.H.51 – that is the machine which Capt de Havilland himself flies. It seems that this engine should be ideal for installing in Service Avros in place of a Monosoupape Gnôme.

The second new product is a Martinsyde F.4 which has been converted to take the 350 h.p. Armstrong-Siddeley Jaguar engine. The mounting of the Jaguar, which has been devised by Mr Kenworthy, is certainly the neatest that one has yet seen.

On its recent tests with full war load the top speed was well over 150 m.p.h. and the climb is quite extraordinary.

On Saturday morning just as Mr Perry was taking off Mr Soden of Austin Whippet fame happened to be passing on a Service machine also with a Jaguar engine and seeing an F.4 taking, off decided to give chase. Although the Service machine had already got up speed by a preliminary dive and Mr Perry was taking straight off the ground the Service machine was unable to catch the Martinsyde and at 10,000 feet it was left well behind. The engine in both machines was identical. Comment seems unnecessary.

Within a short while, it was not just engines that were being modified and given a new lease of life. The acquisition of Martinsyde provided not just the bare bones for development so much as a first-rate British design from the old Woking team – one which could be sympathetically improved upon. Once more, it is to the pages of *The Aeroplane* that we must turn for the first announcement published on November 26th 1924:

THE MARTINSYDE ADC.1

It was announced some time ago that the Aircraft Disposal Co., Ltd., had taken over the entire rights of the late Martinsyde Co and during the last week

Some three hundred Martinsyde G.100 Elephants were built between their introduction at the end of 1915 and their subsequent replacement by the DH.4 between 1917 and the end of the War. The name 'Elephant' was unofficial, but it stuck. This example served with No.27 Sqdn. Pressed into a training rôle, no Elephants survived into peacetime although their spares holding, not to mention 120 hp and 160 hp Beardmore engines, ended up at Waddon.

what may be called the first product of this fusion made its first test flights at Waddon Aerodrome. This was the Martinsyde ADC.1, which is in reality a Martinsyde F.4 equipped with a Siddeley Jaguar engine of 350 h.p.

It will be remembered that the Martinsyde F.4, which was produced just prior to the Armistice in 1918, was a descendant of the F.3 which, when it was designed in 1917, possessed a performance which was far in excess of anything produced during the war 1914-18. The F.3 was fitted with the 275 h.p. Rolls-Royce Falcon engine, and as this was in great demand for other machines, particularly the Bristol Fighter, the machine was not put into production, but was adapted to take the 300 h.p. Hispano-Suiza, and known thus as the F.4 was put into quantity production. Its appearance in sufficient numbers to equip existing and new squadrons was antedated by the Armistice and its adoption as the standard single-seater scout of the post-war Royal Air Force was ruled out owing to the fact that it was fitted with a French engine. In consequence, a large number of Martinsyde F.4s were handed over to the ADC for disposal. Quite recently the ADC decided to modernise one of these machines and the Martinsyde ADC.1 is the result.

With the exception of the fuselage forward of the pilot's cockpit, the engine and the equipment carried, the machine is almost identical with the F.4, but the resultant alterations now make the machine a high speed single-seater aeroplane that is comparable with the most modern example of its class.

The principal alteration to take the Jaguar engine consists of rearranging the main longerons forward from the point of attachment of the rear centre-section struts. From this point forward to the main fireproof bulkhead, the top longerons slope upwards instead of downwards and the bottom longerons are straight. The main engine bearer plate is a standard Armstrong-Siddeley engine plate, except for a slight alteration in the angle of the four engine bolt slots. This plate is attached to the fuselage by a framework of steel tubes as shown in the accompanying sketch.

The whole machine has been practically rebuilt and in its new form the Martinsyde ADC.1 reflects great credit on Mr Kenworthy, who has been responsible for the engine installation and on the ADC, generally for having sufficient faith in producing such a machine and also for the excellent workmanship and finish embodied in the machine.

It is yet impossible to give complete performance figures for the machine as the full tests are as yet in progress, but it is possible to say that with full load, including two Vickers guns, 1,200 rounds of ammunition and 55 gallons of petrol a speed of over 160 m.p.h. has been attained, together with a climb of 10,000 feet in 5 mins. – altogether a very creditable showing.

The Aircraft Disposal Company's changing image was clearly worn with pride that was reflected not just in its regular and copious trade-press advertising but also in the manner in which it conducted itself in dealings with other aircraft and engine manufacturers.

An example of this came on March 17th 1925 when Sir Sefton Brancker's DH.50 piloted by Alan Cobham completed its epic 17,000 mile flight to India and back, landing at Croydon to the cheers of a welcoming crowd. At a Royal Aero Club banquet in their honour held the following week, Tommy

The demise of The London & Provincial Aviation Company, first owners of Stag Lane Aerodrome, created shock-waves throughout the business and drew from *Flight's* Stanley Spooner one of his most barbed editorials. L&P had distinguished itself during the war as a sub-contractor but fell victim not just to the post-war aviation slump but the methods of 'encouragement' extended by the civil aviation department of the Air Ministry. Briefly the company wanted to keep afloat by using its aircraft for joy-riding like everybody else. To this end it prepared five of its two-seater L & P Biplanes but the Air Ministry refused to license them as airworthy because they were powered by 50 hp Gnôme engines. As a corollary, the same authority would not agree to license the airfields it wanted to use, so effectively 'killing' the firm's earning capacity for the 1919 season. It had good cause to complain in the above full-page display advertisement of June 17th. The following month, bitterly disappointed, it broke up and burned its aircraft, moved out of Stag Lane – and got out of the aviation business for good.

How to encourage :: ::

CIVIL AVIATION!

The London & Provincial Aviation Co.

regrets to announce that after between nine and ten years' experience of Practical Aviation on the part of their Principal, after building aeroplanes for 5½ years without a breakage in the Air, and after training 550 pilots for the Flying Services with only one fatal accident, they are compelled to cease business owing to the operations of the Department of Civil Aviation.

The said operations make it impossible for the L. & P. Co. to obtain any adequate return for capital, labour, enterprise, experience or industry. The shareholders therefore consider that it is better to play for nothing than to work for nothing.

A number of highly skilled mechanics will be thrown on an overcrowded labour market.

A number of aeroplanes and engines of proved quality will remain idle.

A number of people will be deprived of the opportunity of flying.

A number of opportunities of increasing public interest in flying will be lost.

A good aerodrome will be left idle.

For further particulars apply—

The London & Provincial Aviation Co.,
:: Stag Lane Aerodrome, Edgware. ::

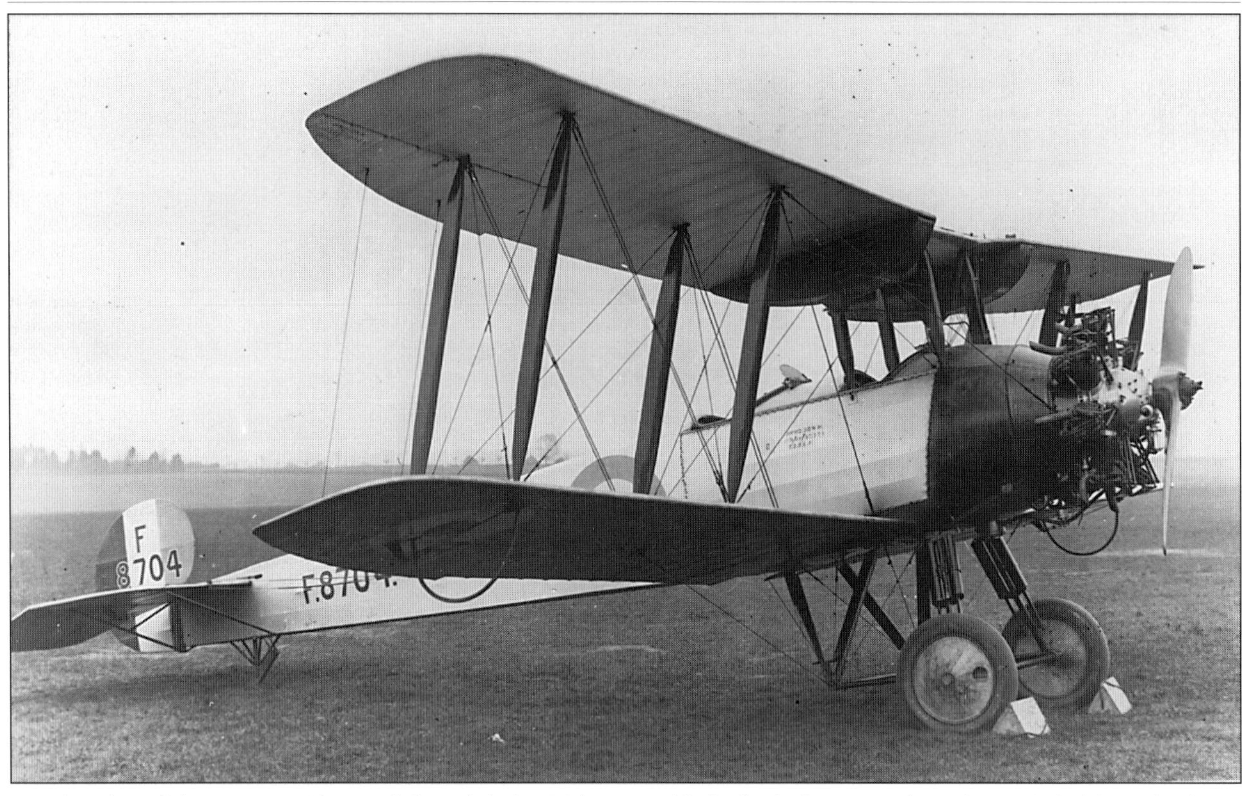

A number of aircraft that were Avro 504 type ended up as hybrids. F8704 was one of the last batch of 250 Avro 504K machines to be built by Frederick Sage & Company of Peterborough. It is thought that many of this batch were cancelled. This picture of F8704 has stencilled just below the cockpit 'Avro 504N' followed by characters that include the letters 'LY'. This confirms that it is indeed an Armstrong Siddeley Lynx II-powered 504N. It has been fitted with tapered ailerons and the 504N undercarriage together with two underwing fuel tanks outboard of the upper centre-section. This particular aircraft is believed to have been sold for £82 at the Hendon surplus sale in June 1919.

Sopwith, chairman of the SBAC, revealed that the Treasury had refused to authorize payment for the flight, so Charles Richard Fairey had guaranteed to raise the money.

> When the proposition was put to the industry not a single firm wavered. Not only did all come in with their whack but others joined. De Havilland paid more because his machine was being used, and ADC paid more because it was their engine. The Anglo-Persian Oil Co and the Wakefield Castrol people also helped. *[19]*

When he came to give his reply to the Duke of Sutherland's toast of the guests, Sir Sefton said:

> I take no responsibility for the performance except for wangling a very small sum from the depressed and somewhat scandalized financial department. I think we have proved that flying is not a stunt. We were not blazing a trail, but following the footsteps of Sir Geoffrey Salmond who did the flight five years ago, but we are the only people who have come back by air as well. All the credit is due to the de Havilland machine, the Siddeley Puma engine, and the pilot and mechanic. The flight was easy with such a crew. We got in and out of many difficult aerodromes, and Elliott spent many unpleasant hours working on the machine. I myself merely sucked in fresh air all day and banquets all night and delivered hot air in many languages.

Later in that same year, 1925, there was to be a curious, ironic twist to the ADC story. Until then there had been activists who were anxious to close down the Royal Air Force and divide any Service flying activities between the Royal Navy and the British Army. And, of course, the dramatic reduction in strength of the Royal Air Force meant that most of its personnel had gone, most of its infrastructure had been dispersed and many of its airfields sold back to their owners for the sums originally paid. As for aeroplanes, well, the RAF had very few. Now, though, it needed to organise itself afresh and this meant getting more aeroplanes and getting them quickly. And there was only one place where it could buy aeroplanes quickly and cheaply – and that was Croydon where the Aircraft Disposal Company (now officially known as ADC Ltd) acceded to an Air Ministry order for 100 DH.9A biplanes (designed in 1917) fitted with American-built Liberty engines from its seemingly inexhaustible store of components. It was now selling its wares back to the people that had originally packaged them up for scrap!

And by the end of that year, ADC Aircraft Ltd had been outstandingly successful in disposing of millions of pounds of stock, re-paying the Government, exclusive of taxation, some £1½-million as its share. It was able to take stock of its operations from a standpoint of success far and away beyond anybody's wildest expectations. The company's premises at Croydon were larger than those of any aircraft manufacturer's. Not only reconditioned aircraft and engines but, as Penrose confirms, machine-guns, Scarff rings, and bomb-sights could be bought – a telling point to countries unable to afford expensive armaments. In short, it was the most profitable business in the world of aviation. On top of its widespread sales it also provided a valuable spares service.

By this time, ADC Engines Ltd was operating as a subsidiary making the Cirrus engines needed by de Havilland for the Moth lightplane. With this work the manufacturing future of the company also seemed assured.

Chapter 9
The ADC Martinsydes and the Birth of the Cirrus Engine

VERY soon after its formation, ADC had begun to make its own modifications to machines such as the DH.9 designed by de Havilland and built by The Aircraft Manufacturing Company (Airco) at Hendon and its sub-contractors. This became known as the Airdisco DH.9, one of the most successful and earliest civilian conversions of this type that clearly traded on the similarity of the respected name 'Airco'. Another type that ADC was to make its own was the Martinsyde F.4, numerous conversions being noted.

Almost from the outset, then, ADC undertook modifications to the machines it handled. Besides the Avro 504K, DH.9 and Martinsyde machines was the company's engine work that eventually made an enormous contribution to the light aircraft business. But not all of the company's work was directed towards civilian use. It supplied many military-standard aircraft, complete with combat weaponry, to foreign air forces plus, it is said, a few mercenaries.

The demand for ADC's reconditioned machines thus included many for overseas and there were numerous visiting delegations from foreign governments that beat a path to Waddon. These resulted in orders from powers such as Finland, Latvia, Portugal and Russia while each of the two sides in the Spanish-Moroccan war were equipped with Airdisco's aeroplanes. Regarding this last-mentioned skirmish, Howson *[16]* relates that:

> With its top speed of 138 mph the [Martinsyde] Buzzard was one of the fastest fighters of its time, but it was not adopted by the RAF. Most of the machines were sold abroad by the Aircraft Disposal Company. Twenty were sold to Spain, and ten of these, (of which five were two-seaters with two-bay wings) were transferred, after service in the Moroccan war, to the Escuadrilla de Combate y Acompañamiento (Combat and Escort Squadron) of the Aeronáutica Naval at Barcelona in 1924. In 1933 the squadron was transferred to San Javier, Cartagena, the aircraft bearing the serials MS-1 to MS-10 (later changed to EA-EAA-1 to -EAI-10, but including -EAJ-8). All of these were officially still in service, although only seven were airworthy, on 18 July 1936.

For the next six weeks a group of naval pilots under the command of Francisco Piedra flew the Martinsydes on protection patrols over the base, which had been the scene of dramatic events before the local Nationalist uprising had been crushed, and over the port of Cartagena without, fortunately, meeting any enemy fighters. When the British mercenary pilot and confidence man Kenneth Apjohn-Carter (alias Charles Kennett...) was ordered to fly one of these, he flatly refused, and even went so far as to allege, in a newspaper article published after his return to England, that this had been part of a Spanish plot to kill foreign pilots.

At the end of August two F.4s were transferred to Málaga, but both were soon grounded by permanent engine failure. In October the remainder were transferred to the Escuela de Vuelo at El Carmolı, and were withdrawn from service as slightly more modern trainers arrived from France. The aged F.4s were flown to the Parque de Reserva (Reserve Park) at San Pedro del Pinatar nearby, after which nothing more was heard of them.

For sheer flexibility in performance and operation, few could approach the amazing Airco DH.9 for versatility. Marketed by the Aircraft Disposal Company as 'the DH.9 Commercial Aircraft', it was available in a variety of Waddon-created styles, this version with three open cockpits to take pilot and two passengers.

Another view of the Aircraft Disposal Company's DH.9 Commercial Aircraft with three open cockpits. It was also possible to fit a 'partially-enclosed superstructure' to house passengers in 'adjustable and removable wicker seats'. Other versions offered were capable of carrying freight and a float-type undercarriage was optional to convert the machine into a seaplane. Normally this machine was offered with the 240 hp Siddeley Puma but by the mid-1920s ADC was offering it with its ADC Nimbus – a completely re-worked Puma that produced 300/330 horsepower. With this motor the cruising speed rose from 110 to 134 mph and the rate of climb to 5,000 feet reduced from 11 minutes to exactly half that time. Meanwhile the standard DH.9 two-seater reconnaissance or light bomber fitted with Puma, Fiat, Galloway Adriatic, Napier Lion or Liberty engines was also on offer.

Besides revamping and selling armed military machines, civilianising aircraft and fitting different engines produced new models and kept alive some aircraft types that would otherwise have been unsaleable in time of peace. It also altered and improved engines, ultimately leading to the production of new types. And de Havilland was able to buy a batch of 90 hp eight-cylinder RAF (Royal Aircraft Factory) engines for 14s 6d each – rather less than 75p apiece in today's money.

The quality of the reconditioned aircraft it turned out was unquestionably very high both as regards the airframes and the engines. Several ADC machines were to be used on record-breaking flights and the company always featured this fact in their advertisements. One such flight was that undertaken in an Airdisco-rebuilt Siddeley Puma-powered DH.9, G-EBDE, by Capt Norman MacMillan who flew his heavily laden three-seater biplane from London to Calcutta starting on May 24th 1922. Intended as a round-the-world trip, the flights was blighted by many problems including illness and several crashes, one of which necessitated a replacement aircraft with the same registration!

De Havilland Aircraft Co Ltd was, at this time, still advertising the DH.9 for sale and advertised 'the new and improved 1923 model'. DH prices, though, could not compete with those being quoted from Waddon.

Barrett-Lennard must have been acutely aware that, after the initial flurry of sales, his remaining stock of aeroplanes, though large, was now becoming positively archaic. To concentrate on engine work against a background of probably declining aircraft sales, it was decided to increase capital and this was done by the issue, on December 31st 1923, of £522,000-worth of debentures. Meanwhile ADC's stock of aircraft and motors seemed inexhaustible and in March of 1924 it advertised for sale the following completed airworthy aircraft: Martinsyde F.4; DH.9A; Bristol Fighter 2B; Sopwith Snipe; F3 Flying Boat; Parnall Panther; DH.9; Avro 504K. As for engines it offered: Rolls-Royce Eagle VIII, 160 hp Beardmore; 110 hp Le Rhône; 400 hp Liberty; 210 hp Viper; 240 hp Siddeley Puma; 200 hp BR.II; 300 hp Hispano-Suiza. Additionally, it offered armament, accessories, cameras, dope, instruments, hangars, engine starters, petrol installations and a host of other war surplus goods.

At this time all aircraft were exhaustively

Huge numbers of Avro 504K machines were to be found stacked at Waddon and, like the Martinsyde F.4 fighters, these were in constant demand for service with foreign air forces. Here, outside the ADC workshops, we see a posed line-up of Avros fitted with 125 hp three-cylinder Bristol Lucifer Mk.III medium compression (5.3:1) radial engines awaiting delivery to one of these customers. Modernised (as the company described them) from the original rotary engines, these were undoubtedly sound changes to a popular aircraft and many were sold to civil operators for joy-riding.

Contractors to the BRITISH AIR MINISTRY and most FOREIGN GOVERNMENTS.
Constructors of "MARTINSYDE" Types of Aircraft
Constructors of "CIRRUS" Aero Engines.
120/140 h.p. "AIRDISCO" Aero Engines.
300/330 h.p. "NIMBUS" Aero Engines.

The Key to Safety in Flying is a Reliable Engine

The MERIT of the "CIRRUS" is evident from the following:—

POPULARITY.

"CIRRUS" engines have been supplied to:—

THE BRITISH AIR MINISTRY.
TWELVE DIFFERENT COUNTRIES.
THE EIGHT ENGLISH AERO CLUBS.
THE ROYAL AUSTRALIAN AIR FORCE.
THE AUSTRALIAN AERO CLUBS.
THE IRISH FREE STATE AIR FORCE.
MANY PRIVATE OWNERS,
etc., etc.

The A.D.C. "CIRRUS" aero engine was the first low-powered aero engine to pass the AIR MINISTRY 100 HOURS TYPE TEST.

RELIABILITY.

"CIRRUS" engines were used for the following notable flights.

LONDON TO INDIA - 5,500 miles.
(2 D.H. "MOTHS," CAPT. T. N. STACK & MR. B. M. S. LEETE.)

LONDON TO INDIA - 5,500 miles.
(D.H. "MOTH," MR. DENNIS ROOKE.)

1st KING'S CUP AIR RACE, 1926.
(D.H. "MOTH," CAPT. H. S. BROAD.)

1st AUSTRALIAN AIR DERBY, 1926.
(D.H. "MOTH," SIR ALAN J. COBHAM.)

etc., etc.

"CIRRUS" ENGINES HAVE FLOWN OVER 1,000,000 MILES

and are fitted in the following machines:—

DE HAVILLAND	"MOTH"
AVRO	"AVIAN"
SHORT	"MUSSEL"
WESTLAND	"WIDGEON"

Manufacturers:

A.D.C. AIRCRAFT, LTD.,

REGENT HOUSE,
89, KINGSWAY, LONDON, W.C.2.
Works and Aerodrome: CROYDON, SURREY.

Telephone: Regent 6240.

Telegrams "Airdisco, London."

The Aeroplane 23 January 1924

test-flown by Herbert Howard Perry who had formerly flown for Handley Page Transport until transferring to ADC in 1922. Other pilots assisted Perry in his task, among these being T Neville Stack who, at one time, was referred to as 'chief test-pilot'.

Because of the later and unique association between ADC and one particular aircraft name – that of a manufacturer which is largely forgotten today – it is worth digressing slightly to paint in the background to a deal which was to prove a long-term lucrative involvement for ADC.

Mention has already been made of Martinsyde and its machines. Woking-based Martinsyde Ltd (originally Martin & Handasyde Ltd), together with its factory at Brooklands, was one of the largest and most important British aircraft manufacturers during the 1914-18 war. Immediately the conflict was at an end the company produced several civil types, mostly derived from the F.4 single-seat fighter *[17; vol.3, p.28]*, a fabric-covered wooden biplane designed by George Harris Handasyde. Around 280 had been constructed of which around 50 had been delivered to the Royal Air Force. Despite the sale by Martinsyde of many machines to foreign air forces, the company was in financial difficulty. Its bankers appointed a receiver and manager on November 2nd 1920.

Efforts to rescue the company were both immediate and sincere, but it remained in receivership, a new receiver being appointed on October 19th 1921. The business diversified but was clearly in the doldrums. In February 1924 it was announced that the manufacturing rights, goodwill, and all the remaining stock of airframes and components had been acquired by The Aircraft Disposal Company. Martinsyde, existing as a shell company, was finished: the Receiver was discharged by July 12th 1924 and the business was formally wound-up by Notice published on January 29th 1926 *[23]*.

All surviving Martinsyde F.4 airframes went by road to Croydon to join the surplus Royal Air Force F.4s already held by ADC. Already four of these had been civilianized and had made public appearances. One of these was G-EAXB (D4279) which was flown in the 1921 Aerial Derby by the Handley Page pilot Maj E Leslie Foot (who later lost his life in the crescent-winged Lucifer-powered Bristol M.1D monoplane G-EAVP which suffered mid-air wing-failure over Chertsey during the 1923 Grosvenor Challenge Cup).

Another civil F.4 created by ADC was G-EATD (D4267). This was raced by Reginald Herbert (Rex) Stocken in the 1922 Aerial Derby: he was forced down with engine trouble and the machine was destined not to fly again.

The acquisition of virtually all of Martinsyde together with its designs and its name was ADC's second best deal after its initial surplus acquisitions, for it gave the company *carte blanche* to do as it pleased with the aircraft and, unlike the bickering that had gone on with some others makers such as A V Roe and Blackburn, there was not likely to be any come-back. How much ADC paid for Martinsyde was not disclosed (it was said to be 'a small sum') but it gave the company the designs and rights for Martinsyde aircraft, large numbers of which it still had on its books. It then proceeded to undertake the design development work that Martin & Handasyde had never had the capital to do themselves.

The hiring of designer John Kenworthy who virtually completed the ADC team was the final piece in the jigsaw. During

Structural details of the Martinsyde ADC.1 as drawn by Leonard Bridgman for *The Aeroplane* in 1924.

The ADC.1, seen here right and below, was the first ADC variant of the Woking-designed Martinsyde F.4-type airframe. It was powered by a 385/425 hp Armstrong-Siddeley Jaguar 14-cylinder two-row radial, a medium-compression engine (5 to 1) that developed 385 hp at 1,700 rpm and 425 hp at 1,900 rpm.

It was expensive on fuel, consuming .53 pints/bhp/hr, and weighed 770 lbs giving a weight per cruising horsepower of just 2 lbs – an impressive achievement for its time. The sales blurb for this aeroplane stated that 'as a fighting scout, the machine has a remarkable performance, comparable with the best examples of other machines in this class, including those fitted with engines of greater power'.

Kenworthy's seven-year tenure with the company it was to produce several derivative designs including the ADC.1 and the ADC Nimbus/Boreas. He actually remained with the business until its demise in 1930 after which he joined the Robinson Redwing organisation.

It really began in 1924 when Kenworthy modernised the F.4 for the Aircraft Disposal Company Ltd, redesigning the front fuselage to carry a 395 hp Armstrong Siddeley Jaguar radial and thereby putting the top speed up to 160 mph. The prototype, G-EBKL, designated Martinsyde ADC.I, was first flown at Croydon by the company's test pilot Herbert Howard Perry on October 11th 1924, and subsequently Lt-Col M O Darby entered the machine for the 1925 King's Cup Race flown from Croydon on July 3rd and 4th. For this event it took the racing number 8 and was piloted by Sqdn-Ldr Walter H Longton.

Sanger *[29]* relates how this offered the opportunity to compare the Martinsyde with machines with the same engine, such as the Siskin, which had been designed since the war. All did not go according to plan:

> Longton got away well and disappeared into thick mist but nothing more was heard of him until much later that night. Apparently some special carburettor jets, which had been fitted to the engine for high rate-of-climb trials, had not been replaced for the event. These gave a very high petrol consumption of about 35 gallons per hour. Consequently, after flying through thick fog around Luton and Bedford trying to find an opening, he ran out of petrol and managed to make a landing on Nottingham Race Course. It was three hours before he could find enough petrol to refill his

BRITISH  AIRCRAFT

SIDDELEY "PUMA" AERO ENGINES

AVAILABLE FROM STOCK.

BRAND NEW.

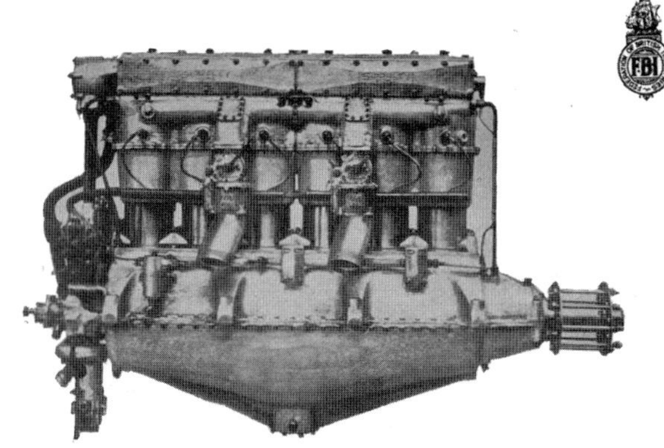

240 h.p. SIDDELEY "PUMA" ENGINE.

BRIEF SPECIFICATION.

Bore, 145 m/m., 5·71 inches	Stroke, 190 m/m., 7·48 inches
Normal B.H.P., 246	Maximum B.H.P., 255
Running Weight, 801 lbs.	Running Weight per normal H.P., 3·25 lbs.
Petrol Consumption, 17¾ gals. per hour.	Oil Consumption, 10·23 pints per hour.

All Engines thoroughly dismantled, inspected, and given a test run, by an expert staff before despatch.

The "PUMA" ENGINE has proved itself to be one of the most Reliable, Efficient and Economical Aviation Engines ever produced, and we have supplied large numbers of these engines to many Foreign Governments, Air Transport Lines and Aircraft Manufacturers.

AIRCRAFT DISPOSAL COMPANY LTD.

REGENT HOUSE,

Telephone: Regent 6240. 89, KINGSWAY, LONDON, W.C.2. Telegrams: "Airdisco, London."

The Aeroplane 23 January 1924

Martinsyde's aircraft were robust and durable and what they lacked in looks was generally made up for in solid utility. Built at Brooklands in the autumn of 1917, the curious lines of the forward fuselage of the F.4 housed a 275 hp Rolls-Royce Falcon engine driving a wide-bladed coarse-pitch wooden airscrew.

> tanks. He got as far as Harrogate before deciding that it was useless to continue as the tanks would not hold enough petrol to enable him to cover the longer stretches of the course.

It did not, nevertheless, require participation in a race to show that the ADC.1 was something very special if not outstanding. Significantly its handling and performance was better than the Royal Air Force's latest fighters, the Siskin and Grebe, for it climbed 10,000 ft in 4 min 50 seconds and had a top speed approaching 160 mph.

For the following year's race, the pilot was Sqdn-Ldr H W G Jones, but again it was forced to retire. Jackson *[17]* relates that just as all Martinsyde aircraft were affectionately known as 'Tinsydes', G-EBKL was inevitably dubbed the 'Disposalsyde'. It was the prototype for a batch of nine that was subsequently sold to the Latvian Air Force in June 1926.

The 1926 King's Cup Race was also the setting for Kenworthy's ultimate Martinsyde F.4 variant. Powered by a 6-cylinder in-line 300 hp ADC Nimbus (which was a redesign of the 230 hp Siddeley-Deasey Puma) this was known simply as the Nimbus Martinsyde. Only two examples were built – G-EBOJ and G-EBOL, originally Puma powered. ADC's own chief pilot Herbert Perry flew the former and Frank T Courtney the latter. In the race a total of four Martinsydes took part – besides the two mentioned above, and the ADC.1 G-EBKL referred to earlier, there was also a Martinsyde F.6 G-EBDK. Of 16 entries, engine trouble claimed nine over the two-day event. These included all three of the Kenworthy machines plus the Martinsyde-built two-seater F.6.

In fairness it should be said that the majority of failures were relatively minor but it only takes a fuel blockage to take out a racing aeroplane.

Kenworthy was convinced that the Nimbus Martinsyde could go even faster and so for 1927 it was re-styled with cylinder-head fairings and undercarriage fairings. This latter consisted of fairing-in the V-shaped legs of the undercarriage and did not extend to wheel fairings. Now named Boreas (although it seems that the name was never actually painted on), the initial showing was to be the 1927 King's Cup Race – the first in which women pilots had entered.

However, the event was a farce due in part to the ridiculous handicap formula that generated theoretical high speeds that were impossible. The Avro 566 Avenger, for example, had a maximum speed of 180 mph, yet the handicappers expected it to compete at 244 mph. Not surprisingly, almost a third of the 26 entrants withdrew in protest. Then came a pre-race accident (Bristol's Type 99A crashed fatally) and finally race-day itself turned out to be meteorologically-challenged: only six fliers

The mainstay of sales at The Aircraft Disposal Company was without doubt the Martinsyde F.4. Known to the newly-formed Royal Air Force as the Buzzard, the 300 hp Hispano-Suiza-powered single-seat fighter was popular because it placed the pilot's cockpit well behind the upper wing which, with its copious centre-section cut-out, offered tremendous all-round visibility. Faster than the Sopwith Snipe (which the Air Ministry preferred and ordered in even larger numbers) it was fully aerobatic. Newly-built but without engines, they cost the taxpayer £1,142.2s each to build. ADC sold many to foreign air forces, in particular to Finland. In this picture we see a line-up outside the workshop awaiting delivery.

The Aeroplane 10 February 1924

finished in rain and heavy overcast. The Boreas was not one of them, having joined the protesters and, wisely, withdrawn.

If Boreas was viewed with suspicion by the King's Cup handicappers, then the Hucknall Stakes High Power Handicap, held a few days afterwards and flown round a tight course, seemed to confirm those nagging doubts: with only three starters in the event, G-EBOJ stormed home at an average 141.2 mph in the hands of Sqdn-Ldr H W G Jones. Scrutiny of comparative performances, though, suggests that despite its appearances, Boreas was not quite as fast as feared, for the Martinsyde ADC.1 with its derated Jaguar III had a maximum speed of 163 mph. The basic F.4, as first built at Woking, could attain 145 mph when pushed in a straight line.

The 'standard' revamped F.4 aircraft were popular abroad and by 1927 ADC had sold a considerable number to foreign air forces around the world while 41 went abroad with civil Certificate of Airworthiness and two others in British civil markings as G-EBDM (which went to the Portuguese air force in June 1923) and G-EBFA also to Portugal in January 1927.

Jackson *[17]* relates that to G-EBMI, one of the last to be made airworthy, fell the honour of becoming the only privately owned F.4. First registered on April 15th 1926, the former D4295 was owned by E D Bigg: five months later, on August 24th 1930, it crashed at Woodley in the presence of Mr Bigg, allegedly following flutter-induced tailplane spar failure, killing flying instructor S W 'Pat' Giddy of Phillips & Powis. Its last-recorded C of A had expired on May 6th 1928.

The three Kenworthy-designed F.4 variants were probably never intended to be sold on the open market and this possibly explains why they remained on the company's books throughout the remaining years of ADC's existence. When the Aircraft Disposal Company Limited finally closed down in 1930, all three ADC prototypes were dismantled and burned along with great quantities of long-obsolete WWI components.

The very last civilian Martinsyde was G-ABKH, a two-seater designated the Martinsyde AV.1. This was erected at Croydon early in 1931 by ADC Aircraft Ltd, successors to the old disposal company. Externally identical to an F.4A, it embodied many airframe and engine modifications devised by the owner, engine designer Charles Amherst Villiers, whose initials provided the marque number. Jackson *[op.cit]* affirms that it was finished in two vivid shades of blue and that it was housed at Brooklands until sold to C B Field in October 1932. Following an accident at Bekesbourne in February 1933, it lay derelict at the owner's private aerodrome, Kingswood Knoll, Surrey, until scrapped in 1935.

So much for ADC and the Martinsyde saga. This aircraft had been very profitable to the firm, but again so had the Airco/de Havillands, the Bristols, the Avros (which after his original attempts to prevent sales, A V Roe conceded would be impossible), the Sopwiths and the Parnalls. The SE.5A and the Norman Thompson NT.2B flying boats had been less so.

In the world of engines, the company began designing and building small engines when it realised that the slow sales of larger motors such as the Rolls-Royce Eagles, the big Beardmores and so on were due to lack of demand rather than price. People wanted smaller engines and only the larger machines and the airlines needed bigger motors. Right through 1924 the company was promoting its huge stocks of 230 hp Siddeley Puma engines and it was obvious that the stocks of these must both be large

The 100 hp six-cylinder Rolls-Royce Hawk engine was introduced in 1916. Curiously although the prototype was produced at Derby, Rolls-Royce contracted out the full 205-strong production run to Brazil Straker, production ending in December of 1918. Although mostly used in RNAS airships where their reliability became legendary (in August 1918 one flight lasted 50 hours and 55 minutes), the Hawks also powered the Avro 504F, some BE.2e aircraft and a few other odd types. A number of Hawks ended up at Waddon with The Aircraft Disposal Company from whence one example made unfortunate history by powering the experimental Cooper-Travers Monoplane that killed its designer during a Croydon test-flight on February 24th 1924.

and immovable.

With a need to develop new engines, initially making use of some of the materials held in stock, Airdisco hired Maj Frank Bernard Halford who had worked for both Beardmore and Ricardo. Among the engines that he designed and which Airdisco now manufactured were the four-cylinder Cirrus, 120/140 hp Airdisco, both these being derived from the 8-cylinder Renault two-bank Vee, and the six-cylinder 300/330 hp Nimbus which was a dramatic re-working of the obsolete Puma. Halford was ultimately to leave and become a valuable part of the de Havilland team where he designed the Gipsy as a rival to his earlier ADC Cirrus.

The birth of the Cirrus was a pivotal moment in British civil aviation. Its story is central to the story of ADC's engines and Frank Halford in particular.

In the preceding Chapter mention was made of Geoffrey de Havilland's conviction in 1924 that there was a possible market for a practical two-seat light aircraft. This was spurred by the rather effete Lympne Light Aeroplane Competitions that had produced a clutch of interesting yet underpowered and hence impractical machines. De Havilland believed that the Lympne trials were centred on engines of too low a power output. At that time he was working on the design for the DH.51 which was nearing completion and he felt sure that the ideal solution lay somewhere between that machine and the DH.53. What he needed was an engine of about 60 hp weighing not more than 350 lbs. This would then also suit a later two-seat design. He approached his friend Maj Frank Bernard Halford who, with his sole assistant John Brodie, had been working for the Aircraft Disposal Company refining the 90 hp RAF.1A so that it could develop 140 hp.

De Havilland suggested that Halford might take four of the eight cylinders and appropriate parts of this 'Airdisco' engine, as it was named, and fit them to a new crankcase with a shorter crankshaft in order to make a practical small and light motor. However, Halford was now busy uprating the Puma to 335 hp for ADC as well as designing an engine for Aston Martin cars. Despite all this, he eventually warmed to DH's idea, but the terms of his contract with ADC prevented his undertaking 'outside' work in the aviation industry.

De Havilland knew only too well that he himself could not afford the cost of

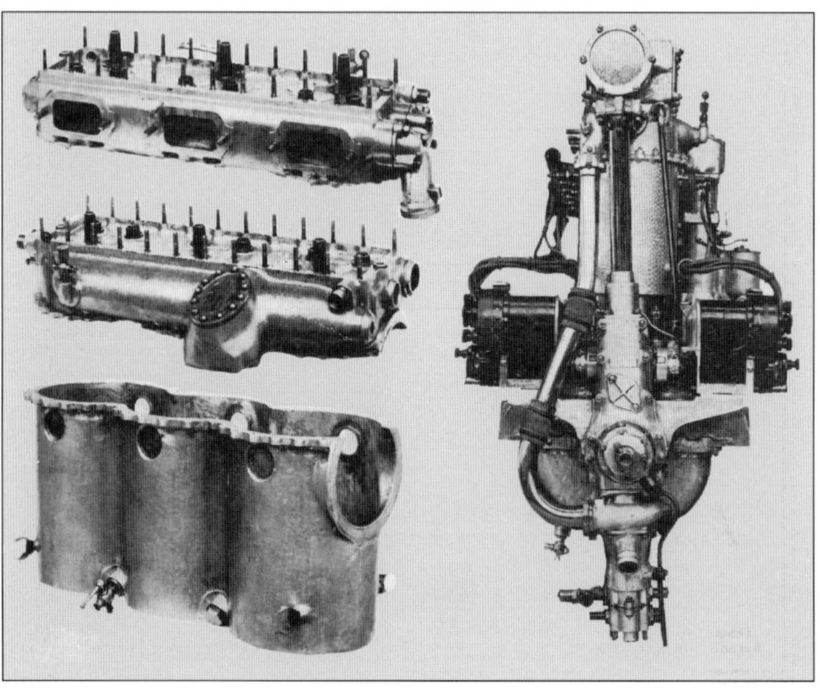

The water-cooled ADC Nimbus engine, as seen in this semi-dismantled view, was an impressive re-working of the original 240 hp Siddeley Puma. Producing between 300/330 horsepower, it weighed 660 lbs and, at only 20 lbs more than the original Puma, it output marginally over 2 lbs/hp at cruising power and consumed 0.49 lbs of fuel per horsepower. This engine successfully passed its Air Ministry 50-hours type test with flying colours and was to prove an undoubtedly impressive economic benefit to the company for a number of years.

ROLLS-ROYCE "EAGLE VIII" AERO ENGINES.

We can supply from stock new Rolls-Royce Engines of the well-known "EAGLE VIII" and "FALCON III" types together with spare parts.

EXTRACT from letter we have received from HANDLEY PAGE TRANSPORT LIMITED, dated 5th December, 1923.

"EAGLE VIII" Engines.

"This type of engine is now used exclusively on our air services between London, Paris, Basle and Zurich.

In the period from the inception of the Handley Page Air Services in 1919 to the present date, 17,000 "EAGLE" engine hours have been flown, approximating 1,360,000 engine miles.

In the period October, 1922 to September, 1923, 5,070 hours were flown, representing 431,000 engine miles, with an engine efficiency percentage of 98.5.

We have now on our charge twenty-eight engines, and the total running time of these engines is 9,500 hours. Six of these engines have each over 500 hours to their credit, as follows, and are still in service:

ENGINE.	HOURS.
8E.3164	790
8E.3704	670
8E.3076	640
8E.2672	611
8E.5224	516
8E.3046	506

All the above flying hours have been carried out with engines supplied to ourselves by the Aircraft Disposal Company."

EVERY ENGINE BEFORE DESPATCH FROM OUR WORKS, IS DISMANTLED FOR INSPECTION, AND AFTER RE-ASSEMBLY IS GIVEN A TEST RUN.

AIRCRAFT DISPOSAL COMPANY LTD.

REGENT HOUSE,

89 KINGSWAY, LONDON, W.C.2.

Telephone: Regent 6240.

Telegrams: "Airdisco, London."

The Aeroplane 9 January 1924

developing a prototype engine, so he resorted to a cap-in-hand approach to the ADC directors suggesting that it would be advantageous to them to take on the development themselves. He successfully pointed out that by undertaking the project at their own expense it would help find a market for ADC's huge stocks of cylinders and pistons.

The psychology was perfect! After much prevarication, the Aircraft Disposal Company accepted de Havilland's arguments and agreed to build the engine for him. The outcome was the first of a long and illustrious line of Cirrus engines. It was a four-cylinder engine to Halford's design and de Havilland's specification, utilizing the 140 hp Airdisco cylinders, pistons, and other parts.

Now would come the turning-point in the development of Britain's light aircraft industry for the Air Ministry's backing of flying clubs encouraged de Havilland to redesign the DH.51. De Havilland went ahead and produced a scaled-down version of the DH.51A and styled it the DH.60. This had a span 3 ft less than the DH.51A, and was intended to have half the weight yet carry two at the same cruising speed of 80 mph so that it could combat head winds. Constructional simplicity, and therefore minimum cost, was to be the keynote. And so was formed the Moth dynasty – a direct descendent from the Aircraft Disposal Company's business.

Years later, Halford would lead de Havilland's own engine design team, producing the Gipsy series of motors including the Gipsy III – the first inverted DH engine. For the moment, though, the Cirrus was the product of ADC's Waddon factory and was marketed as an ADC property.

In February 1927 it was announced that a new company, Cirrus Aero Engines Ltd was to be formed to take over from ADC Aircraft Ltd that part of their business that related to Cirrus engines – in other words ADC Engines Ltd. One of the main reasons given was that hitherto the Cirrus engine had had to bear much of the overhead charges of ADC Aircraft Ltd. This meant that the selling price of the engine was too high. The new firm was registered as a private company on February 16th 1927 with a £10,000 capital. The managing director of both ADC Aircraft and the new company was Lt-Col Maurice Ormond Darby while Lt-Col John Barrett-Lennard, who resigned from Handley Page Ltd in order to concentrate on his ADC work, became general manager.

By 1930 the management structure of ADC comprised M O Darby as managing director and Ernest Stephen Olney as works superintendent. From its foundation until 1925, the works superintendent had been Maj John R Grant. He was replaced in that year by Capt Roy Walker. Grant, plagued by serious infirmity caused through an accident while destroying unused bombs after the Armistice, died on March 15th 1927. The Danish-born Mogens Louis Bramson (*b.* Copenhagen. June 28th 1895) combined the duties of chief test pilot and sales director. He had worked with skywriting pioneer Major John Clifford 'Jack' Savage in the design and development of the Savage-Bramson Anti-Stall Gear launched in 1927.

So it was that The Aircraft Disposal Company Limited prospered and for some years was Croydon Aerodrome's principal user with large numbers of test-flight, sales demonstration flights and delivery flights taking place. During these early years activities and movements were more or less continuous as huge numbers of surplus aircraft were built up and ferried to many parts of the world.

There was one early casualty of the old NAF Waddon complex and this concerned the special single-track branch line that somewhat bucolically picked its way through the back gardens of Croydon, crossed the main road with its tram tracks and entered the aerodrome. Once all the surplus material and aeroplanes had been gathered together in the vast ADC storehouse, the siding became surplus to needs. Convenient in time of war for bringing in materials, and in the immediate years afterwards for bringing wrecked and redundant machines to the Salvage Depot, it had long outlived its usefulness.

It was at best a cumbersome feature to use involving the complexity of what railway people define as 'single-line working'.

The aircraft for which Frank Halford created the first Cirrus engine was Geoffrey de Havilland's two-seat biplane which he named Moth. Registered on February 10th 1925, G-EBKT was the prototype DH.60 Cirrus Moth. With clear-doped wings and unbalanced rudder, the first examples had the exhaust pipe running down the starboard side of the fuselage: later examples took it to the port side. The first flight took place at Stag Lane on Sunday February 22nd 1925. This 'first of the many' Moth survived until August 21st 1927 when it was written off in a crash at Stanmore.

Designer Frederick George Miles also chose the upright ADC Cirrus engine for his Hawk trainer and sporting monoplanes. This illustration shows the necessarily long undercarriage legs needed to provide adequate propeller ground-clearance with the low thrust-line of the type. The arrival of the inverted motor with its higher propeller line allowed shorter, more practical undercarriages and, consequently, better forward view on the ground.

Closing off Stafford Road to allow trains to cross was unusually complex because of the frequent tram service that ran in both directions along this busy thoroughfare. In 1923 this anachronism was 'disconnected' from the main line railway and the tracks removed. However, the old freight loading platforms each side of the track bed were used for engine-testing: one platform still exists to this very day. Here motors were run for ten or more hours after assembly to 'run in' the components. This continual noise is known to have caused complaints from local house owners, in particular since the noise often went on far into the night. Early in 1924 there were even questions raised in the House concerning this nuisance.

By the mid-1920s, Airdisco had been outstandingly successful in disposing of millions of pounds worth of stock repaying the Government, exclusive of taxation, some £1.25 million as its share. The company's premises at Croydon were larger than those of any aircraft manufacturer – an increasing cause for concern throughout the industry. They were even bigger than the premises of its founder Handley Page.

ADC was now established in its rôle as an aircraft supplier. It also played a growing part in the life of the local community. Apart from providing employment for a number of people it contributed to social activities. At the end of 1923 it formed The Waddon Aircraft Sports Club of which the football section was a major part. Under the captaincy of a man named Kerswill of the Rigger's Department, the team succeeded in its first season in winning the Croydon Junior League Cup. At a celebratory dinner held on Wednesday May 4th 1924 in the Dickens Room of Carr's Restaurant in the Strand it was reported that of 16 matches played, 15 had been won and the other match resulted in a draw. Goals scored totalled 95 against 10.

That June ADC took a long-overdue step – and painted their name in large white letters across the top of its huge hangar.

While a significant proportion of ADC's aircraft stock depreciated rapidly into obsolescence (the DH.2 and DH.4, early FE and BE aircraft among others) and had to be 'reduced to produce', ADC had not only succeeded in meeting much of its founding aims and objectives, but it had also generated a surprising amount of goodwill in all aspects of the industry. ADC had achieved a remarkable feat, under the circumstances, of earning the respect of the industry that had suffered so severely at its hands. It had gained this respect by an open and fair business policy under which it dealt with the industry and its needs. It had become a major supplier of parts and components to all and this had earned it a reputation for fairness and dependability.

The business advertised its abilities and its wares widely and every week it took costly full-page display advertisements in the magazines *Flight* and *The Aeroplane*. It also ensured that its advertisements were changed regularly (the same advert seldom appeared more than two weeks running) and ADC took every opportunity to capitalise on the achievements of its aircraft, engines and clients. In this respect, ADC became a most considerate business that took care to fit into its aviation community.

One of its adverts listed the countries to which it has supplied goods: it reads like an atlas of the world! But the company contributed in a number of other ways, some of which it did not shout about from the roof-tops. One was Count Louis Zborowski's racing car, the Higham Special, which was raced at Brooklands. It was powered by a 400 hp 25-lit V-12 Liberty engine supplied by ADC. The car had an unhappy end: sold to the speed-chasing John Godfrey Parry Thomas (who christened it *Babs*), it was making an attempt on the world land-speed record at Pendine Sands in South Wales in 1927 when it crashed killing its owner-driver. Shocked mechanics buried the car where it lay. One cannot blame an ADC engine for that, however.

Curiously, at the 1924 Paris Air Show which commenced on December 5th at the Grand Palais (and remained open until December 21st, ADC was surprisingly coy about its new engines. For visitors to the 9th Salon d'Aeronautique, the British engine-makers were represented only by Armstrong Whitworth, Bristol and the Aircraft Disposal Company, but the ADC stand displayed just three engines – and all of these obsolete. The first was the 230 hp Siddeley Puma, the second the 210 hp Wolseley Viper (a motor based on the 180 hp Hispano-Suiza), and the third the 230 hp BR.II rotary. While the last-mentioned was significant in being the highest-powered rotary that had ever been used to any degree, and although it was virtually unknown outside Britain, it hardly promoted ADC's current thinking.

Even so, a display of stripped engine

BRITISH 

AIRCRAFT

ANOTHER "PUMA" SUCCESS.

A number of "Puma" engines awaiting despatch at Waddon.

The First complete Circuit of Australia by a land type machine was recently made by Col. H. C. Brinsmead on a De Havilland 50 machine fitted with a

240 h.p. SIDDELEY "PUMA" ENGINE

This 8,000 Miles Flight was completed in 25 days Consecutive Flight with an average of 4 hours flying daily in extreme temperatures.

Every engine before despatch from our works is dismantled for inspection, and after re-assembly is given a test run under the supervision of our qualified and approved inspection staff.

AIRCRAFT DISPOSAL COMPANY LTD.

REGENT HOUSE,

Telephone: Regent 6240. 89, KINGSWAY, LONDON, W.C.2. Cables: "Airdisco, London."

The Aeroplane 1 October 1924

Martinsyde produced good, solid, practical aircraft and one was the G.100/102 Elephant, a large two-bay biplane fitted with, initially, a 120 hp Austro-Daimler engine. The prototype, serial number 4735, is shown here at Brooklands prior to testing at Upavon in September 1915: it was fitted experimentally with a three-bladed propeller. Of the 300 or so machines built, none survived into the surplus market, but their reputation undoubtedly boosted the saleability of the F.4 machines that ADC had in abundance. Bottom:- Rare view of G-EBOJ, the Nimbus Martinsyde, probably taken after its first flight. *[Mike Hooks]*

components on the stand showed if anything a better workmanship and finish than was to be found in most of the new French engines in the exhibition. Remembering that all the ADC merchandise on show was war surplus, this must have enhanced the prestige of the British manufacturing industry.

Largely to consolidate this reputation, ADC held a Board Meeting on July 30th 1925 at which it was agreed the name would be changed to ADC Aircraft Ltd with John Kenworthy as chief designer. A second company, ADC Engines Ltd, was also created which would have Maj Frank B Halford in charge of development. The name 'ADC Engines Ltd' was rarely used and the majority of the company publicity for both aircraft and engines was issued under the one title of 'ADC Aircraft Ltd'.

Up to this time, the old Aircraft Disposal Company Ltd had succeeded in selling many aircraft to foreign markets which, had it not been for the bargains offered, would never have thought to even consider buying British. It had sold 2,000 aircraft and 3,000 engines as a result of which more than £1,250,000 had been returned to the Treasury under the profit-sharing scheme. This was an incredible three times more than originally budgeted for.

A curious tale emerges from early in 1927. Still engaged in revamping and revising the Martinsyde stock, ADC produced a new and 'secret' variant that began its test-flying at the start of that March. A Puma-powered two-seater, the machine was the old G-EBOL christened Gugnunc I. The aircraft was subsequently flown to Stag Lane where it was operated by Air Taxis Ltd. On October 7th 1927 it was inbound from France when it became caught in the infamous Surrey fog, crash-landing on Epsom Downs and being damaged beyond repair. The bits went back to Waddon and there it was stored until the cremation ceremony in 1930.

This was thus a full two years before Handley Page's HP.39 machine, also nicknamed Gugnunc, was completed for the Guggenheim Competition. Not that there was anything aeronautically special about that name: it came from the nonsense words 'spoken' by a character in the popular *Daily Mirror* strip cartoon Pip, Squeak and Wilfred. And the appropriation of 'Gugnunc' as a name for the HP.39 came not from Cricklewood but from the editor of *Flight,* the venerable Stanley Spooner. Perhaps he had forgotten ADC's prior aeronautical use of the name!

Perhaps the biggest event to take place in the 1920s was the seventh International Aero Exhibition staged at Olympia. Held from July 16th until the 27th, 1929, as a London show this great event was never to be equalled. Two adjacent stands in the centre of the Main Hall marked the zenith of the Waddon achievement. Stand No. 96 was ADC Aircraft Ltd and Stand 99 was Cirrus Aero-Engines Ltd. Both were opposite the large stand occupied by Blackburn Aeroplane & Motor Company. At this time in its existence both stands showed only engines, ADC displaying the Nimbus and the new and impressive Airsix air-cooled motor. Cirrus displayed the Cirrus Mk. III and the Cirrus Hermes and a further exhibit showed the latter as an installation complete with cowlings and propeller.

It was to be the ADC swansong.

BRITISH **ADC LIMITED** AIRCRAFT

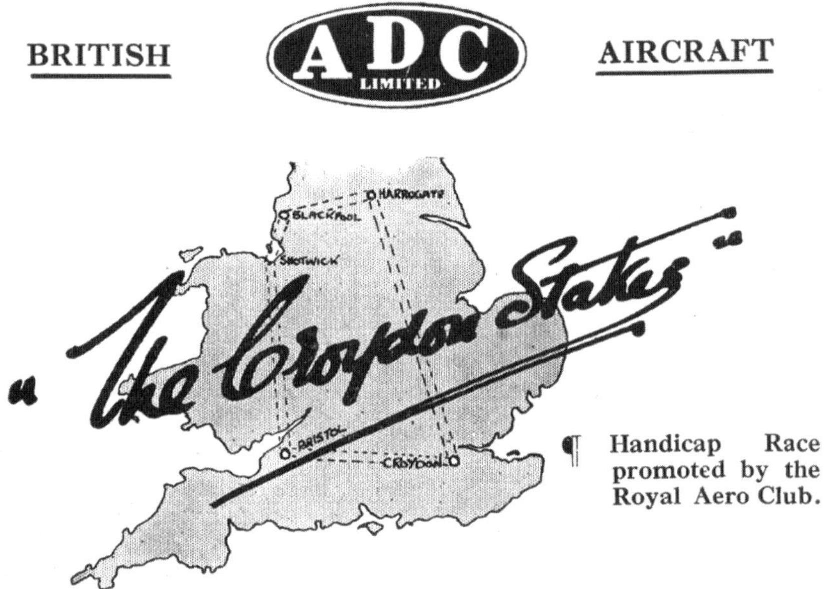

¶ Handicap Race promoted by the Royal Aero Club.

Course: 523 miles in a circuit, CROYDON—BRISTOL—SHOTWICK—BLACKPOOL—HARROGATE—CROYDON.

Col. The Master of Sempill, piloting the winning machine—D.H.51, 120/140 h.p. AIRDISCO engine, averaged 101 m.p.h.

Mr. A. J. Cobham, finished second on the D.H. "Moth," 27/60 h.p. CIRRUS engine, averaged 87/5 m.p.h.

The AIRDISCO and CIRRUS engines, although not designed and built for speed,

AGAIN DEMONSTRATED THE HIGHEST EFFICIENCY AND RELIABILITY.

120/140 h.p. "AIRDISCO" Engine.

27/60 h.p. "CIRRUS" Engine.

AIRCRAFT DISPOSAL COMPANY, LTD.,

REGENT HOUSE, 89, KINGSWAY, LONDON, W.C.2.

'Phone: Regent 6240.

Cables: "Airdisco, London."

Flight 16 July 1925

Chapter 10

The Aircraft Disposal Company runs its Course

AS 1930 dawned, both of the divisions of the Aircraft Disposal Company – engines and aircraft – began to wind down. The greater majority of usable aircraft components acquired at the company's foundation had been assembled into finished aircraft or engines and there was less and less work for the company to get its teeth into. It was no longer justifiable to occupy all of the vast premises that a little over a decade earlier had been Britain's National Aircraft Factory Number One.

All the indications were that the Aircraft Disposal Company had now run its course. The last of its saleable 1914-18 stock having been sold off, the business had ceased to be an economic proposition. By the beginning of 1931, most of the remaining residue of saleable material had been disposed of. On March 4th 1931 a Receiver was appointed expressly to wind up the business.

There were still huge stocks of obsolete engine parts and many old airframe components. Not for the first time would good aviation material be sold off for pennies. The metal went for scrap and the rest was turned out to be burned. Sadly this pyre was topped by the three dismantled but otherwise airworthy prototype Kenworthy-reworked Martinsyde ADC.1

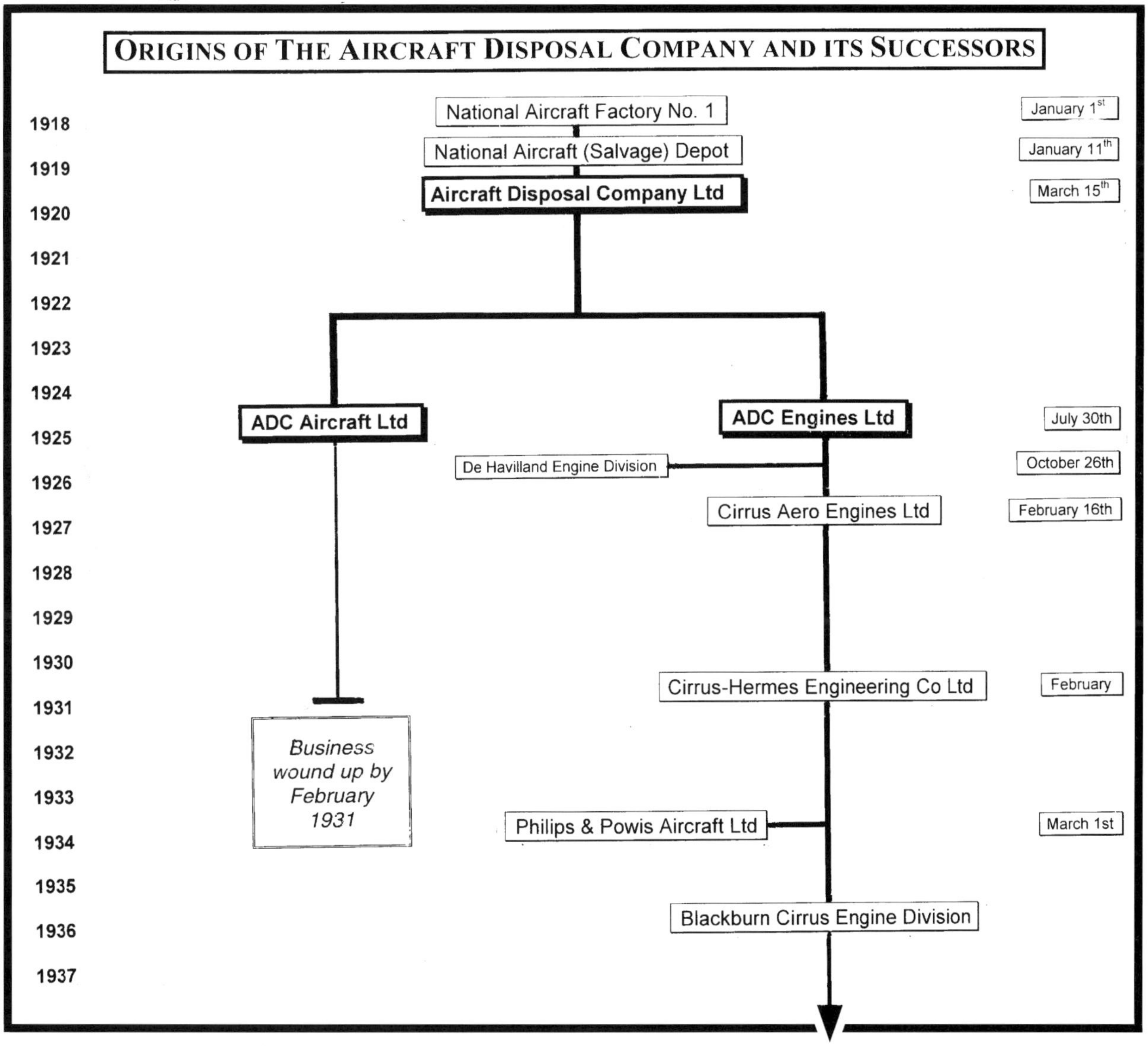

ORIGINS OF THE AIRCRAFT DISPOSAL COMPANY AND ITS SUCCESSORS

Year	Aircraft	Company / Engines	Date
1918		National Aircraft Factory No. 1	January 1st
1919		National Aircraft (Salvage) Depot	January 11th
1920		**Aircraft Disposal Company Ltd**	March 15th
1921			
1922			
1923			
1924			
1925	**ADC Aircraft Ltd**	**ADC Engines Ltd**	July 30th
1926		De Havilland Engine Division	October 26th
1927		Cirrus Aero Engines Ltd	February 16th
1928			
1929			
1930			
1931		Cirrus-Hermes Engineering Co Ltd	February
1932	*Business wound up by February 1931*		
1933			
1934		Philips & Powis Aircraft Ltd	March 1st
1935			
1936		Blackburn Cirrus Engine Division	
1937			

machines, never sold nor proceeded with.

And so in the winter of 1930-31, the vast premises at Waddon that had originally been created for building fighters for the war effort had finally fallen silent and the space cleared. Waddon was at last stilled.

The buildings that had been erected as the National Aircraft Factory No.1 never belonged to the Aircraft Disposal Company but had been leased from its owners, the Air Ministry. ADC's gradual contraction in size began during 1928 and in that year it began to relinquish some of the site back to its landlords who had found new short-lease tenants for the buildings as they became vacant. It appears that once ADC had closed down or otherwise departed the old National Aircraft Factory premises, the Air Ministry would dispose of the site as a whole.

Now the remaining stocks of AGS parts (Aircraft General Stores, meaning nuts, bolts, washers, turnbuckles, shackles and so forth) were disposed of by the Receiver to engineers' shops, yacht chandlers, model-makers, surplus stores – in fact to anybody who wanted to buy them. These stocks were still to be found in circulation forty years later and the first post-Second World War generation of amateur aircraft builders could still buy brand new AGS parts that had been made around sixty years earlier.

One particularly large specialist surplus outlet (K R Whiston of New Mills, Stockport) was selling one-time ADC stock right to the end (1970s) while R J Coley & Atkinson Ltd (originally Coley & Barnett, later simply Coley's) of Hounslow still had propellers and engine parts, as well as gimp pins and huge stocks of special cement-coated brass woodscrews for aircraft woodwork for sale at their warehouse as late as 1955.

Coley published regular catalogues in the 1930s from their original premises, Ordnance Works, Queen Elizabeth Road, Kingston-on-Thames. Their 32-page list for November 1931 makes very interesting reading. 'Aeroplane landing wheels (only sizes now in stock – 800 x 150 and 900 x 200) £2 10s per pair.' These were actually DH.2 and DH.4-size. Airspeed indicators were 4/- and 10/- and altimeters 10/6d. Lucas aero dynamos (250 watt, 12-volt) cost £1.

There was also a good choice of aircraft engines, the 160 hp 6-cylinder water-cooled Beardmore complete with two magnetos and carburettor was £12 10s. For the same price you could buy a 75 hp Rolls-Royce Hawk, also with carburettor and magnetos ready to run. More expensive was the American-made 12-cylinder 400 hp Liberty which, ready to run, would set you back £15.

This late catalogue includes oil gauges (2s and 3/6d), revolution counters (17/6d), two-bladed propellers ('approximately 10-ft long') 4s, safety belts (2s) and elastic shock-absorber cord which, in a choice of three thicknesses, could be had from 3d to 5d a yard. Five different types of sparking-plug (from 6d each), four sizes of turnbuckles (from 2s each) and so on. The firm did a special line in domestic barometers which were 'Converted from Aero Altimeters and mounted in polished mahogany or walnut boss, cut from actual aero propeller: A Very excellent and novel instrument – £1 10s'. A special note at the end advises that there is also 'A very large quantity of Machine Spares, Avro, etc., Main Planes, Skids, Axles, Cowlings, etc: Send for Separate List.'

Not long afterwards, the magazine *Air and Airways* published the following news story in its edition for June 1932. Remember it was then just fifteen months since the residue from ADC's warehouses at Croydon had been acquired for scrap:

> **WHERE OLD AIRCRAFT GO**
>
> At last I have discovered the secret of where old aircraft go to when they die. The address of this aerial Valhalla is Coleys of Kingston, a firm who, in Air Ministry parlance, have 'reduced to produce' over 6,000 aeroplanes and some 5,000 aero engines.
>
> When an extra large batch of 'write-offs' has been brought in for scrapping their yard resembles an insurance broker's nightmare, and recently 400 tons of damaged propellers alone were smashed up for firewood. On another occasion 50,000 new sparking plugs for obsolete types of aero engines were purchased as junk and later resold to a popular 'sixpenny' store.
>
> Scrapping an aero engine at Kingston has been reduced to a fine art. Nuts, bolts and ball bearings are all carefully salvaged, aluminium crankcases and phosphor bronze bearings are sold to foundries for re-melting while magnetos and instruments are reconditioned and bought up by motorists.
>
> A worn-out aero engine, costing £1,650 new is worth, I was told, only £2 as scrap, but obsolete types, especially of low power, are much more valuable, for they can be adapted for use in fast motor-boats, cars, and hydro-gliders. A 75 hp Rolls-Royce airship engine may, if in new condition, fetch as much as £12 10s.
>
> Among the many aircraft which have fallen victims to this aerial 'knacker's yard' were the Titania, once the world's largest flying-boat and the Short Crusader which, built for the 1927 Schneider Trophy Race, crashed and sank off the Lido on a practice flight due to the aileron controls having been crossed in assembly.[1]

Twenty-one years later this famous yard would house the tortured remains that had originally been the two Brabazon airliner prototypes: scrap-dealers Coley had been summoned to Filton to do the dastardly deed.

Meanwhile the properties branch of the Air Ministry now found itself back in untenanted possession of the vast Waddon site – surely the last-remaining World War One surplus property on its books. The War Office, as the ultimate owner, decided to dispose of this burden (which, remember, had cost the taxpayer £1m to build) by public auction and so, in March of 1931, auctioneers Herring, Son & Daw offered the property on the market.

By now it was the height of the 1930s Depression, the market was pancake-flat, and nobody was buying any space for industry, certainly not on the scale Waddon had to offer. The result was that bidding failed to meet the reserve price and the premises remained unsold; they were bought in at £100,000 by the Government over a bid of just £74,000.

The matter of site ownership rumbled on all through 1931 as, faced with the ailing economy, the War Office saw the old ADC buildings declining in value. At the end of November, however, it was unexpectedly announced that a purchase deal had been struck between the War Office and Mr A Maitland Kish, chairman of a property investment group called Town Investments Ltd. Although the Government had clearly been holding out for the best possible deal and while some sources claimed that the undisclosed sale price was not less than £100,000, informed opinion in the industry later suggested that the actual sum realised was well under that figure.

In reporting the event under the headline 'The Sale of a War Relic', *The Aeroplane* for December 9th 1931 commented that:

> The buyers intend to put all the buildings into substantial repair and sell or let in sections... The factory covers an area of about 25 acres and has

1. Titania was a Fairey-designed variant of the N.4 flying boat and was built on the Clyde by Fyffes. She flew in 1925 as N129 but was scrapped within four years. The Short-Bristow Crusader N226 crashed on September 11th 1927 and spent a week on the sea-bed, memorable for the fact that during its time under water its magnesium engine crankcase almost completely dissolved.

In October 1927 ADC Ltd obtained a DH.60X from de Havilland in order to act as a flying test-bed for the Cirrus engine development. De Havilland was one of the biggest customers for the Cirrus and G-EBUF was first fitted with a Cirrus II and later a Cirrus Hermes as seen here. By the time this picture was taken, ADC had closed, disposing of the Moth in June 1930 to Smiths Aircraft Instruments at Heston where it was flown by Capt Neville Stack as a communications machine for the firm. Later sold to France (July 1934), it became F-ANHN. In this congested snapshot, Stack runs up the engine in very close proximity to a crowd of curious onlookers. At this time the majority of men still wore hats as this assortment of trilbys and caps ably demonstrates.

> 415,000 square feet of floor space. Sidings to the Southern Railway form the outlet for heavy goods.
>
> Some idea of what these buildings housed may be gathered from the fact that one big shed, in which the stock of aero-engines taken over by the Aircraft Disposal Co Ltd from the Air Ministry were housed, contained some years after the war engines which cost the Air Ministry £3,000,000.
>
> A large proportion of the stock of engines, aeroplanes and accessories was unsaleable because the types were completely obsolete, and there would be much interest in learning what has become of so much material which, in its time, was the product of the best brains of the day.

The reference to the railway sidings at this late stage is curious since, while they still existed as features, the track connection to the main railway line had long since been abandoned and the rails lifted.

As mentioned earlier, prior to this sale, some of the space had found new short-lease tenants as little by little, the factory bays were divided up into hangars and rented to other firms. One of these was The Robinson Aircraft Company, later to be re-named the Redwing Company. The prototype of its delightful side-by-side two-seater Redwing biplane, the ABC Hornet-powered G-AAUO was completed in one of these hangars by the Spring of 1930. The leases all seem to have been of short duration, for Redwing's occupancy finished at the beginning of 1932 following the sale of the site to Town Investments.

Other tenants included the original General Aircraft Company, formed on February 27th 1931, before it moved from Croydon to Hanworth two years later. Other users included Rollason Aircraft Services while Imperial Airways rented had hangar space. A non-aviation tenant was Trojan, the car and van-makers. Despite the Recession, Trojan was selling well and needed temporary vehicle storage space: early in 1931 it took a short lease on three ADC Aircraft sheds at an annual rent of £60 in order to store fifty vehicles.

By this time, the era of the Aircraft Disposal Company was over and its activities and achievements were being consigned to history.

And so the business that had virtually milked the industry dry during the first half of its eleven-year existence was mourned across the industry even though it had operated very much as a cuckoo in somebody else's nest. While after around 1924 it found itself able to contribute some design and manufacturing expertise back into the industry through sub-contract work and especially in engine design and manufacture, it was not until that year that the manufacturers themselves began to be able to fight back.

But Airdisco was not all bad news. It succeeded in putting British aeroplanes, engines, materials and accessories into practically every country in the world at prices that we should never have got had we only been able to offer brand-new goods. By concentrating on its job of selling aeroplanes, it probably performed far better than any ordinary aircraft manufacturer could have done. The true value of that exercise remains a moot point.

Airdisco's structure and marketing was, nevertheless, considerably better organised

The Cirrus-Hermes, developed from the original work of Halford at Waddon, became a light-plane mainstay in the 1930s. Here Sqdn-Ldr H R A Edwards swings the propeller of his Avro Avian Mk.IV at the start of the Hatfield-Ronaldsway Isle of Man air race on May 27th 1939. His wife is seen in the cockpit. The race, routed via Blackpool's Stanley Park aerodrome, was won by the DH/TK.2 G-ADNO which picked up the £100 first prize. This Avian, G-ABEE, survived the Second World War and was flown by the present author at Denham in the 1950s.

than similar activities in other countries. In both France and Italy, for example, sample war-surplus aircraft were initially given away to anybody who showed the slightest interest in them and after that these countries sold off brand new aeroplanes at prices with which Britain could not possibly compete. Many were bought, unwisely, by people who tried to teach themselves to fly them. The outcome was predictable.

Interestingly, comparatively few of these foreign aircraft attracted foreign buyers who found British machines of greater attraction in terms of performance and reliability.

The Aircraft Disposal Company had begun as a means of satisfying the Exchequer and the taxpayer in putting to use the huge stocks of surplus aeroplanes and parts. As it progressed through its eleven-year existence, the company gradually changed its emphasis from Treasury-refunder to the position of a more conventional aircraft business. Its operations and activities progressively impinged more positively on those aspects of aviation which existed outside the gates of what was by then Croydon Aerodrome.

As we have seen, one of the most important of these ways was in the matter of engines. Production of the Cirrus engine in particular was an entirely new operation which, while initially using up surplus components, ultimately developed into an original design that sold on its own merits all over the globe. ADC Cirrus, Nimbus and Hermes engines were exported in huge numbers and flew in many aircraft, establishing a favourable reputation in almost every corner of the world.

While Croydon Aerodrome formed the backdrop for one of the most controversial aircraft businesses ever to have existed, it also spread the message that British-made aircraft were a sound proposition as regards performance and reliability. That message was to survive as other British manufacturers struggled to surmount the obstacles placed in their path by the Aircraft Disposal Company. The overseas reputation gained by our aircraft, British designed and built, both military and civil, was to sustain our industry through the bad years of the Depression and prepare us for the events of September 1939. In that respect, ADC operated as a commendably-good ambassador for the whole of the industry.

If ADC was a terrible child that demoralised the legitimate aircraft industry, was the problem at any level avoidable? The answer has to be no, not really. It is part of the dreadful waste that is war. The nature of war does not conform to any plan and you cannot operate a battle by supplying weapons and machinery on the 'just-in-time' principle. No, you have to keep an ever-expanding reserve of weaponry 'just-in-case'. And had the war continued, naturally all these goods and more would have been needed and needed urgently.

The Armistice came suddenly. It caught everybody by surprise. Both sides were battle-weary yet none were to know that suddenly it would stop at the eleventh hour of the eleventh day in the eleventh month. ADC was created as a necessity, and the future was bound to be turbulent.

So what is there to be seen of the National Aircraft Factory Number One, the Number One Aircraft Salvage Depot and the Aircraft Disposal Company today? Sadly, the short answer is hardly anything.

One of the level-crossing gates that originally blocked off the main Stafford Road when a freight train was making a delivery into the National Aircraft Factory site via the special spur track from the main London-Brighton railway line, remained in existence right up to around 1955. It had been seconded to the job of closing off the Purley Way entrance to the Southern Foundry premises.

Progress and development are today's 'in-words' for destruction and obliteration. Just as Croydon Aerodrome became a building site soon after its closure, developers cast their beady eyes on the old ADC buildings several years ago. With no good reason to preserve the old buildings, they were razed and in their place an industrial estate has risen. Because in this modern age buildings are expected to be functional and to shock rather than to be practical and attractive to the eye, one need not expect the new structures to offer anything to the benefit of the site. In that respect they do not disappoint. But to those that remember other days, their presence cannot obliterate, let alone replace, the great history that once was made upon that site. And somewhere there is still the shadowy image of that great sign that spanned the side of a black building. It read ADC AIRCRAFT LTD.

Appendix 1

The Handley Page Aircraft Deal

This article, written by the editor Stanley Spooner, first appeared in the issue of the weekly magazine Flight *for April 29th 1920. It reveals some of the background to the horny subject of the disposal of surplus war goods and is reprinted here in its entirety – obvious 'warts and all' – with grateful acknowledgement to the present proprietors of that aviation journal. In preparing it for republication, the over-long blocks of type that formed the original have been broken into shorter paragraphs in order to make it less tedious to the reader.*

AN extremely impressive and interesting visit to Waddon Aerodrome was organised by Messrs Handley Page, Ltd, last Friday for the purpose of disclosing – if only to a small extent – the vast nature of the undertaking of the Aircraft Disposal Company Limited. The gathering of visitors was worthy of the event, consisting as it did of representatives of many industries and many countries.

As a display of magnitude, this visit to Waddon was a marvel in itself, not to be easily forgotten, but the mind almost failed to grasp the situation when it was casually pointed out to us that the material we were seeing was only a fraction of the whole purchase from the Government. There were similar depots scattered in sundry parts of the country, and presumably even the world.

It is impossible to convey in words all that was seen. Suffice it to say that we passed – following an apparently endless white line! – through numerous 'sheds' in which were stacked, packed and piled literally acres of aeroplanes, aero engines, airscrews, landing-gears, rev. counters, compasses, and other instruments, magnetos and starters, carburettors, wire strainers, bolts, nuts, pins split and pins not, sundry other accessories not recognised at the moment, airship and kite-balloon materials, etc, etc – all to the Nth power!

Amongst the aeroplanes we recognised many well-known and successful types, such as Handley Page bombers, DH 9's, DH 4's, DH 6's ('Sky-Hooks'), Avro 504K's, Martin-sydes, Bristols, Sopwiths, SE.5A's, FE.'s, Vickers, Beardmores, etc. It seemed that all known types of engines were represented, but we were 'moved along' too often to allow a complete inventory being made. We noticed that all those engines that had seen service had their log-books hung neatly round their necks, so that no one need buy a 'pig in a poke.'

Following this impressive inspection, details of plans of the Aircraft Disposal Co were briefly entered into at a luncheon – a welcome solace for our dazed brain – at the Savoy, at which Lord Londonderry, Under-Secretary of State for Air, presided.

The Marquess of Londonderry said they were com-memorating an arrangement of very far-reaching importance. While he could lay no claim to being an expert, and while he was what was termed a politician – and politicians were usually regarded with thinly-veiled suspicion – there was nothing lacking in his enthusiasm to do his best to further the great science of aviation, which had potentialities which we could hardly envisage. The transaction which had taken place was one of which they had every reason to be satisfied.

While they were all in favour of private enterprise, and while they believed that the Empire had been built up by the initiative and enterprise of individuals, there was a position which the State could take up which would assist those individuals rather than hamper them, and in the arrangement which had recently been made they saw the best principles of that theory. The Government, as the disposer of property, was always in a difficult position, and therefore, in his official capacity, he welcomed the advent of an organisa-tion which was prepared to carry out the undertaking in the best interests of private enterprise.

The transaction was one of immense

An 80 h.p. Renault-engined three-seat Airco DH.6 takes off on a joy-ride from a stretch of foreshore. The aircraft, G-EAUS, belonged to Blackpool Flying Services. Originally carrying the military serial number C7763, this was acquired from Air Ministry surplus and registered on July 9th 1921. It was withdrawn on the expiry of the C of A on July 2nd 1923 when it was sold to Manchester Aviation Co for use as spares. Observe that the aircraft is taking off over the seaso that, if the engine should fail, the falling aircraft will not damage the sand.

magnitude. The handing over had consisted of 10,000 aeroplanes, 30,000 aero engines, and large quantities of material and accessories. This monument erected by the War represented 100 years development in the ordinary course. The whole of these stores had been handed over for the sum of £1,000,000 and 50 per cent benefit accrued to the Government for any profit which resulted on the under-taking. This, he felt, was an arrangement of which he, as the representative of the Government, had every reason to be satisfied. That was not all. The Government was not altogether indifferent to the other 50 per cent. The long arm of the Treasury touched all profits and all income – and they might rest assured that the Government were not losers on the transaction.

The Government might be criticised for having handed over to a company something in the nature of a monopoly, but he was prepared to con-tradict that absolutely. They had handed over to a firm, which was capable of disposing of aircraft and accessories, property which any Government would have had great difficulty in disposing of. The arrangement had many advantages; it provided opportunities for circulating through-out the world the product of British industry, and it provided an opportunity for advertising British machines and the enterprise of the British constructor.

In this venture they owed a debt of gratitude to Mr Handley Page. The Air Ministry perhaps had come in for a greater degree of sus-picion than any other department, but there was no hanging back on their part. The Ministry were not wondering whether aviation was going to be a success. They were convinced that it would be, and they wanted to establish the science on the lines on which it could progress as thoroughly as possible. It had such a great future before it that it was not possible for most of us to envisage. It was quite a mistake to imagine nothing was being done by the Civil Aviation Department. On the contrary, it was often difficult for the Ministry to keep pace with what was being pushed forward by Sir Fred[eric]k Sykes and his department. The chairman concluded by proposing the health of Mr Handley Page.

Mr Handley Page, having expressed the regret of Mr Godfrey Isaacs, chairman of the Aircraft Disposal Company, at being unable to be present, said that they had seen at Waddon some small portion of the material acquired from the Government. It was difficult to visualise the whole amount. That depot was but one of six which had been taken over and which were equally full, and the contents of 130 more stations, crammed full of the result of British brains, had to be sorted out and turned over to the company. Whilst the material was originally destined for aircraft work, enterprising business men and manufacturers had found that it was readily adapt-able for other purposes. Such things as the 500 to 1,000 tons of ball bearings, 350,000 sparking plugs, 100,000 magnetos, bolts, nuts, and small accessories were finding a ready sale with the present shortage of manufactured goods. Out of the enormous stock of instruments which they had, instrument sets for motors were easily made up. The revolution counters could be changed into speedometers, and the aneroid barometers for registering height into baro-meters for telling the weather.

The steel tubes previously used for aircraft had been bought up by enterprising bedstead manufacturers to change into bedstead frames, and the RAF wires for bracing the planes were being used for the cross-slats of a bedstead frame. Propellers had been widely used for hat stands and clock cases, and discarded instrument cases for the family cruet. The greatest enterprise, however, had been shown by a firm who had solved the housing pro-blem and the provision of facilities for summer travel by purchasing under-carriages from aircraft, and fitting on top of them a light caravan body, furnished with the material available from the stores.

In engineering work a great quantity of material was also being utilised. Engines which were designed for aircraft work ran most satisfactorily on town gas. For instance, the Sunbeam 'Arab' engine, which developed 200 hp as an aircraft engine, with its gearing removed was running at a slower speed as a most efficient electric plant engine developing 50 hp. Such a unit took up but a small space, and thus enabled the small electric light plant to get over its period of bad load without unduly taxing the normal capacity of the other plant. Such an engine could be purchased at a very small price compared with the large slow-speed gas engine which would otherwise be required.

But all these were but side issues to the main problem of the disposal of aircraft, and it is to this that the company had directed their ends. Machines could now be purchased at a cost which was only a small proportion of the original cost to the Government, and a country inaugurating a national air programme could thus get through the development period at a very low cost. The military side of aviation did not exhaust the possibilities of air work.

Today air transport was slowly but surely taking its place among the many facilities for the carrying out of quick commercial transactions. There was no question to his mind as to the certainty of air transport occupying a prominent position in future business development. On the Handley Page service between London and Paris, for instance, they had carried 67,811 lb. of freight, and flown 97,428 miles without injury to a single passenger or loss of a pound of freight; and this was but a beginning. They, therefore, looked with great confidence to the opening up of further facilities and the use of machines such as they had for carrying out the services. His company was not tied down as a government to conduct its business in a stereotyped way. They could extend greater facilities for payment and start perhaps new enterprise which would not be otherwise possible. It would be their endeavour to work in the most harmonious relations with all those firms whose machines will be dealt with by the company, and this question had been frankly and freely discussed with them and an outline of the way in which they could work laid down.

Today the prestige of British aircraft stood higher than any in the world, and even nations who had had foreign aircraft, pushed by expeditions, sent to their shores, and foreign demonstrations conducted regardless of expense, had realised that the machines offered were not so good as those from this country. It was early to give the results of the sale of aircraft by the new company, but he could state that in the short period of their existence they had sold many more machines than the Aircraft Disposal Board during the whole period of its existence. It would be their endeavour to push still further the sale of British aircraft abroad, and to remove the impression that sometimes existed that Britain lagged behind in selling efforts abroad.

Major-Gen Sir Frederick Sykes, Director-General of Civil Aviation, proposing the health of the chairman, said his department wanted to get as much as possible of this British aircraft throughout the world in the quickest time. The whole essence of the question was speed. The disposal of this aircraft must be done quickly, and, in his opinion, it was impossible for a Government Department to get rid of it sufficiently quickly.

Facing page: The original page of pictures as printed in *Flight* for April 29th 1920. Despite poor definition, the give added insight to how the birth of ADC was presented to the world.

"Flight" Copyright

SCENES AT THE AIRCRAFT DISPOSAL CENTRE AT WADDON AERODROME.—1. A heap of old metal parts waiting to be sorted. 2. A corner of the store for De H. 9 machines, showing the method of stacking. 3. A few of the propellers which are available. 4. Various types of engines being cleaned up and classified. 5. The method of stacking spare wings. 6. One of the workshops where the dissembling and sorting are carried out

Above: ADC Martinsyde G-EAXB was formerly D4279 and was an Aircraft Disposal Company demonstrator. It raced in the Whitsun Meeting at Croydon on April 17th 1922 when it collided on landing with SE.5A G-EAXU and was damaged beyond repair. *[via Richard T Riding.]* Left: A standard ADC Nimbus Martinsyde single-seat fighter. *[Janes AWA.]* Below: This Martinsyde F.6, G-EBDK, was owned at one time by skywriting pioneer Major Jack Savage and was scrapped as late as 1930. Too late for military use, the F.6 was a rare bird and only three entered the Civil Register. *[via Richard T Riding.]*

Appendix 2

The Aircraft Disposal Company's Aircraft

WE have seen that from its inception The Aircraft Disposal Company dispensed a degree of largesse in its conversions of surplus aircraft into saleable machines to suit the specific needs of its ever-increasing portfolio of world-wide customers. From creating fresh airframe-engine combinations to providing extra seats for joy-riding aircraft, the Waddon workshops never allowed thoughts of originality and its preservation to deter them and indeed this unrestricted mandate was to prove extremely beneficial. Many of the machines that were unwanted with their original engines quickly became highly desirable with a different or more powerful motor. The fact that the company developed its own engines was initially beneficial although gradually they were forced to at least be able to offer a wider choice of power units.

ADC's 'variations on a theme' were widespread and were in truth little different from those offered elsewhere in the industry. A V Roe converted its own machines into three and four-seaters, so did de Havilland and a host of maintenance contractors. These modifications, then, cannot with honesty be described as changes that were of sufficient magnitude to warrant listing as a new aircraft type. Admittedly some were quite major: getting acceptable passenger accommodation into a fighter or a trainer aircraft would today be thought of as a major modification. In those days, though, it was generally little more than a carpentry job.

However, under the aegis of chief designer John Kenworthy (who had earlier designed the Austin Whippet before joining ADC in 1924, and would much later make his name afresh with the Robinson Redwing), ADC made a small number of aircraft that incorporated so many changes that they became new types where the name of ADC was listed as 'manufacturer' on the airworthiness documents. It is this clutch of machines that forms the nucleus of this Appendix. They have been introduced in their historical context in Chapter 9 and now we will look at them in somewhat greater detail.

The first ADC-Martinsyde conversions of the F.4 were in general merely cosmetic, one involving the substitution of the forward radiator of the 300 hp Hispano-Suiza H with two underslung Lamblin radiators so allowing the nose to be cowled with less induced drag. This variant was exported, among others, to Spain. The first proper variant, though, came with the ADC.1.

In the details and specifications that follow it is anticipated that the reader is already aware of the basic type and method of construction and the equipment of the Martinsyde F.4 (*see* Sanger *[24]*): this material will not be repeated here.

Martinsyde ADC.1

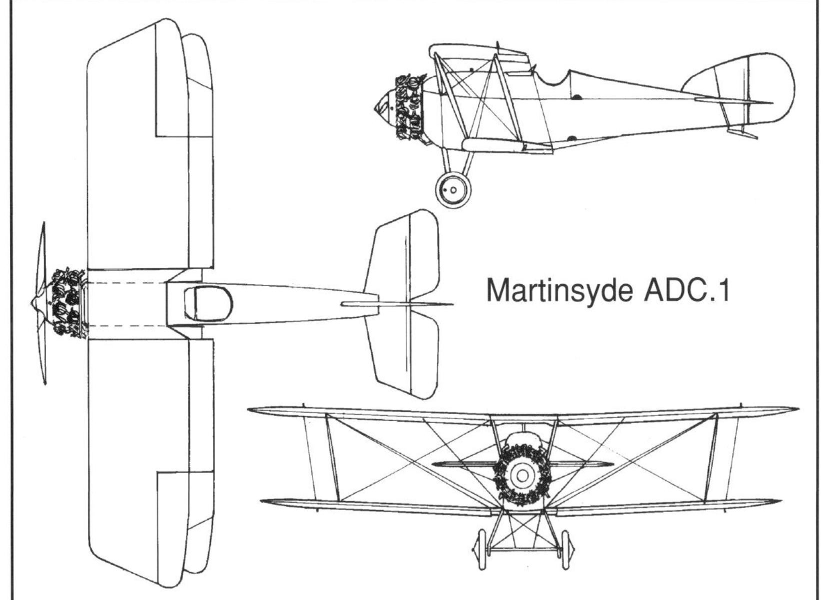

First revealed in November 1924, the ADC.1 was to be the second variation of the Martinsyde F.4 to be produced at Waddon. This time, though, the modifications to the original Martinsyde design warranted the creation of a separate model number. As with previous F.4 variants, the rectangular section fuselage was of wire braced wooden construction with curved turtle deck. The single-bay wooden wings were built around two spruce spars of routed-out beam form with wooden ribs. Ailerons were fitted to all four wings, the usual half control circuit being in each lower and upper wing, completion being by aileron trailing-edge cable tie. Apart from the plywood decking forward of the cockpit, the whole was fabric covered. While the appearance of the aircraft was almost identical to that of the F.4, the fuselage from the pilot's cockpit forward was different as was some of the equipment carried. This change to the fuselage structure was dictated by the switch from the original 275 hp V-twelve Rolls-Royce Falcon inline powered original to the two-row 14-cylinder 395 hp Armstrong Siddeley Jaguar III radial. Instead of narrow and low side truss mounts, the

The prototype Martinsyde ADC.1 G-EBKL fitted with a geared Jaguar 14-cylinder radial engine. *[Flight]*

engine now required a circular mount and to achieve this the upper longerons swept upwards somewhat while the lower longerons, instead of curving up to the engine from the lower wing centre-section, continued straight from a point aft of the seat so creating a deep engine bulkhead. At this time, the provision of the firewall was sometimes seen as separate from the engine bulkhead and in the ADC.1 this was the style adopted. The firewall, comprising two faces of aluminium with an asbestos sheet core, was attached close to the rear of the engine and in front of the engine mounting structure. A feature which at that time was still novel was the provision of the engine unit as what would later be termed 'a power egg'. The engine attachment comprised a conventional welded tubular-steel circular truss 25-inches in diameter to which the engine was fixed using 16 bolts each 3/8-inch in diameter. This whole assembly terminated in a simple four-point fuselage bulkhead attachment so allowing quick removal and exchange of the entire engine and its accessories by disconnecting all fuel and oil lines and electrical leads plus push-rod driven magneto and carburettor controls. The whole motor might then be lifted off complete with its mounting. The gravity fuel system was fed from a 55-gallon capacity tank positioned immediately behind the firewall. Dispensing with a conventional oil-cooler, Kenworthy fitted the oil tank beneath the fuselage floor and directed the return flow from the engine through an air-cooled matrix at the bottom of the tank. Intended as a fighter aircraft, the ADC.1 was provided with twin Vickers guns that fired through the propeller disc using the interrupter gear devised by George Constantinesco. Because these guns ran either side of the fuel tank and to protect against a breech failure, armour plating separated the guns from the tank. Bearing the civil registration G-EBKL, the Jaguar-engined ADC.1 made its first flight at the hands of ADC test pilot Herbert Perry on October 11th, 1924. With more than 100 hp – and even more at full-throttle – Kenworthy's creation quickly demonstrated its exceptional performance. In terms of rate of climb, operational ceiling and cruising speed it proved to be significantly better than the new Gloster Grebe fighter then about to enter service with the Royal Air Force. The climb to 10,000 feet was five minutes. ADC's excellent sales and marketing team lost no time in spreading the message with the result that considerable interest was generated abroad. However, despite demonstrations to overseas buyers from Argentina, Japan, Portugal and Spain, only one order was to be forthcoming: the Latvian Air Force ordered nine machines. Note: the Armstrong Siddeley Jaguar III was rated at 395 hp continuous output at cruising power (1,620 rpm). The power curve produced an output of 425 hp at 2,000 rpm. This engine incorporated a basic form of supercharging using a fan which was driven at engine speed. The prototype ADC.1, G-EBKL, remained at Waddon and was burned as scrap when the company closed in 1930.

BRITISH

AIRCRAFT

MARTINSYDE A.D.C.1.

The Martinsyde A.D.C.1. with "Jaguar" Engine.

This machine is a very fast single-seater Fighter, fitted with the SIDDELEY "JAGUAR" Engine. The machine itself is of very strong construction and possesses an extraordinarily good performance in the air as regards climb, speed, manœuvrability, etc.

We shall be pleased to supply details of the performance on request.

In addition to the above machine we can supply the following MARTINSYDE types:

MARTINSYDE F.4. 300 h.p. HISPANO, single-seater scout.
MARTINSYDE F.4. SEAPLANE, 300 h.p. HISPANO, single-seater seaplane.
MARTINSYDE F.4.A.. 300 h.p. HISPANO, 2-seater fighter or training machine.
MARTINSYDE F.4.A.. SEAPLANE, 300 h.p. HISPANO, 2-seater seaplane.

AIRCRAFT DISPOSAL COMPANY, LTD.

REGENT HOUSE,

Telephone Regent 6240. 89, KINGSWAY, LONDON, W.C.2. Telegrams: "Airdisco, London."

SPECIFICATION

395 h.p. Armstrong Siddeley Jaguar III

Span overall	Length overall	Height overall	Wing area [sq.ft.]	Wing loading [lbs/sq.ft]	Empty weight	All-up weight	Max speed	Cruising speed	Landing speed	Range [miles]	Climb to 20,000ft
32 ft 9¼ in	25 ft 0 in	9 ft 6 in	320	8.28	1,865 lb	2,650 lb	163 mph	138 mph	52 mph	410	17.5 min

Nimbus Martinsyde

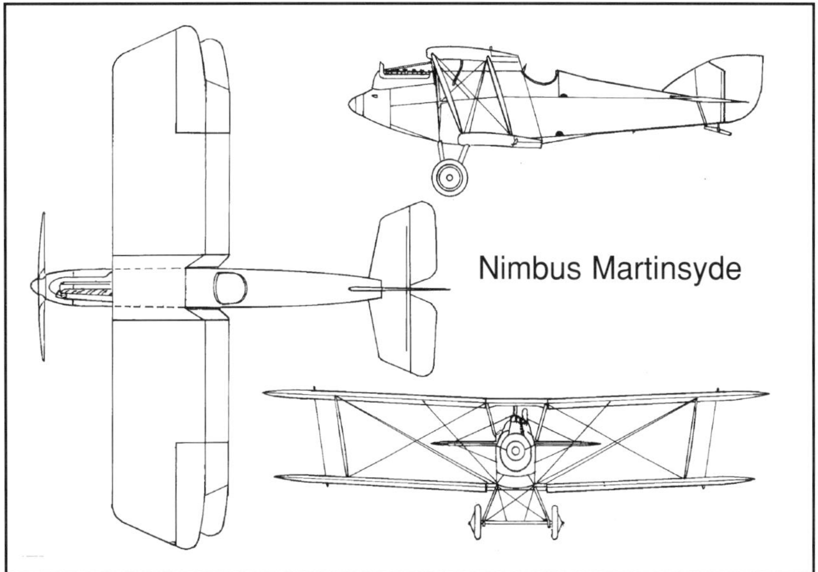

In 1926, a further variation on the Martinsyde F.4 formula was created by John Kenworthy. Intended as a fast twin-gun fighter, the Nimbus was powered by the 300 hp six-cylinder in-line water-cooled ADC Nimbus engine. This motor was a fairly extensive reworking of the old and obsolete Siddeley Puma that was originally rated at 250 hp. The airframe construction was identical to the ADC.1 with the exception that a modified fin with a horn-balanced rudder was fitted. This rudder was to become something of a Kenworthy hallmark and when, after ADC Aircraft closed down and Redwing Aircraft took over the same buildings employing Kenworthy as chief designer, he used the same rudder profile for the side-by-side two-seater Robinson Redwing. However, despite their close-cowled engines and undoubtedly clean lines, the overall performance was below that of the standard F.4. Only two Nimbus-engined Martinsydes were ever built and these were allocated civil registrations G-EBOJ and G-EBOL. This second machine was named Gugnunc I in March 1927. On October 7th that year while operated in-bound from France by Air Taxis Ltd it crashed on Epsom Downs while attempting a forced landing in fog. Damaged beyond repair, it was returned to Croydon and stored until burned as scrap in 1930. The Nimbus was a brave failure simply because it had the wrong engine. Although records of the Nimbus motor give us no reliability doubts, its origins in the Puma were most probably its downfall. ADC's enormous stock of these motors and their spares quite likely encouraged this airframe/engine combination but since the Puma had earned something of a war-time reputation for demonstrating reliability problems, even a redesign and change of name could not redeem it. Long-memoried potential buyers gave it a collective 'thumbs-down'. This probably played a major part in dissuading otherwise interested parties from placing any orders. The Aircraft Disposal Co's armed Nimbus combatant with its planned Vickers guns was destined never to be built.

Nimbus Martinsyde G-EBOJ. Formerly a standard Martinsyde F.4 with the military serial number K1001, it was registered on July 2nd 1926 and was flown in the King's Cup Race by Herbert Perry. Along with the other Martinsyde G-EBOL which was flown by Frank T Courtney, he was forced to retire. *[Mike Hooks.]*

SPECIFICATION
330 h.p. ADC Nimbus

Span overall	Length overall	Height overall	Wing area [sq.ft.]	Wing loading [lbs/sq.ft]	Empty weight	All-up weight	Max speed	Cruising speed	Landing speed	Range [miles]	Climb to 20,000ft
32 ft 9¼in	26 ft 10 in	9 ft 6 in	320	8.33	2,014 lb	2,665 lb	150 mph	131 mph	50 mph	327	25 min

Martinsyde Boreas

After the hiatus of the Nimbus, ADC and Kenworthy must have concluded that the chances of Nimbus becoming a fighter aeroplane were to say the least a bit limited. Both the Nimbus machines had been entered into the 1925-season races and had looked potentially adequate. That they were forced to retire for various reasons was not seen as a reason to rule out any future race participation. The possibility of selling more Martinsydes as fighters had also not yet been discounted, even though the airframes were now six or more years old. Racing was a very good way of promoting an aircraft and getting free publicity for its performance. Kenworthy considered that the Nimbus could be pushed that little bit further and so took G-EBOJ and gave it a special racing/speed makeover. The changes were all aimed at streamlining the airframe as much as possible without recourse to major redesign and new structure. First was the engine which was improved with fresh cowlings and close-fitting cylinder-head fairings. The V-truss of the undercarriage legs was faired in. Searching for a name for this confection, ADC came up with Boreas. According to Greek mythology Boreas was the god of the North wind and the son of Aeolus, King of the Aeolian Islands who was appointed by Jupiter as keeper of the winds. Boreas flew like the wind in the High Powered Handicap at Hucknall on August 1st 1927, clocking an average of 141.2 mph. Unfortunately, the wind did not blow favourably for Boreas and ADC for nobody clamoured for production and so G-EBOJ was retired into store, only to be burned as scrap in 1930. No reliable performance figures have so far been traced: the following data are therefore derivative.

Two views of the ADC Nimbus Martinsyde G-EBOJ when it was revamped for the 1927 King's Cup with cylinder head and undercarriage fairings. It was unofficially named Boreas after the North Wind but there is no evidence that it ever carried this name. It did, though, win the High Powered Handicap at Hucknall on August 1st 1927 at 141.2 mph piloted by Sqdn-Ldr H W G Jones. The large-diameter curved downpipe between the centre-section struts visible in the picture below is the fuel feed pipe from the with centre-section tank. Note the covered-in undercarriage legs, also the complex wing rigging array.

SPECIFICATION
330 h.p. ADC Nimbus

Span overall	Length overall	Height overall	Wing area [sq.ft.]	Wing loading [lbs/sq.ft]	Empty weight	All-up weight	Max speed	Cruising speed	Landing speed	Range [miles]	Climb to 10,000ft
32 ft 9¹/₄ in	26 ft 10 in	9 ft 6 in	320	8.44	2,050 lb	2,700 lb	152 mph	135 mph	50 mph	325	7.30 min

AV.1

The AV. I G-ABKH seen here at Brooklands, was the last-ever ADC-built aeroplane. *[Richard T Riding]*

The very last Martinsyde to be built at Waddon was G-ABKH. Erected in 1931, it was constructed by ADC Aircraft Ltd, the company founded in 1925 to succeed The Aircraft Disposal Company Limited and represented almost the last act before the business was wound up. The registration was allocated early in March 1931. Built to the order of the engine designer Charles Amherst Villiers, the AV.1 was a tandem two-seater having two separate cockpits. Externally similar to the F.4A, it embodied many detail airframe and engine modifications devised by its owner, one of which removal of the normal fuselage fuel tank and its substitution by a pair of F.6-style streamline-ended cylindrical tanks mounted either side of the upper wing centre section. Villiers, who was director of the Villiers-Hay Development Ltd and the designer of the outstanding Villiers Maya four-cylinder inline engine *[14]*, had the machine finished predominantly in dark blue and two lighter shades of the same colour and called it, appropriately, *Blue Print*. Sanger *[20]* describes Villiers as a man 'of an inventive mind without being entirely practical or worried about technicalities' and relates that on one occasion he was apparently experiencing difficulties with high oil consumption, 'and as a result was having difficulty in getting a certificate of airworthiness or permit to fly. In order to check this, the inspector asked Villiers to fly the aircraft for an hour or so. According to his story, the engine cut shortly after taking off from Heston and [he] was lucky to find a field in which to land. After a few minor adjustments to the engine, he persuaded several youths to hold the aircraft down while he swung the propeller. The engine started first time and he flew back to Heston. By this time the required hour had elapsed and on his return it was found that the oil problem had been miraculously cured.' The aircraft spent some while hangared at Brooklands until sold to C B Field in October 1932. Field specialized in building up aircraft (mostly Avros) for joy-riding operators from his base airfield, Kingswood Knoll in Surrey. On February 5th 1933, the AV.1 struck a telegraph pole and crashed at Bekesbourne in Kent. Returned by road to Kingswood Knoll, it remained derelict there until it was scrapped in 1935. Few performance figures exist for the AV.1 but it is likely to have had a similar flight performance envelope to the Woking-built production F.4 machines.

SPECIFICATION
330 h.p. ADC Nimbus

Span overall	Length overall	Height overall	Wing area [sq.ft.]	Wing loading [lbs/sq.ft]	Empty weight	All-up weight	Max speed	Cruising speed	Landing speed	Range [miles]	Climb to 10,000ft
32 ft 9¹/₄ in	25 ft 5¹/₄ in	9 ft 1 in	328.5	7.0	1,811 lb	2,300 lb	142 mph	115 mph	44 mph	295	8.5 min

Two rather hazy but nevertheless rare snapshots which are actually fuzzy and tiny images enlarged from the centre of 127-sized Box Brownie negatives of the G-EBOJ, the Nimbus-engined Martinsyde, probably taken at the time of the first flight. Formerly a standard F.4 with the military serial number K1001, it was registered on July 2nd 1926 and Herbert Perry flew it in the King's Cup Race. *[via Mike Hooks]*

SEPTEMBER 30, 1926

"CIRRUS"

SUCCESSES

ARE BEST EXPRESSED

IN

SALES, & MILES FLOWN

"CIRRUS" ENGINES HAVE NOW FLOWN ONE MILLION MILES.

Mark II. Power Curve Readings taken during Type Test.

70. b.h.p.	@	1,600 r.p.m.
81.5 b.h.p.	@	1,900 r.p.m.
84. b.h.p.	@	2,000 r.p.m.
88. b.h.p.	@	2,200 r.p.m.

"CIRRUS" (Mark I.).

Normal h.p. @ 1,800 r.p.m.	60
Maximum h.p. @ 2,000 r.p.m.	65
Weight, less Fuel and Oil	268 lbs.
Petrol Consumption @ Normal h.p.	0.66 pts./h.p./hr.
Oil Consumption @ Normal h.p....	0.013 pts./h.p./hr.

"CIRRUS" (Mark II).

Normal h.p. @ 1,800 r.p.m.	75.
Maximum h.p. @ 2,000 r.p.m.	80.
Weight Complete with Boss and Magnetos ...	256 lbs.
Average Petrol Cons. during Type Test	.62 pts./h.p./hr.
Oil Consumption	.02 pts./h.p./hr.

For full particulars apply to the Designers and Manufacturers:

A.D.C. AIRCRAFT, LTD.,

REGENT HOUSE,

89, KINGSWAY, LONDON, W.C.2.

Works & Aerodrome: CROYDON, SURREY.

Telephone: Regent 6240.

Cables: "Airdisco, London."

When communicating with advertisers, mention of "Flight" will ensure special attention.

viii

Appendix 3

The Aircraft Disposal Company's Engines

JUST as the Aircraft Disposal Company never set out with the intention of creating 'new' aircraft types, so it was never intended for it to do anything other than overhaul and recondition war-surplus aircraft engines. It never occurred to anybody to seek a specific mandate for engine design and manufacture. That event caught up with the company almost by accident and it rapidly developed into something of such magnitude and importance as a separate profit centre that when the company decided to change its name, the two-way split into ADC Aircraft Ltd and ADC Engines Ltd was both logical and practical.

ADC's move into 'new' engine design was by far the most important development the company ever undertook. The effects of this move remain to this day for it is true to say that the British light aircraft industry was kick-started from the Waddon factory. The whole dynasty of British light aircraft would have been very different had it not been for ADC.

This is because the work ADC put into building the first Cirrus engine led directly to the Gipsy engine of the DH.60 Moth and the ultimate creation of Geoffrey de Havilland's engine division.

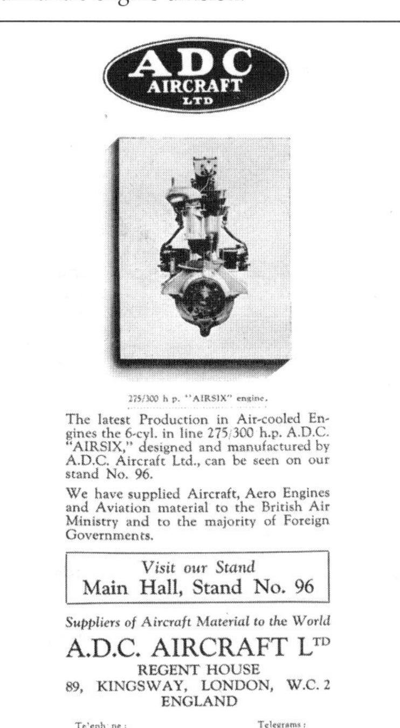

The Aircraft Disposal Company's Rolls-Royce aero-engine erecting and assembly shop at Waddon.

On the one hand, this development was to be sustained into the 1960s with the Blackburn Cirrus series while on the other a comparable path into relatively modern times was pioneered by the Gipsy. Both stemmed from the hand of designer Frank Halford and the buildings that once housed the National Aircraft Factory No. 1 at Croydon.

Very soon after its formation, ADC's engine division was confronted with great quantities of 80 hp Renault engines for disposal. They were 8-cylinder upright 90-degree Vee air-cooled direct-drive motors. The problem with these motors was that not only were they heavy but they also had a high fuel consumption. By 1923, ADC directors were becoming concerned at the almost non-existent rate of sales for these now very obsolete engines that were occupying a large storage space.

Engine designer Frank Halford, who had recently established himself as an independent engine design consultant, was asked if he could think of a way of making this engine more attractive to the market. He believed that by incorporating relatively minor changes this could be achieved.

As a direct result, Halford joined ADC in 1924 to take charge of the project and make whatever use possible of the large number of engines left over after the war.

His move coincided with the approach to ADC by Geoffrey de Havilland who persuaded the company and Halford to produce a small four-cylinder air-cooled in-line motor. The outcome was the first Cirrus engine designed by Halford to the requirements of Geoffrey de Havilland. The story is told that Halford laid out all the components of the 80 hp Renault 8-cylinder engine and took away those parts that he could use to make a four-cylinder motor.

Provided with a new crankcase and crankshaft, the new engine became the first of a highly successful dynasty that would also spawn the later de Havilland Gipsy engines. The first upright Cirrus, with its cast-iron cylinder barrels, developed 60 hp. Halford now applied the experience gained with the Cirrus to revamp the 80 hp V-8 Renault engine in its own right. He immediately designed aluminium cylinder heads, made a deeper and lighter sump, increased the compression ratio and fitted a new carburettor. The most radical change, though, was the halving of the propeller drive speed through a 2:1 spur-driven reduction gear. This gave a 50 percent increase in power at the same rpm while the engine was five percent lighter in total weight. Now developing a healthy 120 hp, the new upright motor was named the Airdisco and entered the market in 1925.

The next Halford revamp was to the Siddeley Puma and this was the 300 hp Nimbus of 1926. A 6-cylinder water-cooled upright inline, it featured direct-drive and proved itself moderately successful in a number of aircraft. While based on the Puma, there were numerous alterations to the principal components and it had a slightly larger capacity following the increase of the cylinder bore from 145 to 152mm. The compression ratio was also raised and the claim was that it was the lightest engine in terms of pounds-per-horsepower in its class.

From this was a most advanced derivative that deviated from the original by forsaking water-cooling for air-cooling. It was thus possibly unique in the world of aircraft engines in changing its fundamental cooling system. Also a revision of the Siddeley Puma, this was known as the Airsix but for some reason its development was shelved and there is no record that it ever flew. A probable explanation is that by this time Halford was transferring his services to de Havilland at Stag Lane and ADC no longer had an ace engine designer on its books.

The Airsix remains undoubtedly one of the most important and significant engines of its age yet today it seems to have been completely forgotten. Frank Halford's experience with this motor is reflected not just in the Gipsy series of inverted air-cooled engines he went on to design for de Havilland, but specifically in the Gipsy Six.

While it is all-too easy to describe ADC's whole output as simple variations on somebody else's theme, even a cursory examination of the engines that the company developed reveals that in their development not only were they wholly innovative but also they were close to the cutting edge of current thinking. That in the main they failed is largely because they were for the most part associated with the original engines from which they derived. Such simplistic thinking – which, both curiously and fortuitously, was never directed towards the Cirrus and its later derivative, the Gipsy – must have been a bitter return on ADC's great creative investment in its engines.

On February 16th 1927, Cirrus Aero Engines Ltd was registered as a separate £10,000 private company to take over the manufacture of the Cirrus range of motors. It shared its registered address at Regent House, 89 Kingsway, London, WC2, with ADC and its production facility was based in the self-same ADC buildings at Croydon, the new business merely representing a name-change. In charge of the business as general manager was William Henry Peak with John Vivian Holman as sales manager. Works manager was Ernest Stephen Olney and chief designer was the capable Alfred Henry Caple. The last product of the company was to appear in 1929 and was the first Cirrus Hermes.

At the International Aero Exhibition held in July 1929, Cirrus Aero Engines showed three engines, including the 90 hp Cirrus Mark III (with a bore of 110mm and a stroke of 130mm) and the new 105 hp Cirrus Hermes (bore 114mm, stroke 140mm). At this same event, ADC Aircraft Ltd displayed what *Flight's* reporter referred to as the 'evergreen' watercooled Nimbus and the Airsix. Significantly these were the only two 'normal' petrol engines of the in-line six type amongst the British exhibits; survivors of a type which had at one time been extremely popular but which, by then, were being superseded by more powerful engines of the 'V' and radial style. The 'six-in-line' would, however, be revived in due course by Halford's Gipsy Six.

Almost the last act of the Cirrus Aero-Engines company was the presentation of 'The Cirrus Trophy' to the New South Wales Aero Club for open competition. This was the second and last time it was given, the first being on December 13th 1930 to the winner of a light aeroplane race at Sydney. Winner in 1931 was Cirrus Mk.II-powered Westland Widgeon owned by Milton Kent.

The final phase came after the dissolution of The Aircraft Disposal Company Limited in the early part of 1931. Cirrus Aero Engines, increasingly operated as a separate entity within ADC Aircraft Ltd, no longer had a parent and went into voluntary liquidation to pave the way for a wholly-new business.

Cirrus-Hermes Engineering Company Limited was set up that February to take over Cirrus Aero Engines Ltd and the rights to the Cirrus engine and its latest version, the Hermes. Many of the senior staff of the former company also made the changeover. One of the directors of the newly-named Cirrus company was Robert Blackburn, founder of Blackburn Aeroplane & Motor Company Ltd of Brough, Yorkshire.

Three years later, Cirrus-Hermes Engineering Company Limited decided to discontinue the already-obsolete upright Cirrus engines and concentrate their efforts on the new inverted range. The early Cirrus uprights had been specified by F G Miles in the first Miles Hawk monoplanes built by Phillips & Powis at Reading. In a rather shortsighted move to secure supplies of their chosen engines, Phillips & Powis bought the rights to the upright series (Cirrus I, II and III) together with all the production tooling from Cirrus-Hermes Engineering.

It was only a short time after this strange event that F G Miles appreciated the opportunities offered by the inverted motor. As a builder of sporting and racing machines as well as trainer-touring aircraft, Miles adapted to the idea of the inverted motor. Besides offering less aerodynamic drag, the higher thrust-line of the engine permitted use of shorter undercarriage legs since it allowed more propeller ground clearance. It is not thought that Phillips & Powis ever made any engines themselves and the business must have rapidly faced up to the humiliation of having to write off the cost of a bad management decision.

It was in 1934 that Robert Blackburn became chairman of Cirrus-Hermes Engineering and moved the whole production and headquarters to Brough. Here the business operated as a separate entity under the control of Caryll Napier, son of Montague Napier (1870-1931) who founded the famous Napier engine and car company (which, coincidentally, had strong ties with Cirrus-designer Frank Halford: it was building his 16-cylinder Rapier 'H'-form engine at the time).

The company name was finally changed in 1937 to The Cirrus Engine Division of Blackburn Aircraft Ltd under which aegis the company produced a new 90 hp engine called the Cirrus Minor followed by the 150 hp Cirrus Major. The Cirrus name was thence carried forward well into the 1960s. In post-Second World War years this division blossomed making engines including new versions of the Cirrus Minor and Major series as well as the Bombardier that were widely used by British aircraft manufacturers, predominantly Auster Aircraft Limited. The name was now Blackburn Engines Limited following the name-change of the parent company to Blackburn Aircraft Limited in 1936.

The whole era of the inverted inline aircraft engine can be said to have begun in the workshops of The Aircraft Disposal Company at Croydon from which it expanded to see out its days with the de Havilland and Blackburn companies until finally it was effectively killed off by the mass adoption (by manufacturers) of the flat-four and flat-six format.

ADC Cirrus

The 4-cylinder Cirrus was created using components from the 8-cylinder 80 hp Renault and marrying them to a new crankshaft and crankcase. Featuring a single induction system, the Cirrus had cast-iron cylinder barrels with aluminium heads and steel connecting rods. Like the Renault from which it was descended and its larger derivative the Airdisco, the first Cirrus was a long-stroke engine having a bore of 4.13 inches and a stroke of 5.12. The Cirrus engine was installed famously in the DH.60 Moth but was also fitted in the Avro 543 Baby and 581E Avian, the Short S.7 Mussel I, and the Westland Widgeon III. The Mk.II was introduced in 1926 and was very similar to its predecessor except that it used duralumin forgings for its connecting rods and duralumin tubes as push rods. The induction system had two independent induction passages, one for the two central and one for the front and rear cylinders each fed from a dual Zenith carburetter provided with a separate choke and adjustments for each pair of cylinders. This was claimed by the makers to avoid the 'irregularity of distribution usual in 4-cylinder engines with a common induction pipe'. The Mk.III appeared in 1929 and was the last variant to be produced by under the aegis of the ADC company. This engine had improved cylinder head cooling and revised valves and rocker gear. The carburettor was a single Claudel-Hobson mounted on the starboard side feeding all four cylinders through a welded steel manifold. An exhaust-heated jacket was fitted above the carburettor to combat icing to which earlier models of the Cirrus had been prone. It was available with two different compression ratios; normal was 5.1 giving 90/94 hp, while to special order one could have a compression ratio of 5.4 giving a power output of 92.5/97 hp. Further development of this motor was carried out by Cirrus Aero Engines Ltd, the ADC spin-off company set up on February 16th 1927. Engines produced after that date were known as the Cirrus Hermes series of which the Hermes IIB was the first inverted example. The first Cirrus Hermes had cast iron cylinders deeply spigoted into the crankcase to avoid distortion. Special Y alloy heads were fitted. Details of subsequent developments can be found in Ord-Hume *[22]*. The illustrations below show the Cirrus Mk.1 of 1924 with BTH magneto and impulse couplings.

ENGINE SPECIFICATIONS

Name of model	No of Cylinders	Cylinder Layout	Cooling System	Comp. ratio	Cubic capacity	Super-charged	Gear ratio	HP rating	Max Take-off [hp/rpm]	Continuous [hp/rpm]	Weight [lbs]	Lbs/ hp
Cirrus I	4	Upr In-line	Air	4.7:1	4.5 lit	No	Direct	60	65/2,000	60/1,800	268	4.46
Cirrus II	- do -	- do -	- do -	4.9:1	4.94 lit	- do -	- do -	75	85/2,000	75/1,800	280	3.73
Cirrus III	- do -	- do -	- do -	5.1:1	- do -	- do -	- do -	90	94/2,100	90/1,900	285	3.16
Cirrus Hermes	- do -	- do -	- do -	5.1	5.717 lit	- do -	- do -	105	115/2,100	105/1,900	310	2.95

ADC Airdisco 1

When the original announcement was made in November 1924 upon the conclusion of its 10-hour Air Ministry type-test, this engine was referred to by the name of ADC-Renault. First flown in an Avro during November and December, it allegedly took the aircraft to 10,000 feet in half the time possible with any rotary engine. The next installation was to the DH.51 that de Havilland himself flew. By the time this was complete, the decision had been taken on obvious commercial grounds to change the name of the motor to the Air-Disco, later becoming simply Airdisco I. It was the second engine the company produced and it owed much of its success to the experiences gained developing the 4-cylinder Cirrus. Also derived from the direct-drive 80 hp Renault, the 8-cylinder Airdisco was an upright 90-degree Vee air-cooled engine provided with a 2:1 reduction gear. The bore and stroke remained unaltered – 105 x 130mm – but in place of the original cast-iron head with a side inlet and an overhead exhaust valve, aluminium cylinder heads with two overhead valves of the same type as the Cirrus were used while the connecting rods were of the main and articulated type. The steel pistons of the original were replaced by aluminium ones while the crankshaft bearing arrangements were also similar to those of the Cirrus save for the provision of an extra ball race fitted beyond the pinion of the reduction gear. Other refinements included two Zenith carburettors – one on each side rather than just one at the rear of the crankcase – and revised ignition system. The outcome was an engine that was flown successfully in a number of contemporary aircraft including the Avro 548A, DH.51 and civil conversions of the SE.5A. Cockpit-starting was possible. The Cirrus engine had a hand-starter lever that could be connected to a lever in the cockpit and worked rather like a motor-cycle kick-starter. The Airdisco had a similar system using a small flywheel on the crankshaft. Fuel comsumption at cruising power was 79 pints/hour.

ENGINE SPECIFICATIONS

Name of model	No of Cylinders	Cylinder Layout	Cooling System	Comp. ratio	Cubic capacity	Super-charged	Gear ratio	HP rating	Max Take-off [hp/rpm]	Continuous [hp/rpm]	Weight [lbs]	Lbs/ hp
ADC Airdisco	8	Upr V-8	Air	4.6:1	9.000 lit	No	2:1	120	140/2,000	120/1,800	452	3.53

ADC Nimbus

If the Airdisco was considered a Renault by another name, then the Nimbus also owed its origins to another engine, this time the 230 hp Siddeley Puma. The original motor was initially plagued by reliability problems that were only beginning to be sorted out by the end of the War: it came into its own very much as the conflict concluded and became a popular and respected motor. The Nimbus, with its larger bore and higher compression ratio, was in detail a somewhat different engine, the only similarity claimed to be that it fitted into the same engine-bearers as the Puma. Bore was 152mm and stroke 190mm. The cylinders had steel liners with closed heads in aluminium block castings, three cylinders to each block. A watertight joint was made at the bottom of each block using a split bronze ring screwed onto the liner and clamping a rubber ring between jacket and liner. Trunk-type aluminium pistons were fitted, each with four rings and a floating gudgeon pin. Two Zenith carburettors were attached directly to flanges on the cylinder head castings and fed inlet valves through passages in the casting. Two six-cylinder magnetos with horizontal transverse axes were mounted on brackets at the end of the crankcase. As with the Puma, there were three valves per cylinder – one inlet and two exhaust. The imlet valves were operated by short rockers while the exhaust valves were moved by using and overhead camshaft. Frank Halford expended a great deal of time and effort in perfecting this engine but when completed it proved to be an exceptional performer. Unfortunately this engine was only ever to be produced in small numbers. It did, though, fly in at least half a dozen types of aircraft including Airco DH.9 series, DH.37A, DH.50, Martinsyde Nimbus, and the Vickers 133 and 157.

ENGINE SPECIFICATIONS

Name of model	No of Cylinders	Cylinder Layout	Cooling System	Comp. ratio	Cubic capacity	Super-charged	Gear ratio	HP rating	Max Take-off [hp/rpm]	Continuous [hp/rpm]	Weight [lbs]	Lbs/hp
ADC Nimbus	6	Upr In-line	Water	5.4:1	20.353 lit	No	Direct	300	335/1,600	305/1,450	670	2.19

ADC Airsix

Perhaps the most exciting of the ADC engines was this radical second reworking of the 230 hp Siddeley Puma. This was also one of the most important and significant aircraft engines of its age to be designed and produced in Great Britain. Its originality of concept was to herald seminal changes in future engine design While the ADC Nimbus had preserved the water-cooling of the original, the Airsix was a wholly air-cooled engine having new cylinder barrels and heads offering a bore of 137mm and a 190mm stroke. The first six-cylinder in-line air-cooled engine to be produced in this country, the Airsix was designed to present a minimum frontal area and to this end it had its two Zenith carburettors, each feeding three cylinders, positioned at either end of the manifold. Slipper-type pistons machined from 'Y'-alloy forgings were provided with floating gudgeon pins contained in bosses that were continued up into the piston crown so as to ensure heat dissipation. Steel cylinders with integral fins were matched with bolted-on cast aluminium cylinder heads of the 'poultice' type. Each was fitted with two inlet and two exhaust valves and, unusually, operated by an overhead camshaft fitted in a cam-case bolted to the cylinders in order to reduce variations in clearances that occurred when the engine was hot. Dual ignition was standard and lubrication was of the dry-sump type. Cooling consisted of six air chutes so arranged that each chute projected slightly further into the airstream providing excellent cooling for each cylinder. The oil pump was fitted directly to the underside of the auxiliary gear housing. ADC claimed that the saving in weight per horsepower over similar-powered engines was 'considerable'. That Airdisco succeeded in getting more power per litre capacity in so light and radical an engine (for its time) remains a triumph of aero/motor engineering. Unfortunately the Airsix came into being too late in the existence of the company to make a great impact on the aircraft engine world and Frank Halford's departure for de Havilland seems to have marked finis to an otherwise exciting development that surely represented the pinnacle of ADC Engines Limited's achievements. The Airsix was far-reaching in its improvements over its contemporaries, yet it appears to have been too quickly forgotten by most historians who condescendingly dismiss it merely as 'another derivative'.

ENGINE SPECIFICATIONS

Name of model	No of Cylinders	Cylinder Layout	Cooling System	Comp. ratio	Cubic capacity	Super-charged	Gear ratio	HP rating	Max Take-off [hp/rpm]	Continuous [hp/rpm]	Weight [lbs]	Lbs/ hp
ADC Airsix	6	Upr In-line	Air	5.4:1	17.403 lit	No	Direct	270	300/1,950	273/1,750	620	2.27

Endnote: On July 10th 1929, a quite separate and unrelated business was established as Sidarblen Engines Ltd with a registered address at 4, Old Burlington Street, London. With a share capital of £500, this company revealed its as directors A A Sidney of 22, Barnes Road, Croydon, Maurice O Darby and J Barrett-Lennard, both giving their address as Regent House, Kingsway. Eponymously named to develop a Diesel-type compression-ignition engine devised by Sidney, the involvement of the two prime movers of ADC Aircraft Ltd is of particular interest. However, the Sidarblen appears to have been stillborn and nothing further was heard of the enterprise. Perhaps an even more curious event was the registration of a new private company on December 15th 1932. This was called ADC Engines Limited – a revival of the old and, by that time, defunct name. With a £1,000 share capital and with both Darby and Barrett-Lennard listed as directors, the stated objectives of the new ADC-named company remain unknown and there is no trace of its subsequent activities. It seems that the directors believed there was the opportunity to trade off the old company's name.

Unmarked and unadorned, the main office premises at Waddon for the Aircraft Disposal Company Ltd. With its main business address in London, the Croydon premises did not need to advertise their presence as a headquarters building. While the hangars were all prominently marked 'Aircraft Disposal Co' for the benefit of the 'airside' visitors, these buildings, formerly the offices of the National Aircraft Factory Number One, remained largely anonymous. Along with all the other buildings that once formed the ADC empire, they are no more.

Postscript

WITH hindsight it is clear to see that the Aircraft Disposal Company was a unique business that existed to serve a political need. Generally speaking, the formation of a company is normally associated solely with the generation of profit for its founders and backers. Certainly ADC assembled and sold aeroplanes, and in so doing earned profit for its founders, but its real purpose was to serve the Government of the time. Astonishing though it may sound, perhaps even its founders did not realise that at the outset.

Most contemporary observers would have seen little further than ADC being a new business to deal in old aeroplanes.

While Handley Page had the notion of entering the surplus business as a means to an economic end for himself and his company, was he astute enough to foresee the true position that ADC would quickly adopt? It is a question that will forever be unanswered. The Cricklewood Bomber-builder may have been an adroit and clever businessman but one may doubt that his commercial chess-playing manoeuvres included so much as an insight into the wiles of the National Purse.

Its real task was far and away beyond that, for its purpose was to placate the population of a nation that had been heavily taxed and seen the public coffers bled dry by the enormous cost of war equipment. An enormous sigh of relief must have greeted Handley Page's suggestion and there is evidence to support that the deal was moved through with undue if not indecent haste. Somebody possibly gritted teeth and crossed fingers, praying that the deal was done quickly before HP might change his mind… ADC, then, was not just another business enterprise: it was the salvation of a nation that demanded that the costs associated with the huge surpluses of war be redeemed for the benefit of the impecunious man in the street.

So long as the Aircraft Disposal Company prospered, awkward questions were less likely to be raised in Parliament. And questions about surplus aircraft that had hitherto being sold off for pennies, could be answered assertively as, with chest puffed out and confidently grasped lapels, the ubiquitous spokesperson could say, with little fear of being challenged, 'We have already sold the lot for a good lump of money!' And any further embarrassing queries could be countered by saying 'They are all being turned into revenue-earners, many going for export to bring in much-needed foreign currency – of which sales we will take a goodly percentage!'

We should all have been thankful that the aeroplanes business was capable of being tidied up so neatly! After all, there was also the embarrassment of all the questions regarding Army equipment and our Navy's fleet!

The Army business had already cropped up on several occasions in the House of Commons but fortunately (for the persons expected to offer explanations) military equipment could easily be explained away by (a) either being lost in battle, or (b) returned to army stores. There was no need to account for 'wastage' because there wasn't any. At least, none that anybody wanted to talk about. And 'stores' covered a multitude of sins, not the least of which was the widely-feared complexity of time-consuming 'stock-taking'.

Quite legitimately, keeping Army (meaning Government) property fully accountable, especially in time of war, was virtually impossible. Expensive and largely irreplaceable equipment (such as field telephones, medical equipment and leather map-cases) all-too frequently were destroyed by enemy action. Field guns occasionally suffered catastrophic breach or barrel-failure, or simply sank in mud and had to be abandoned. Even rifles and ammunition were readily lost in the heat of battle.

The Navy was in a similar position although here the accounting was a bit simpler. Ships and their accounting of was a sort of binary equation. Stores, meaning Navy (Government) property, could only be in one of two places – on the surface of the sea or on the bottom. The surface was accountable, the bottom of the ocean was not. Anything that could not be found in the first environment could be accounted for by claiming that it had entered the second. And nobody thought to question the facts associated with the strength of the Navy! After all, we were in the position of having the greatest, strongest and largest Navy in the world! We knew that for we had all been told about it, therefore it must be so. The fact that it was probably untrue didn't enter into it. You could never have enough ships and so the Navy, like the Army, was off the hook.

Well, not entirely, because there was still the question of supplies. Ships were one thing, but the bits that go with them left plenty of scope for potential public revenue fraud to be exposed by those who relished in exposing such things. In general, anything that went missing could be explained as having accidentally (meaning irretrievably) fallen over the side. Valuable chronometers are known to have legitimately been lost to the deep, while damaged aeroplanes were pushed over the side to avoid both costly repairs and awkward questions. Nevertheless many were the questions regarding quite silly things. These went on for many years after the war had ended.

Not that the Air Ministry could escape entirely scot-free from the war surplus rumblings. Aircraft and bits of aircraft were one thing, but there were other items in AM stores that were less easy to explain away. Take rope, for instance! After the great linen scandal, another, albeit lesser, tangle concerned an inexplicable and on-going demand for the stuff. One might say that given enough rope, somebody was guaranteed to hang himself. And so it was!

In the House of Commons on May 5th 1924, the Under-Secretary of State for Air responded to a question by Major Leslie Hore-Belisha (later famed as the inventor of the 'Belisha beacon' for pedestrian road crossings) that the Air Ministry used about 65,000 fathoms of rope a year, war stocks of rope were still held and new supplies were obtained by requisition on the Admiralty. How the Air Ministry used its 74 statute miles of rope a year was neither asked nor answered...

Clearly a legacy from the days of observation balloons and blimps, somebody must have forgotten to cancel a standing order – or maybe simple didn't know how! There was clearly enough rope for the whole Government to hang themselves: some said it was a pity that they didn't put it all to such good use.

As for this rope fiasco, rope had been a

valuable military necessity for millennia: even Roman soldiers used rope for things to do with horses and carts, while the Navy historically used enormous quantities of the stuff for rigging sailboats and tying ships either to bollards or to each other. Rope was also useful for chucking out to retrieve careless sailors who had fallen overboard. If the Army and the Navy found rope so indispensable, then so must the RAF! To begin with, it did use a lot of rope on balloons and airships as well as, much later, barrage balloons. But 65,000 fathoms?

It was these parliamentary nosey-parkers that could make life tough for a politician. With nothing better to do than examine some fatuous stores issue such as the number of bath-plugs in use in military establishments in the Sudan, they left politicians plenty of reason for establishing and encouraging an accountable means of coping with surplus war goods. It was important to show that all the investment in public money was not lost and that what could be salvaged was being salvaged for turning back into money.

A good example of this was Bourbourg in the Calais region of France. This became infamous as an Army Ammunition Depot and, being one of the last to be planned, was actually still under construction when the Armistice was declared. Now it was hastily finished as an Ordnance Salvage Depot where salvaged ammunition (including enemy goods) could be reclaimed.

> Salvage operations were specially onerous in the case of ammunition of which many thousands of tons were scattered over the face of the country... The ammunition thus collected was next sorted out. What was worth keeping was sent down the line and the rest blown up bit by bit after brass, copper and other valuable by-products had been saved.*
> *[* Forbes, Maj-Gen Arthur: A History of the Army Ordnance Services, London, Medici, 1929, Vol.III, p.181]*

Bourbourg was thus one arm of the Army's salvage campaign. As for vehicles, many tanks were purchased cheaply as war memorial mementos by well-meaning village communities up and down the country. Many village greens sported the disintegrating rusted remains of WWI tanks standing on stained concrete plinths well into the late 1930s, survivors even making salvage for the WWII war-effort.

Few other military vehicles found civilian homes and so, along with many of the guns, they were melted down – to create a glut on the steel market. This was boosted by the volume of surplus tonnage of shipping left by the Navy. Many ships were successfully sold abroad: many more (in particular the older vessels refitted at the outbreak of war) went back into the melting-pot via the breakers' yard.

I have shown that indecision and ineptitude created a situation where, in 1919 and 1920, we were ill-prepared to be custodians of the spoils of war and, as a corollary, to govern ourselves and our aircraft industry adequately in time of peace. In case that sounds a bit harsh, remember that 1920 proved to be a year of disillusionment on more than just one front. If the sum total of our efforts at emasculating the Luftwaffe ended up being unquantifiable, there were some dismal revelations regarding the war for the American tax-payer (*see* page 58).

Idol-shattering is a seemingly inevitable consequence of the immediate vacuum that follows war as aims, objects and achievements are all called to question.

As for The Aircraft Disposal Company, very early on in its existence – and certainly by 1924 – the principal reason for its existence had long passed and it settled down to being a trading company making and selling aircraft around the world and was less driven by the question of satisfying the public via the Chancellor of the Exchequer.

What seems remarkable is that independent industry (that which was once superciliously described as 'the Trade') should have been allowed to set up such a business in the first place. It was, after all, Government's responsibility. The only problem was that the Government had already tried to do the job through the Aircraft Disposal Board – and if not exactly failed, then spent a good deal of time and money to get rid of only a few hundreds of aircraft.

The Aircraft Disposal Company was thus a curious solution to a public problem. It was created under most unusual circumstances, operated under peculiar conditions and wielded a far greater hidden power than its founders ever imagined. Certainly we are never again likely to see such an operation.

A useful comment and summing-up of The Aircraft Disposal Company's transition from scrap-dealer through aircraft broker to ultimate acceptance in the world of the British aircraft industry is to be found in the 1924 edition of *Jane's All The World's Aircraft*. Here, for the first time, the business is admitted to that exclusive coterie – the list of manufacturers that make up the British Aircraft Industry. This, then as now, is an alphabetical list of all the

SIR DOUGLAS HAIG'S MESSAGE TO MUNITIONS WORKERS

GENERAL HEAD QUARTERS,
BRITISH ARMIES IN FRANCE.

24th November 1918.

Dear Mr Churchill.

Now that the Armistice has been signed, I wish to express my thanks to you personally, to the Heads of your Departments and to all Munition Workers, men and women, for their continuous labours to provide the war material necessary for the success of operations and the final defeat of the enemy.

The British Armies in France under my command thoroughly appreciate the great efforts that have been made by your Ministry.

Believe me,
Yours Very truly
D. Haig.

Right Hon. W.S. Churchill,
Ministry of Munitions of War,
Whitehall Place,
London, S.W.1.

The Nation's gratitude to the war workers was demonstrated by this poster, a copy of which was hung up in the old National Aircraft Factory at Waddon. Up and down the land, thousands of munitions workers had worked day and night six and more days a week. Now top man Sir Douglas Haig was saying thanks for the effort. Within weeks, most of those who read this, especially those at Waddon, would be out of work. This poster, 29-ins by 20-ins and with a print run of 70,000 copies, went to factories and workshops all over the country.

companies beginning with Air Navigation & Engineering of Weybridge and ending with Westland. The Aircraft Disposal Company is permitted to 'rub shoulders' with the elite, being allocated a spacious entry of three full pages – curiously placed after Westland at the very end of the British section.

In his introductory notes to the entries, editor and compiler (as well as *Aeroplane* editor) C G Grey explains the logic of ADC's inclusion and observes:

> Since their formation, the Company has done a very large business both in Britain and abroad in supplying customers of all kinds with aircraft and aircraft material. Of the stocks taken over, a very large volume consisted of obsolete aircraft and equipment, useless for any aeronautical purpose, and a very big proportion of such material has been disposed of at very low prices, either for purposes other than aeronautical or admittedly as scrap.
>
> But in addition to this type of material there still remains a large stock of serviceable aircraft, engines, and accessories of types still in use in the British service. The Aircraft Disposal Company, from this stock, has supplied many hundreds of machines, both to private concerns and to foreign Governments in all parts of the world.
>
> At their works at Waddon they maintain a large and competent staff. Further, they undertake modifications of standard machines to meet the requirements of users and maintain an adequate designing staff for that purpose. They do not manufacture aeroplanes, and for this reason they have not been included in the foregoing pages which relate to British aeroplane manufacturers as such.
>
> In no case do they deliver machines except after thorough overhaul, re-conditioning and test.
>
> No guide to the present state of the British Aircraft Industry would be complete without a reference to this firm…

But ADC had made it, so to speak. Its aircraft are well provided for with illustrated entries for the Martinsyde F.4, Avro 504K (110 hp Le Rhône), DH.9 (230 hp Puma), DH.9A (360 hp Rolls-Royce and 450 Napier variants), Bristol Fighter (300 hp Hispano), SE.5A, Sopwith Snipe (230 hp BR.II), DH.9C, Felixstowe F.3 flying boat (2 x 360 hp Rolls-Royce), Norman-Thompson NT.2B flying boat, and the Parnall Panther (230 hp BR.II).

After World War II things were very different. While the Americans had a firm and avowed policy of scrapping as distinct from selling off military equipment, it was with some reluctance that Britain took the decision to follow suit. True, some Halifax and Lancaster bombers that were in adequate condition went through a form of face-lift in order to provide first-generation post-war airliners, but they were relatively few and far between.

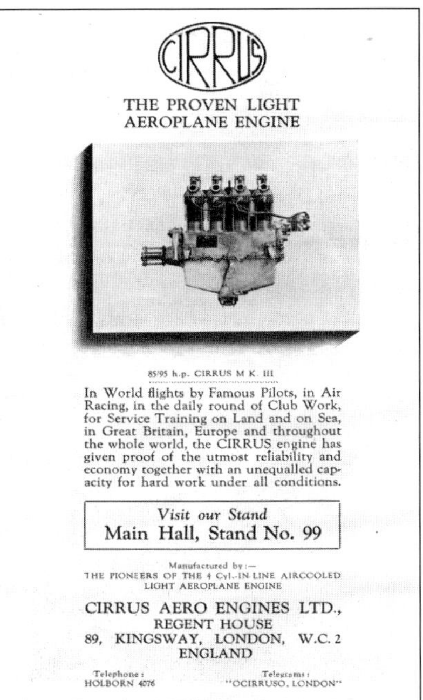

The company Cirrus Aero Engines Ltd was formed on February 16th 1927 to take over the Cirrus range of ADC motors. Two years later it took this advertisement in the programme for the Seventh International Aero Exhibition staged at Olympia in London. It was promoting what was to be the last of the uprights – the Mk.III. The Cirrus Engines stand, No. 99, was right next to ADC Aircraft's stand at No. 96.(*see* page 123)

Huge numbers of aircraft were parked at disposal sites on now-redundant airfields mainly around the southern half of the country and from here they were sold off in batches to the scrap contractors through a process of sealed postal bids. The secret was for the scrap contractor to know the true weight of the empty aircraft and then accurately deduce the various total weights of the many materials that made up that weight. This gave him a precise scrap value. A knowledgeable and careful dealer could thus bid wisely for aircraft and so ensure that, while the Government got a fair price, he might still profit from the transaction.

This approach was often very accurate and, certainly as far as aircraft engines were concerned, the calculations went into many decimal places. The present author was one of the numerous qualified aircraft design engineers frequently hired by the scrappers to prepare materials break-downs for aircraft and components. This approach was a far cry from, say, the burning fields of the defeated German air force in 1918-19, and even from the bulk-buying basis of The Aircraft Disposal Company Ltd.

Recent years have seen the final obliteration of the buildings that once formed National Aircraft Factory Number One. It was these that had become the home of ADC, a company that few can recall today. ADC lived out its entire existence at Croydon. It had started out in the far-off days of Waddon and Plough Lane, was then absorbed into the new airport established off Purley Way. Now integrated into Croydon Airport, the twilight days of ADC marked but another change of occupation on the site. Its buildings now went on to house other businesses such as Redwing and General Aircraft, and its products literally went all over the world. Built originally as the most modern factory for the mass-production of military aircraft in time of war, it is to be regretted that nothing remains today.

And so finally what about that dramatic comment from Charles Grey Grey, founder editor of *The Aeroplane* until September 1939, with which I prefaced the *Introduction* to this book? Well, the problems of 1945 were similar to those of 1919 save that of the 125,000 aircraft built in Britain during the 1939-45 War, very, very few were usable in time of peace. But was the irascible 'CGG' correct in his comment on 1919 surplus disposals? I think not. As CGG grew older his pen became ever more fluent (some would say verbose) while his content increasingly became what we might best describe as 'poetically-licensed'. His memories of 1919, then, were more coloured by his urge to promote a message of the current time than in offering the account of the historian. His recollections of times past became notorious for their little inaccuracies.

Mind you, as regards what he wrote, I can't prove it; nor can I disprove it, but merely comment that the circumstances he so graphically described do sound just a little unlikely. I have shown earlier how isolated instances of aircraft destruction created ripples in Westminster. Although possible, we may conclude that CGG's account cannot have been indicative of a widespread practice. CGG was ever one to write what he thought best in everybody's interest, not necessarily what was totally true – and in this regard he could always make people sit up and think. That, I feel, was the underlying message here. Communicating an idea was, after all, CGG's forte.

Bibliography

1. [anon]: *A Short History of the Royal Air Force.* Air Ministry Publication 125, 1920, rev. ed. 1936
2. Barnes, C H: *Handley Page Aircraft since 1907.* Putnam, London, 1976
3. Bruce, J M: *British Aeroplanes 1914-18.* Putnam, London, 1957
4. Cluett, Douglas [edit]: *The First Croydon Airport 1915-1928.* Sutton Libraries, Surrey. 1977; 2nd rev. ed. Croydon Airport Society, Surrey, 2001.
5. .. .. : *Croydon Airport: The Great Days 1928-1939.* Sutton Libraries, Surrey. 1980
6. Courtney, Frank T: *Flight Path.* Kimber, London, 1972
7. Davis, Mick: *Airco: The Aircraft Manufacturing Company.* Crowood, Marlborough, Wiltshire, 2001
8. .. .. : *Sopwith Aircraft.* Crowood, Marlborough, Wiltshire, 1999
9. Gilbert, Bentley B: *Britain since 1918.* Batsford, London, 1967
10. Goodall, Michael H: *The Norman Thompson File.* Air-Britain Historians, Tonbridge, 1995
11. Grey, C G [and others]: *Jane's All The World's Aircraft.* Sampson Low, Marston, London, 1919-1930
12. Harber, Olivia: *The National Aeroplane Factories: Government Intervention in Airframe Manufacture 1917-1918.* Unpublished dissertation, University of Leeds School of History, 1993
13. Hare, Paul R: *Aeroplanes of the Royal Aircraft Factory.* Crowood, Marlborough, Wiltshire, 1999
14. Hooks, Michael J: *Croydon Airport. Archive Photo Series,* Tempus, Stroud, 1997.
15. .. .. : *Croydon Airport: The Peaceful Years.* Tempus, Stroud, 2002
16. Howson, Gerald: *Aircraft of the Spanish Civil War 1936-39.* Putnam, London, 1990
17. Jackson, A J : *British Civil Aircraft 1919-1972* [3 vols]. Putnam, London, 1973
18. Jones, H A: *The War in the Air* [6 vols; 1922-37: vol. 6]. Clarendon Press, Oxford, 1937 [*see* also Raleigh]
19. Londonderry, Lord: *Wings of Destiny.* Macmillan, London, 1943
20. Lumsden, Alec S C: *British Piston Aero-Engines and their Aircraft.* Airlife, Shrewsbury, 1994
21. McMillan, James: *The Way it Happened 1935-1950.* Kimber, London, 1980
22. Ord-Hume, Arthur W J G: *British Light Aeroplanes.* GMS Enterprises, Peterborough, 2000
23. .. .. : *British Commercial Aircraft.* GMS Enterprises, Peterborough, 2003
24. Penrose, Harald J: *British Aviation, The Great War and Armistice: 1915-1919.* Putnam, London, 1969
25. .. .. : *British Aviation: The Adventuring Years: 1920-1929.* Putnam, London, 1973
26. Popham, Hugh: *Into Wind: A History of British Naval Flying.* Hamilton, London, 1969
27. Raleigh, Walter: *The War in the Air* [2 vols with H A Jones: vol. 1]. Clarendon Press, Oxford, 1922; 2ed Hamilton, London, 1969*
28. Redman, Ronald N: *Yorkshire's Early Flying Days.* Dalesman, Clapham via Lancaster, 1981
29. Sanger, R: *The Martinsyde File.* Air-Britain (Historians) Ltd, Tunbridge Wells, Kent, 1999
30. Sinnott, Colin: *The RAF and Aircraft Design 1923-1939.* Frank Cass, London, 2001
31. Thomson, Lord: *Air Facts and Problems.* Murray, London, 1927
32. Wackett, Lawrence James: *Aircraft Pioneer.* Angus & Robertson, Sydney, Australia, 1972
33. Wainwright, David: *Broadwood by Appointment: A History.* Quiller, London, 1982

* Sir Walter Raleigh's projected great work, sub-titled *Being the Story of the Part Played in the Great War by the Royal Air Force,* was interrupted by his death after this first volume appeared. It was subsequently continued by H A Jones *[qv]* to a total of six volumes plus a volume of appendices, an enterprise spanning 15 years. Vol. II = 1928; Vol. III = 1931; Vol. IV = 1934; Vol. V = 1935; Vol, VI = 1937. All, including the volume of Appendices, were reprinted in 2002 by Naval & Military Publishers, Sussex.

Periodicals consulted *(the dates shown refer to relevant issues only):*

The Aeroplane, *1918-1930 (founder and first editor: Charles Grey Grey)*
Flight, *1917-1930 (founder and first editor: Stanley Spooner)*
Aeronautics, *1907-1921 (editor: John H. Ledeboer)**
Croydon Airport Society Journal, *Croydon, Surrey, 1982-2004*
The Royal Air Force and Civil Aviation Record, *London, 1920-c.1921***

* This began life in 1907 as a supplement to *Knowledge & Illustrated Scientific News* published by Benn Brothers and edited by Maj B Baden-Powell, but after three issues quickly became an independent and respected 6d weekly periodical solely edited by John Ledeboer that survived until 1921 by which year it had produced 21 volumes. Ledeboer, of Dutch descent, was an early aviation author and translator of European books on aeronautics.

** This seems to have been a short-lived, quality magazine that appeared first in April 1920. No issues seen or recorded after mid-1920 suggesting that this was also a victim of the aeronautical recession that characterised the immediate post-war years.

Index

Page numbers in **BOLD** type indicate a photograph

N

BRITISH ADC AIRCRAFT
SUPPLIERS of AIRCRAFT to the WORLD
AEROPLANES
ENGINES
SEAPLANES
ACCESSORIES
We have had the pleasure of supplying aircraft material to the following countries:—
ARGENTINE
AUSTRALIA
BRAZIL
BELGIUM
CANADA
CHILE
CHINA
CZECHO-SLOVAKIA
DENMARK
DUTCH EAST INDIES
ESTHONIA
FINLAND
GERMANY
GREECE
GUATEMALA
HONDURAS
HOLLAND
INDIA
IRISH FREE STATE
ITALY
JAPAN
LATVIA
LITHUANIA
NEW ZEALAND
NORWAY
PERU
POLAND
PORTUGAL
ROUMANIA
RUSSIA
SIAM
SOUTH AFRICA
SPAIN
SWEDEN
SWITZERLAND
URUGUAY
UNITED STATES AMERICA.
AIRCRAFT DISPOSAL COMPANY LTD.
REGENT HOUSE,
89, KINGSWAY, LONDON, W.C.2.

O

P

R

S

T

U

V

W

Y

Z